Dogs, Houses, Gardens, Food

& other addictions

Dogs, Houses, Gardens, Food

& other addictions

Sondra Gotlieb

McArthur & Company
Toronto

This paperback edition published in Canada in 2003
by McArthur & Company

First published in Canada in 2002 by
McArthur & Company
322 King St. West, Suite 402
Toronto, ON M5V 1J2
www.mcarthur-co.com

National Library of Canada Cataloguing in Publication

Gotlieb, Sondra, 1936-
        Dogs, houses, gardens, food and other addictions
        Sondra Gotlieb.

        ISBN 1-55278-310-3 (bound). – ISBN 1-55278-370-7
        (pbk.)

        1. Gotlieb, Sondra, 1936-. 2. Authors, Canadian
        (English) – 20th century—Anecdotes. 3. Ambassadors'
        spouses – Canada—Anecdotes. I. Title. II. Title:
        Dogs, houses, gardens, food, and other addictions.

        PS8563.O838Z53 2002   C818'.5409   C2002-903347-0

Composition + Cover: *Mad Dog Design Inc.*
Printed in Canada by *Transcontinental Printing*

The publisher would like to acknowledge the financial support of the
Government of Canada through the Book Publishing Industry
Development Program, the Canada Council, and the Ontario Arts
Council for our publishing activities. We also acknowledge the
Government of Ontario through the Ontario Media Development
Corporation Ontario Book Initiative.

10 9 8 7 6 5 4 3 2 1

To Allan

Contents

1

Food Came First

WHEN I WAS SIXTEEN I didn't know much but I knew what I liked: food, flowers, our house, our dogs (an English setter, two cocker spaniels and a Scottie) and a milkman's son.

Food came first (it was readier at hand than the milkman's son), especially my mother's food. Mummy's friends called her Fanny the Feeder—she had more things in her fridge than anyone in Winnipeg, all homemade. My brother and I used to stare at the inside of her fridge as if it were the *Ed Sullivan Show*. Knowing our fondness for her show of shows, she would put warning signs on her specialties like Russian butter cake, such as "Children do not touch. I made this for Aunt Zora."

Russian butter cake had chocolate pudding (her recipe, not Jell-O's), between the five layers, but it was covered by a separate chocolate icing and topped with a hardened caramel shiny enough to reflect my face. Mother was the only person who could cut the first slice without damaging the cake. I never helped her in the kitchen.

My father believed that the only way you could judge a woman's worth was by her cooking. He used to say, "The better the cook, the better the woman." Not that my father believed in following the precepts of Brillat-Savarin or ever heard of him. His taste was strictly Eastern European: what he liked was food wrapped in dough or cabbage and dry cookies made with poppy seed. He needed two different kinds of soup a day and meat had, of course, to be well done. Needless to say, my father was not a salad man. My mother's fancy pastry was not for him, but for the many ladies' charity teas so prevalent in those days. These were the years when ladies never went out to tea without a hat and gloves. My mother could bake any kind of cake— angel cake, chocolate cake, coffee cake, cinnamon bundt cake— but she was careful not to tred on another woman's culinary turf. Everyone had their signature cake for which they were justly renown. Mrs. Birnboim had her angel cake, my future mother-in-law had her lemon sponge (although there was always some question whether her housekeeper baked it), and Mrs. Sokolov was celebrated for chocolate-honeyed nuts and sour cherry jam (although everyone knew that her sister, Mrs. Brownstone, had really made them). I knew about deception even then.

As a result of this intense emphasis on food, I was a plump child. My father did not see this as a bad thing in a marriageable female. His philosophy was: "Plump is good." Also, I had no pimples. "It's the skin that counts" was his equally firm belief.

I liked flowers, but knew only those I saw in Winnipeg—one of the coldest horticultural zones for any major city in the world, including Moscow. This means freezing that lasts from October until Queen Victoria's birthday in late May. The flowers that appealed to me were the fragrant ones—lilacs, sweet peas and wild roses—but I nearly swooned when I saw my first delphiniums in the public gardens in Clear Lake, Manitoba, where we used to go on holidays in July. My father never grew delphiniums, but he dug the sweet pea seeds very deep in the ground when the frost lifted in May. In early June he planted annuals, red salvias (I hate them to this day), snapdragons and marigolds in stiff rows along the beds in our narrow backyard. All the backyards in North Winnipeg where I lived were laid side by side in narrow plots, with garages and lanes for the deliverymen. Even though mother asked, I never helped with the gardening either.

My mother used to run out of the house in her bathrobe every spring when the first peony bloomed—the only time she appeared outdoors undressed. My father forgave her. Like every young girl, I loved *Anne of Green Gables* but what caught my curiosity most in the L.M. Montgomery books was the description of the flowers in Prince Edward Island—narcissus, tulips and anemones, snowdrops, bluebells—all of which didn't grow in my Manitoba.

The only amazing garden I knew belonged to my uncle Rex Winograd, or Lord Rex Winograd, as he liked to call himself when he signed a hotel register or made a reservation at a restaurant. He had a sprawling ranch-house on the Assiniboine River on Wellington Crescent in the South End—it was the finest street in Winnipeg. He supervised a grand planting of annuals, a gaudy mixture of sizes and brightly coloured plants that grow so brilliantly in the Manitoba climate. The reds, yellows and blues jumped out at you and grabbed your eyes, despite the fact that the flowers were set back deep in the huge lot in front of his house. In the back, going down to the river, he grafted apple trees with the help of his Ukrainian gardener and gave me various bites of new breeds, which he constantly bragged about to his bored relatives.

In our circle, Uncle Rex's house was considered unusual. It was the grandest that I knew. One wall was sixty by thirty feet and devoted entirely to live and dead fish. The walls were covered with ten-foot-high glass containers of tropical fish—"the aquarium room." Above the cases he displayed large dead salmon caught up North. During long Winnipeg winters he paid as much attention to feeding and cultivating his flickering fish as he devoted to his apple orchard in the summer. His wife, my aunt Edith, was always silent, always bitter, perhaps because she never had a voice in the design and furnishing of his house and garden. Lord Rex delighted in Chinese jade objects and Hong Kong–airport lacquered chinoiserie, exquisite to my eye at the time, as well as in a vast accumulation of Asian carpets of dubious vintage. One wall of his living room was devoted to a gigantic mural of himself—in the style of Ferdinand de Lesseps building the Suez Canal (Uncle Rex was in the construction business). He stood ten feet higher than his construction site, a rolled blueprint in his hand. Uncle Rex had an overblown ego like most rich men who have passed through my life. But he was the first. Although Rex was small time, in a small town, he had flair. His manner was the same as a Donald Trump or a Walter Annenberg—men who love to have their surroundings reflect their egocentricities. Uncle Rex also had a mania for driftwood lamps and tables, several of which he tried to fob off on my mother as wedding presents for me and Allan, my future husband. She dissented and settled for an oriental carpet.

Uncle Rex's garden was not, even then, to my taste. He never grew perennials like delphiniums, and like most Winnipeggers, he stuck to the safe annuals. His display of annuals—a jumble-jamble of snapdragons, marigolds, petunias, bachelor buttons, coleus, dahlias and zinnias—reflected a lack of any colour sense and design. Even I could detect this. His house did not appeal to me either. Although it was, as my mother pointed out, easier to clean than the old Victorian and Edwardian mansions that lined Wellington Crescent and the neighbouring streets of the South End (where I didn't belong), I knew that I would rather live in one of those grand old houses than in the sprawling flat-top California-style ranch-house that I doubted belonged on the street. "Don't be so critical," my father would say, as he drove us on our Sunday afternoon excursions through the neighbour-hoods where the rich people lived.

I loved Leonard, the milkman's son—handsome, shy and intensely interested in politics. I wished he was more intensely interested in me. Daddy allowed me to go out with Leonard but disapproved of his father's occupation—Leonard's dad was a Jewish milkman. It goes without saying I had to marry some-one Jewish. But my father had his own social caste among Jewry, and Leonard's father didn't make the grade because of his occupation. There were many working-class Jews in Winnipeg at the time and my father considered himself a member of the professional class.

In the schools I went to in the North End, about half the classes were Jewish. About two-thirds of the Jewish children came from families where the father was a shopkeeper, busi-nessman, lawyer, doctor, dentist or accountant. The parents of the rest of the Jewish kids were working class. The general ethos among the Jewish families was that the children had to do better than the parents. One day a teacher asked the children what they wanted to be when they grew up. One Jewish girl stood up and said, "I want to be a presser." The teacher, startled, said, "What do you mean, a presser? What's a presser?" "You know," the girl replied, "like my father and mother. They press clothes and I want to be like them." (There was a very large garment industry in Winnipeg at the time.) The Jewish kids in the class were silent. Why did she not want to better herself? I knew that my milkman's son wanted to become an economist. He never talked about delivering milk. With the presser's daughter very much in mind, I made sure that my father knew that my milkman's son would be no milkman. It made no difference. My father didn't want a milkman, father or son, in the family.

Among the Jews who immigrated to Winnipeg, my father put German Jews at the top, because they were the most educated, but he disliked them because they had no sense of humour and were too assimilated, like the Czech and some Hungarian Jews. Russian Jews, like himself, were best, especially if they came from Lithuania, where many of the Hebrew scholars belonged to an older tradition that despised Chassidim. My father thought the Chassidim were devoid of rational thought, far too emotional, and sang and danced "like crazy people." Daddy regarded Polish Jews as vulgar (all the girls had thick ankles), but the worst were the Romanian Jews who were thieves and murderers. Their women, however, knew how to cook. Daddy had struggled hard to reach his social status and he certainly didn't want his daughter to slip four notches down the ladder to marry a milkman's son. "His father is Russian," I told my mother, but she just said that Leonard was too young for marriage.

My father was born in Russia and described himself as a Kerenskyite. He told me that Kerensky was a democratic-liberal politician, "Canadian-style, not Russian-style." "How come he didn't win?" I asked. "People like that get nowhere in Russia," he said. Daddy came to Winnipeg in 1917 to escape from the Communists: "Hooligans, all of them, hooligans." The Tsar wasn't a particular favourite either because of the pogroms. I think the Tsar wanted him to join the army to shoot the Communists—but as he understood it, this was a twenty-year contract. Why did he choose Winnipeg? Because as with most immigrants, he emigrated to a place where he had relatives. But in time he came to regard Winnipeg as a latter-day Athens. In my father's eyes, Winnipeg was the cultural capital of the world.

I had a happy childhood except for two things. I had trouble passing exams and I had refused to speak directly to my father since I was four years old. I would only relent if my mother begged me to "have a little conversation with Daddy, because he feels hurt." I loved my mother, and never wanted to leave her or her house. It was her house because she picked out all the furnishings, and to me it was the best house in the world. If only some television person would come into our home and live with us, he or she would show everyone that we were the ideal family, not only in Canada but in the United States too.

My father loved me deeply, I knew that, but he spoke with an accent and tended to become overwrought about trifles—a trait I unfortunately inherited from him. The man never lifted a finger to me, barely ever drank, but he had such an awkward way about him when he had to deal with people. It's funny how you can become a snob at the age of four. My mother, who was born in Winnipeg, spoke without an accent and possessed that rarity, true charm. She was pretty, warm-hearted and had a wicked sense of humour. Her sense of duty, sadly, always over-rode her devilish streak. Some of my aunts called her Fanny the Martyr because of my father.

"Why did she marry your father?" her sisters would moan. "Dave plucked the finest flower in the field. Why Dave, of all men?" Nobody really liked my father except my mother. He was a good honest man, and he supported his mother-in-law and even her youngest sister before she married. He needed my mother to organize his life (except for his work) and to be his emotional interpreter to the world. And she needed to be needed. My father was not a mild man—he was bossy and sarcastic to everyone, especially my mother. But she never minded. She knew that he was blind and deaf without her.

Back to the house I loved. Two storeys, turn-of-the-century in North Winnipeg, imitation Chippendale furniture and other Eaton's furnishings, and a piano. When the husband of a couple who were my parents' best friends committed suicide, my mother bought their bedroom swag-curtains and their bedspread for my very own bedroom. They had been a little more flush than my parents, and the reason Sam committed suicide, according to my father, was that he got into debt because he was "too sure of his buyers." (Sam had a pricey line of ladies dresses that he sold to the top shops.) My father never lived beyond his means. Sam had bought a bigger house on the river. Daddy looked down on salesmen—unless they were really successful. "I would never stand behind a shop counter," he said. "I was supposed to go to University in Vienna before the revolution." My father considered himself an intellectual but I never caught him reading books. Occasionally, my mother would read out loud to him selections from the book being studied by her Bible club, lively books such as *Joseph and His Brethern* by Thomas Mann. These readings to my father would last about five minutes because he had had a hard day at the malting plant where he was superintendent and needed his early evening snooze. When he came to Winnipeg at the age of eighteen, he supported himself and his sister as an agricultural worker in Manitoba, stooking wheat and working on dairy farms. Then he saved money and went to the agricultural school (a leading centre of learning in the province at the time), and instead of farming became an agricultural chemist. He even developed some kind of barley during the thirties that withstood the Manitoba winters. My mother displayed the provincial plaque he received in honour of his discovery until her death. The barley, of course, had long been surpassed.

I loved dogs. My parents would buy them for me but none ever survived for long. They became my second lesson in deception.

I liked Duke, our English setter who was a large dog. My mother sold a lot of war bonds during the forties and the *Winnipeg Free Press* wanted to take a picture of her. Modest beyond the realms of reason, she suggested instead that they take a picture of me hugging Duke. Shortly afterwards, Duke disappeared. My parents told me that dogs didn't have rationing cards and Duke ate a pound of meat daily. "Don't worry," Mummy said, "Daddy found a nice farmer near the plant where he works, who has lots of meat. Duke will come back to us after the war." Of course, Duke never showed up.

I complained continually, so they bought Timmy, who was pretty smart for a cocker spaniel. One day Timmy was chewing on a bone on someone else's lawn where we were all playing. One of the younger kids, stupider than Timmy, tried to take the bone away from him. I knew that you're never supposed to take a bone away from a dog. Timmy snapped at this rotten spoiled rich kid, and broke his skin, without drawing any blood. That was enough for the kid's parents and my parents. Timmy had turned into a werewolf in my parents' eyes and was promptly put down. I knew it wasn't Timmy's fault and I became

Timmy's defence lawyer, to no avail. But dogs that snap at rich kids even for a good reason had no place in my father's world. That was the first time I learned that life wasn't fair.

The second time I learned this lesson was when the same thing happened again. Trixie, the new cocker spaniel, was also chewing on a bone while we played baseball in a corner lot. Another rich kid (my father classified everyone as either richer or poorer than he and he judged them accordingly) tried to take Trixie's marrowbone, which my mother had given her. Even though Trixie was a female and should therefore have been a calmer dog according to my father, she growled and bit the kid on the lip—he ran off crying and told his parents. Trixie went the same way as Tim.

Finally, my parents bought me a Scottie named Sport who loved to chase the horses drawing the Eaton's vans that would drive up to our house from time to time to make a grand delivery of a pound of coffee. The dog ran after the van, my grandmother ran after the dog shouting "Sport, Sport, come back" and I ran after my grandmother. Sport, a bad-tempered Scotch terrier, never listened. We saw him fly high in the air, turning cartwheels after the horse kicked him. He landed on his head and lay stone-dead on the street when my grandmother and I reached him. "Enough dogs," my grandmother told my father. "I refuse to remove any more corpses." For the first time I remember, he nodded in agreement with his mother-in-law.

A year after Sport's demise, when I was eighteen, I found myself in Oxford, a married woman. It wasn't to Leonard, the milkman's son, because he was too poor to marry. I married Allan, son of the owner of a Portage Avenue radio and auto-supply store and a strong-willed mother active in the cause of Zionism. Allan was an Oxford don, I was a high school gradu-ate, and neither of us was in love with the other. Allan's mother wanted him to marry a potential Hadassah girl from Winnipeg and I wanted to leave home because I couldn't live in the same house as my father anymore. Also, I didn't want to write my first-year university exams.

When we got engaged we had known each other for only ten days. Three months later, Allan returned a week before the wedding for a sit-down dinner with five hundred people he didn't know. We barely recognized each other. When I complained to my Aunt Anne before Allan arrived for the wedding that I shouldn't marry him because I couldn't remember what he looked like, let alone love him, she answered airily that my Uncle Manuel (her husband) had been away five years during the war and although she already had a child with him, she couldn't remember what he looked like either. "So don't worry," she said with a laugh, "as long as he shows up for the wedding."

Little did I know that this life—with its Rex Winograds, Aunt Zoras, untouchable Russian butter cakes, dead dogs and bright Manitoba annuals—would soon be over for me forever. I was sure that after a year at Oxford with Allan, I would get back to my old life again in Winnipeg. I would live in a different house from my father but never separated from my beloved mother. I would visit Uncle Rex in his aquarium room, go to Clear Lake in the summer where I first saw delphiniums, attend my mother's tea parties, gossip with my bridesmaids and other girlfriends, cleverly avoid university because I was a married woman, and live with the strange man I'd married who would be assisting his father selling radios and auto parts.

I never lived in Winnipeg again.

It was only when I was in my mid-thirties in Ottawa and trying to write a memoir about my growing up and marriage in Winnipeg, that several of my friends asked me why I married so young to a man I didn't love. So I turned the book into autobiographical "fiction" and explained how it all happened. For the reader who might inexplicably want to know more, it's in the book, which some people thought funny—including the jurors of the Leacock Prize. It's called *True Confections*. I am still married to the strange man I wrote about in that book, and as I write, forty-seven years have elapsed since that hideously cold evening late in December when we married.

Today, forty-seven years after I left, Winnipeg to me is not a real place but a cemetery, an infinite source of memories and an unwritten book of rules, values and prejudices that I cling to, for better or worse.

2

Honeymoon Blues

M Y FIRST INTRODUCTION TO FOOD outside my native Winnipeg occurred on the second day of my honeymoon. I insisted on getting out of Winnipeg the very night of our wedding. The idea of spending the first night of my marriage in Winnipeg (needless to say, I was a virgin) horrified me. I could see my parents, my brother and his friends watching me doing it (whatever it was) in the honeymoon suite of the glorious Royal Alexandra Hotel (long since destroyed). Allan was very excited about our honeymoon because (a) his father was paying for first-class passage on the finest ship sailing the South Atlantic and the Mediterranean, the *Christoforo Colombo*, flagship of the Italian Line, (b) his father had also paid for a room at the Waldorf Astoria

Hotel in New York, from where the ship was sailing, (c) he was going to see his beloved cousin Ron in New York, and (d) as a wedding present, Ron and his wife were taking us to the most famous restaurant in Manhattan (or so they said). None of these things would have happened to Allan if he hadn't married me.

We arrived in New York in the middle of the night and checked into the Waldorf Astoria. My father-in-law had reserved the smallest room in the hotel. It was even smaller than my bedroom in my home on Machray Avenue. Allan was horrified, but I didn't care. I was too exhausted. My mother had bought me a honeymoon special, a pink negligee and nightgown that I duly put on, locking myself in the bathroom—and then crawling into bed, barely alive. Then Allan went into the bathroom, locked the door and came out in what he said were new pyjamas. He instantly fell on top of me and tried to do something between my legs. I said, "What are you doing?" "It's our honeymoon," he replied. "We're making love." I pushed him and told him to get off. He complied and fell asleep.

The wedding night didn't seem to please Allan but he was looking forward keenly to seeing his beloved cousin and going to Mama Leone's restaurant. Although I began to weep nonstop, I was also intrigued about eating in the famous New York establishment. Unfortunately for Allan, the tears never stopped. "After Mama Leone's," I said, "I don't think I'll go to the boat. I want to go back to Winnipeg." Allan asked, "Would you like to make a long-distance call to your mother?" In those days long-distance calls cost a lot of money and I thought it was a damn decent thing for him to offer.

I got hold of my mother on the phone. She wasn't crying like me but was in a high-anxiety mood because her sisters and friends told her right after the wedding that she had let her daughter marry too young.

My father didn't agree. "What do Dolly, Annie and Zora know?" I'm not sure whether he said that because we couldn't live in the same house anymore or whether he really did believe, as he always said, that "when you marry a daughter, a hump is off your back." He certainly didn't want me home again. He spent more money on the wedding than at any time in his life, except for the house he bought before I was born. I told my mother on the telephone from my Waldorf Astoria hotel room, with Allan listening in, that I was deeply unhappy and wanted to come back. Just what she wanted to hear. Urged on by my father, whom I could hear breathing on the other line, she said, "Give it a try dear, and I promise if you really want to come home, you can. We will always love you." She spoke to Allan, who said, "She'll sort herself out." I knew it would be pretty hard for me to take a rowboat and disembark from the *Christoforo Colombo*, which was to sail early the next morning. "You can fly back from Sicily after the voyage," my mother said. "Your father-in-law spent all that money on the boat. You might as well take advantage of it. That would be the most sensible thing to do."

After the telephone call, weeping uncontrollably, I carefully put on my new rose-coloured tweed suit with a gored skirt and round leather buttons on the jacket. It was the nicest suit I have ever owned—to this day. Allan cheered me up. "Your mother really picked out a beautiful suit. It looks like it comes from Harrods, not Eaton's." He hadn't been crazy about my wedding gown (even though, years later, both my daughters wore it at their weddings—without the crinoline).

Despite my tears and regrets about marriage, I was anxious to meet Allan's cousin. He was, my husband said, a writer for *Reader's Digest*. But more important, I had to go to Mama Leone's, which his cousin, who knew everything, told him was the finest Italian restaurant in New York. To that date my sole experience with Italian restaurants had been with a Northern Italian establishment in Winnipeg whose owner was indeed Italian and married to a local Ukrainian lady. Unfortunately, one never knew if the restaurant was open or closed because the owner did not fully understand that in Manitoba restaurants could not serve wine, even with meals. Occasionally, when a good customer came in, he would open up a bottle of his own Chianti and soon after the RCMP would close him down for a while. The restaurant was, in fact, more closed than open, notwithstanding the sympathy of his customers. Even I knew that his food was far more sophisticated than the spaghetti and meatballs widely available in Winnipeg. The restaurant had shown me that there was something better in Italian food than I normally ate. Now I was ready for the best of the best. We were to meet Cousin Ron and the wife for drinks before dinner in his Manhattan apartment.

All I knew of Manhattan was what I saw in the movies. Fred Astaire, Betty Grable and Esther Williams lived in two-storey apartments with grand stairways and marble entrances and bedrooms bigger than my parents' house. I was ready for glamour. For some reason Ron and his wife, who had set out some hors d'oeuvres—cheese balls, I noted with disappointment—lived in quarters smaller than the house in which I grew up. What kind of salary does *Reader's Digest* pay its writers? I wondered. While I sobbed throughout the cocktail hour, sipping my first martini, Allan, who at this period drank only German hock, complained to Ron about the dinginess of his room at the Waldorf. But my spirits picked up when we arrived at Mama Leone's.

Not only did we receive an extraordinarily warm reception from the waiter (Ron had tipped off the restaurant that we were a honeymoon couple), the restaurant even put a pound or so slab of Parmesan on our table. "This comes free," Ron said, "and so do the peppers, olives and bread." I was deeply impressed. My non-stop crying was interrupted when I picked up the menu. It was huge, bigger than any I had seen in my life. While Allan and Ron were deep in conversation, I dared to ask the waiter on my own what I should have to eat. He replied, "The bay scallops—they are wonderful." I had never eaten scallops in Winnipeg, let alone bay scallops, but I decided that the waiter was right. When I announced my selection to Allan and Ron, they told me about the thousand other things I should have ordered but I wouldn't listen. Allan, by this time, was getting on my nerves. He seemed far more interested in catching up in gossip with his beloved cousin than he was in his sobbing bride.

Allan ignored Ron's wife. Why, I don't know. Maybe he'd been influenced by his father. "Not a looker" my father-in-law told him, "not a looker." My father's test of a desirable woman was whether she was a good cook. For my father-in-law, there was also only one test: she had to be good-looking.

Mama Leone's was famous for its colossal portions, and Cousin Ron and his wife, people of girth, saw no reason to warn me about this. All sixty of the bay scallops on my plate looked and tasted delicious. Even Allan shifted his attention from Ron long enough to spear a number of scallops off my plate. But my destiny overwhelmed me. Bay scallops could only assuage my grief briefly. How many bay scallops could I eat? I burst into tears again and ran to the ladies room, bolting through a vast array of statues of naked woman, grottos, waterfalls and fountains in an endless series of rooms in what must also have been New York's largest restaurant. Ron's wife, older than me by some years and feeling responsible, decided she should join me in the ladies room to find out what was wrong with me.

"Things will get better," she yelled to me in my toilet booth, and then she left me alone. Much later, Ron told me he and his wife thought our marriage would end before the boat sailed and they were wasting their money taking us to Mama Leone's for a honeymoon dinner.

The next morning we sailed on the *Christoforo Colombo*.

3

Crying over the Noodles

NOT ONLY WAS I A VIRGIN, the only thing I knew about sex was in a little book my mother had given me when I became engaged. It was very basic. I learned that the man's penis had to be inserted into the woman's vagina in order to have babies. The book also had another nugget of information. It said this process could be painful for a woman because we were virgins and it was a good idea to ask a gynecologist to spend some time stretching the labia or something else in there to enlarge the passage to prevent a painful penetration by the husband. Well, I certainly didn't want pain.

Someone in my mother's bridge club had recommended the book to her and I don't thing she read it all the way through.

She dropped the book into my lap and told me that she had made an appointment for me with a gynecologist, who would fit me with a "pessary." When I asked her what that was she explained it was a round rubber disk that would keep me from having a baby too soon. "You have to be measured for it by a gynecologist." This made sense to me. I was measured for my wedding dress and I certainly didn't want to have any babies. Babies always bored me; I never played with baby dolls when I was little.

Unfortunately, mother was unaware that the doctor, recommended to her by her sister Dolly, was a strong Catholic and did not believe in birth control.

After my first gynecological examination, the doctor told me I was fit and fertile. "Can you fit me for a pessary?" I asked. At first he didn't understand and then he said, "You mean a diaphragm." He lied, and said it was impossible to fit a virgin with a diaphragm. "Oh, no," I said, thinking what I had read in the book, "can't you stretch me with your finger until a diaphragm could be fitted?" He looked horrified and embarrassed, and sent me packing with a curt no. What did I say that was so upsetting? I was just repeating what it said in the book. At first, when I learned he was a Catholic, I thought it was his religious sensibilities. Now, of course, I realize if he specialized in hand stretching virgin labias he might be stricken off the medical record.

When we boarded the *Christoforo Colombo*, Allan, who had crossed the Atlantic tourist class many times back and forth to Oxford, was dazzled by our first-class quarters. I was not as impressed as he was. After all, I had my standards set by the Hollywood movies I had seen in Winnipeg. They featured luxurious ocean liners with Xavier Cougat and his fifty-piece orchestra, Esther Williams in a hundred-foot swimming pool surrounded by beautiful aqua girls, and never-ending decks and lounges filled with rich and famous people who were always friendly. So, in fact, I was rather disappointed. The orchestra and the pool lacked Hollywood dimensions and even though the people dressed for dinner, they didn't fall all over Allan and me. It just wasn't the same as portrayed by MGM. The more my husband exulted over the luxurious appointments of the ship, the more irritable I became.

The waiters and the maid service helped change my mind. Since we were going to spend at least a year at Oxford immediately after our honeymoon, we were accompanied by a dozen pieces of luggage, six of which were unpacked by the cabin maid. My same honeymoon nightgown and negligee were laid out on the bed with the waist carefully pinched, ready for my deflowering (which did not take place on the ship).

Even I was impressed by the food and the service in the first-class dining room. I wore a pink peau de soie dress with petticoats that came down to my shins, and every time I leaned over to fork up some fettuccine Alfredo (prepared at the table by the maître d'hotel, and the best I ever tasted), my napkin slithered off my lap and onto the floor. The handsome Italian waiters vied to pick it up, no matter how many times I dropped it. Every night we ate the same thing—first course, beluga malassol caviar; second course, fettuccine Alfredo with homemade noodles covered with cream and butter and freshly shaven Parmesan cheese; third course, tournedos Rossini with wine sauce, real black truffles and foie gras; and some evenings, soufflé made to order by the chef. This was the era of tableside flambé. We had noodles tossed over a flame at the table and tournedos brought to us sizzling in copper pots. Dessert, if not a soufflé, would be one of my other new-found favourites, crêpes Suzette à la Grand Marnier, tossed in butter at the table by a more senior and less cute waiter. And for the first time in my life I tasted baked Alaska and cherries jubilee, also prepared tableside. I concluded that any food prepared in the kitchen was pas chic.

Flambé and burners were not particularly popular in North Winnipeg and my mother and I did not know what to do with the three identical brass fondue pots and burners that I had received as wedding presents. Mother knew they would not be used in Winnipeg and promptly shipped them to Oxford in case we needed what she must have considered formal dining equipment fit for an Oxford don's table.

We were the only honeymoon couple on board ship. Everyone else seemed to me to be over eighty, so unlike in the Hollywood films about shipboard romances. I didn't mind because the waiters adored me. One of them even told me that I was the most beautiful woman aboard the ship, something I had yet to hear from my husband. When I would say shyly, every time an Italian hunk would dash to pick up my napkin, "lovely noodles," Allan would laugh. "You've said that a hundred times, and they still keep coming."

My palette was improving, if my sex life wasn't. The first time I tasted caviar, I knew this was going to be one of my most favourite foods in life. However, my appetite for caviar could not compete with that of a solitary Brazilian lady at the next table. Named the Countess of Caviar by the passengers, she consumed only caviar at every meal, scooping it from a fourteen-ounce tin at the table. A small dark woman with a moustache, she was covered in diamonds and wore backless and sleeveless velvet gowns. I learned from one of the older guests who adopted us, a Mrs. Wix whose husband manufactured du Maurier cigarettes, that a woman over forty should never go backless and sleeveless or, she added, "travel alone aboard ships." Mr. Wix, a kind, florid, rotund sybarite, said nothing about the lady's bare back but was delighted to introduce me to my first and favourite alcoholic mixture—the champagne cocktail. He encouraged me in my affection for it. My husband was delighted because he didn't have to pay for the drinks. His daddy was not underwriting the bar bill.

I was still terribly homesick and something was happening to my husband, the nature of which I did not understand. The first few nights (before my projectile vomiting began), I felt something like a big stick when Allan snuggled up to me in bed. My mother's sex book did say that the penis was supposed to go into the vagina. But why did Allan's penis feel so uncomfortable? "What are you rubbing against me?" I asked. "It's me," he said. "It's an erection." I'd never heard that word before except for Meccano sets or constructing a building. But what did an erection have to do with a man's private parts? "If you get that down," I said, "you can go in."

He sounded stupefied. "I can't go in without an erection," he replied. "Why not?" I asked. "It's impossible to have intercourse without a man getting an erection in his penis," Allan explained. I hated the idea of pain. "It's going to hurt. Can't you go inside without being so stiff?" I asked in my most sophisticated, sarcastic manner.

"Sondra," he explained, "you can't have sex or babies without an erection." "It doesn't matter," I said. "I don't want to have a baby yet. We can have a nice marriage without sex." I was beginning to enjoy his company, although I didn't quite believe the erection theory. And my greatest fear was becoming pregnant.

Happily, the whole question of sex on the boat became moot. As we sailed into the Atlantic, the seas grew extraordinarily rough and my projectile vomiting began as I was sipping champagne cocktails in a bar. The voyage took twelve days. I was curled up seasick in my cabin for four days and when the sea calmed as we reached the Mediterranean, I started a long menstrual period. Sex on the ship may have happened for Doris Day, but it didn't happen for me. My husband, however, was not pleased with my comforting solution of a *mariage blanc*. "It's impossible," he said. I couldn't see why. All I wanted was a tourist guide. He had to be one of the most erudite tourist guides a girl who didn't care about sex could get.

4

The Mafia Ball

ON THE BOAT I BECAME VERY FOND of Italian waiters and ship officers because they paid so much attention to me. I began to be more enthusiastic about visiting Italy. Our plan was to go to Taormina for a week or so, arriving in time for New Year's Eve. We planned to spend only a day in Naples. Allan's father told him he had reserved a grand room for us—grander, Allan hoped, than our room at the Waldorf Astoria—at the Palazzo San Domenico Hotel in Taormina where anyone who was anybody visiting Sicily stayed, including Winston Churchill.

Allan could not stop talking about our good fortune. I wasn't looking forward very much to the grand hotel, or for that matter, to Taormina. I was looking forward to the fact that I was going to encounter a little bit of Winnipeg in Taormina where a couple we knew, who were now living in Oxford, were spending their Christmas vacation. An adored friend, popular Carol, my age, got married six months before me to Ronnie, whose father was said to be the richest man in Winnipeg. Although I envied Carol and Ronnie because of their style, sophistication and money, there was nothing more that I wanted in life at this time than to see familiar faces. The fact that our marriage had not been consummated was of no importance to me. I had already told Allan that since I didn't want any babies, I was perfectly satisfied with a *mariage blanc* (I knew what the phrase meant because I heard my mother whisper the words to her sister about a childless couple they knew). Allan's face became inexplicably dark when I mentioned the phrase.

We got off the boat at Naples with our dozen pieces of luggage and entered the customs shed. In the two hours we were in the building, Allan had problems with the overstaffed customs officials. The more there were of them, the more difficult it became for him to deal with them. They kept asking, why do you need a dozen pieces of luggage on your honeymoon? I, on the other hand, was treated like a princess. Some good-looking customs officers who spoke a little English took me aside and told me I would loathe Taormina—"very boring"—and that I should trust them to take us to the most wonderful New Year's parties in Naples, which was definitely the place to be.

No fool, I told them that I was married. "But," they said, "your husband can come too. We don't want to separate you from your husband. We are not like that. We are officers. We are not like the scum over there (pointing vaguely in the direction of the customs shed). We just want you to be happy in Naples. We know you, and of course, your husband, will have a much better time with us." I believed them and went over to Allan who was not having as wonderful a time with the customs officers as I was and I told him I had discovered some startling news. "The New Year's parties here in Naples," I announced, "are much better than the parties in Sicily." "How do you know?" he asked. "You've been here an hour." Pointing to my new group of friends, I replied, "They told me. They know. They are local and they promised to take us to the best Neapolitan parties." They were looking hopefully in our direction. Allan ignored them and me. "We're going to Taormina," he said, his teeth clenched, "if they will release all your bags." I began to cry. At that moment, I truly hated him and wished I had married an Italian customs official.

In the overnight train to Taormina, my menstruation finally stopped and our marriage was consummated. I told my husband, "If this is sex, it hurts like hell." "It won't hurt for long," he replied, turned over and went to sleep.

It was the day before New Year's and the sun was shining brilliantly when we arrived in Taormina. To my joy, Carol and Ronnie met us at the railway station. Carol eased my apprehension about the pain of sex and giggled openly in front of Allan and Ronnie about her own soreness. "It goes away and then you'll like it." Ronnie also put in a good word for sex. "You have to hit the G spot," he told Allan, who pretended he knew what he was talking about. More important, Ronnie and Carol bragged about the wonderful *pensione* that they had found. "The fettucine is delicious and the shrimps are caught by the local fisherman," they said. "You should stay at our place," Carol proposed. "I already asked," Ronnie said, "but it's full." Allan was disdainful. "We're staying at the San Domenico," he said, which he knew would impress Ronnie.

We arrived at the San Domenico with our grand pile of

luggage and with Ronnie and Carol in tow. I was in awe. I had never seen anything like it anywhere, not even in the movies— tall orange trees in pots, blooming shrubs and flowers I had never seen before, grottos and fountains scattered through the patios, arches, arcades and corridors—all part of a huge and sprawling former monastery—and great cascading gardens running down to the Mediterranean. I had had the same sensation when I saw my first delphiniums in Clear Lake, Manitoba. The flowers and trees were blooming on December 31, I noted with astonishment—something beyond my Winnipeg imagination. It was the Garden of Eden and I thought I was in paradise. But, like Adam and Eve, we were in the process of being banished. I could hear Allan protesting to the receptionist, "My father sent a letter of reservations six weeks ago." "Indeed he did," the receptionist said icily, "I have the letter before me. Unfortunately, it arrived only today and we are fully booked. This is New Year's Eve and all Sicily comes to the San Domenico." Allan looked at the letter and envelope. His father's secretary had sent it bearing a sea-mail stamp. She had been with my father-in-law for twenty-five years and was always careful about his pennies. There we were, standing in the middle of paradise, with a dozen pieces of luggage and no place to go. I started to cry. "You should have listened to the customs officer and stayed in Naples," I said. "They knew all the best places."

Seeing me cry (my new specialty), the receptionist took pity and offered to telephone around for a room. We did end up in an ordinary but adequate hotel on a dark little street in Taormina, with no flowers, no blooming trees or gardens. The price, Allan noted, was the same as at the San Domenico. Before leaving the San Domenico, the receptionist apologized again. "Everything is totally sold out," he explained to Allan once more, "but the four of you should come here to celebrate at the New Year's Eve Grand Ball. There are no tickets available, of course, but because of the unhappy circumstances and being on your honeymoon, we will find a place for you and for your friends. Of course, it is very expensive." The four of us were thrilled and agreed to pay the enormous sum required for our tickets.

Although the ball was formal—white or black tie—and although both Carol and I had our fanciest dresses with us, we both decided for some inexplicable reason, and after a three-hour discussion about what to wear, not to put on our formal dresses. I had with me a pale-blue lace concoction with a satin bow in the back. I thought it might look a bit showy. Carol actually had an ermine stole with her that her father-in-law had given her, along with a beautiful black long dress that Ronnie had bought her in London. We had never worn long dresses in Winnipeg and Carol had not yet worn hers anywhere. She was keen to wear the long dress and the ermine wrap but I put my foot down. "Too showy," I declared. "They won't be that dressed up. It's only a hotel. We'll just wear our short cocktail dresses and even then," I said with my great knowledge of the world, "we will be overdressed." Carol looked dubious, but I always felt that Carol overdressed for the occasion in any case.

At the New Year's bash, Carol wanted to kill me, which was okay because I felt suicidal. The women were all in long dresses, the elegance of which I had only seen in the movies. They were covered with jewels and many wore ermine stoles, which made Carol grind her teeth. Too many jewels I reassured Carol. There was also something strange about the men. Notwithstanding the white ties, they were a rough-looking lot, often huddled together and leaving the women alone. Allan and Ronnie were furious at us for not wearing our formal clothes.

They wanted to show us off. After all, we were eighteen and pretty good-looking girls. For some reason, I selected a brown-coloured suit. "Twelve suitcases," Allan muttered, "and you look like you're wearing your best Salvation Army outfit." The evening was not a success. All of the five hundred Italians were having a marvellous party but we weren't part of it. I refused to go into the crowd and dance because I felt so dowdy.

Some years later we were talking to an Italian diplomatic colleague of Allan's about our experience at the San Domenico New Year's Ball. He asked incredulously, "They let you in? Were there any guns?" "Guns, why guns?" I asked. "That's the famous Mafia ball," he replied. "All the boys from Palermo and Catania meet at the ball. If you're not well connected to them, you are not welcome. It's for the family. You didn't know?"

A few days after the New Year's Eve Ball, we checked out of our dismal quarters and left for Rome, hoping for better things. Unfortunately, once in Rome I fell very ill, with what I did not know. I had to run to the bathroom every fifteen minutes since my bladder hurt like hell. This must be the sign of the pregnancy I so much dreaded. We were having too much sex.

Nevertheless, the four of us on our honeymoons kept our schedule and went on to Paris. Allan, realizing after two weeks of marriage that he could stop my tears by promising something new and delicious to eat, had made reservations for us at the grand three-star-Michelin-rated restaurant in Paris, Laperouse. His Oxford gourmand friends said it was the greatest restaurant in France. He was still totally on his father's ticket and seemed to be indifferent to the cost of French grande cuisine. He knew that Sunday lunch was the best time to feed in France and so he reserved for the four of us.

Laperouse was famous not only for its food but also for its small rooms off the main ones, where men and their mistresses could dine discreetly behind closed doors on which the waiters always knocked before opening. Since the maître d'hotel considered, correctly, that the four Winnipeggers were not quite ready for that type of thing, he led us through a series of interlocking rooms to the centre of the restaurant where he seated us. Fresh young girls were, no doubt, always given prominent tables in Laperouse, no matter were they came from, so they could be seen from all sides.

Of course, as soon as we sat down I had to go to the bathroom and, of course, Carol had to accompany me, in the manner of teenage girls. I whispered to Allan to ask directions to the ladies room, being too shy to inquire myself and speaking no French. Allan stopped a passing waiter. *"Pardonnez-moi, monsieur, où est le W.C. pour les dames?"* The waiter gave a huge grin and said at the top of his voice, flinging his arm in the direction of the next room, *"La toilette."* Carol and I cringed but got up and walked in the direction signalled by his thrusting arm. The call *"la toilette"* was repeated thunderously by strategically placed waiters as we walked through each room—and there were many rooms—as if Marie Antoinette and her lady-in-waiting were promenading through the restaurant. All the diners and waiters were smiling, if not smirking, as we continued our procession, blushing very deeply. Our husbands were hugely amused. Once we completed our interminable journey to the unisex toilette, I couldn't relieve myself because (a) there was a man in the booth, (b) there was a female attendant eating a hot meal and waiting for money and I didn't have any, and (c) I couldn't pee anyway because of my strange malady. We left immediately and were ushered by the waiters with great ceremony back to our table and still-laughing patrons and husbands.

By this time we had scrutinized the menu, which contained

many dishes unknown to me and about which I was too reticent to ask. There were items like *oeufs en meurette, chartreuse de pigeons, boeuf en daube,* and *andouillettes*. There was only one phrase on the menu I could understand, *poulet au curry,* and I noticed that it had the least amount of francs beside it. I had already begun to argue with Allan about his overspending and I was terrified the restaurant would bankrupt us. I knew it didn't matter what Ronnie and Carol spent because Ronnie's father was the richest man in Winnipeg and I knew that Allan's father wasn't. So there I was in the greatest restaurant in France and ordered the least desirable and cheapest thing on the menu.

Allan, Ronnie and Carol were horrified by my willful austerity and tried but could not talk me out of my choice. Even the waiter said in English, "It's not good enough for you, Madame. This is not a specialty—order one of our specialties." Suspicious, I just thought he wanted the tourists to spend more money. While Allan, Ronnie and Carol gasped in delight over their rich and refined three courses, I was stuck with a curry that I thought was not up to the standards of Mrs. Margolis, who was famous for her chicken curry in Winnipeg. Allan handed me a spoonful of his first dish—*oeufs en meurette*, and I knew at that moment that I would never again follow my mother's instructions and order the cheapest thing on the menu, as she had told me to do when on a date. When I tasted them, I knew that those poached eggs cooked in wine sauce were the best thing I had tasted in life, better than anything that even my mother made.

I was bitterly angry with myself and even angrier with Allan. I told him he should trade his *oeufs en meurette* for my chicken curry and he refused. "You could have ordered it," he said. "But you have three courses and I only have one," I responded. "That is not my fault," he said. "It was your decision." "I was saving you money," I exclaimed. "I didn't ask you to save me money," he replied. I felt that I was being punished for my virtues and I swore never to be good in a good French restaurant again. I shed, at this time, a large part of my North Winnipeg morality.

Allan had made arrangements to have lunch the next day with a friend of an Oxford friend at a country restaurant just outside Paris. The Oxford pal turned out to be round and chubby and a very intellectual Texan rare books dealer who, as I discovered years later, was a good friend of Larry McMurtry of *Lonesome Dove* fame.

Not long before our lunch outside Paris that day, Allan's friend had picked up a stray dog and, being an animal lover, brought it into the inn where we were going to eat. Allan strenuously objected to the dog being in the restaurant. He made a scene. "You shouldn't do that," he said. "You can't bring a dog into a restaurant. It's not allowed." This was the first time since our marriage I realized that my husband could be truly wrong. I had already noticed that in France dogs eat when, where and what the humans eat—served to them by waiters with good grace. I loved dogs and didn't mind eating with them in a restaurant. After all, we were in a country inn. I thought it was delightful that Allan's friend was having his stray dog lapping up *potage aux légumes*. Allan refused to sit at the same table as the bookseller and his dog. He ceremoniously marched off to another table with me in tow. It was only fifteen years later in Ottawa when we bought a dog of our own, Hector the Protector, that Allan conceded that my attitude towards dogs was at that early time in our marriage more sophisticated than his own.

What happened to me on my honeymoon was, to my astonishment, recounted to me by Larry McMurtry thirty years later in Washington, when Allan was Canadian ambassador to the United States. Larry McMurtry said he was keen to meet me because our mutual acquaintance, the Texan bookseller, had told him that Allan had a gorgeous child-bride from Winnipeg and that he was jealous and madly protective of her. This astonished me. There was no animal at all in McMurtry's story, except for Allan who, the Texan had told him, was "behaving like an alpha dog, beating off all others coming near his female favourite." Whatever looks I had at the time of my honeymoon had vanished. I was well aware that I must have been a big disappointment to Larry McMurtry who talked a lot about the beauty and insecurity of his then girlfriend, Cybil Shepherd. "Great beauties are all terribly insecure," he said.

I felt insecure because I was now a matronly ambassadress who wished she could transform herself back into what she had been and didn't know it. "You surprise me," I told Larry McMurtry. "Your friend never even attempted to flirt or make a pass at me." McMurtry paid me no compliments but gave one to Allan. As a hobby, McMurtry ran a rare bookstore in Georgetown (he still does). "In the long years I have owned this bookshop," he said, "your husband was the only ambassador in Washington ever to visit it."

5
—

The Sleeping Princess

A S FAR AS I WAS CONCERNED, our honeymoon voyage across
the Atlantic to Italy and France was an unsettling, strange
and painful experience. The pain in my bladder was getting
worse and was particularly disturbing because of my conviction
that it was a sign of pregnancy. Fortunately, Allan got an
appointment for me the day after we arrived in England with a
doctor at the Radcliffe Infirmary. The doctor examined me,
told me he thought I was allergic to rubber contraceptives
(which proved to be correct) and that I had "honeymoon cystitis." "You have to be fitted with a diaphragm," he said. "Are you
sure I'm not pregnant?" I asked. He was a nice, easygoing
doctor, and he burst out laughing. "Pregnant?" "What a silly

goose you are," he said. He asked me why I had not used a diaphragm from the beginning of our marriage. I told him about my doctor in Winnipeg and what he had said. "I know him," the doctor declared. "We were at medical school together. He's a barking-mad Catholic. Of course, he wouldn't fit you with a diaphragm." I felt the first sense of relief and happiness since my marriage.

Allan had rented a flat in Oriel Square in the centre of Oxford and we settled in that day. It was a small place owned by a respected German Jewish professor and his wife, a philosopher. They greeted us warmly and then led us through each room taking an inventory of the contents. What did they mean by inventory? They mentioned a lot of Oxford names, told us their closest friends were Enid Starkie and Iris Murdoch, and warned me not to break anything . . . and that, after some months absence from Oxford, they would be returning and living nearby. The implication was that they would be keeping a close eye on us. When I thought of this couple being friends of Iris Murdoch, whose fame had reached even as far as Winnipeg, my image of Oxford got its first spot of tarnish.

After the intimidating professor and his wife left, Allan broke the news that we were invited to dine that night with the Warden of Wadham, just the three of us, in his lodgings at the college. Allan had talked so much about Sir Maurice Bowra, his brilliant wit, vast knowledge of the ancient world and poetry, his conversational prowess and sophistication, that I was nauseated with anxiety. Bowra was a friend of Evelyn Waugh, Angus Wilson, Isaiah Berlin, Cyril Connelly and all of Bloomsbury. There was no one in literary or scholarly England who was not part of Bowra's circle. Even I had read about him in Virginia Woolf's diaries. I felt incipient projectile vomiting coming on, as if I were back on board the *Christoforo Colombo*. The only poets I had ever studied in any depth at school in Winnipeg were William Butler Yeats and Thomas Hardy. What was I going to talk to him about?

Maurice Bowra was extremely fond of good food and Allan had told me that under his stewardship, Wadham's high table, where the dons (but not their wives) ate, was recognized to be the best in Oxford. Of course, the chef prepared even better food for the Warden when he dined at the lodge. We began with a soufflé made of sweetbreads, followed by gamey partridge (the first time in my life I tasted a wild bird) with puff potatoes, then meringue filled with coffee mousse and covered with heavy English cream, and finally a savoury—Wadham's specialty, green butter. I was warned by Allan not to be taken aback by the savoury. It might be angels on horseback (grilled oysters wrapped in bacon), sardines, scrambled eggs on toast or any number of other tidbits that in North America or elsewhere would normally be served, if served at all, at the beginning of the meal or for breakfast. Green butter was the delicious end to our meal. The chef mashed butter with chives, parsley, perhaps spinach and definitely anchovies. Mounds were served on buttered toast and washed down with Sauternes. There was no port and no nuts at our dinner with the Warden. This is because I was the only woman present and Sir Maurice would have thought it impolite to ask the sole female to withdraw while the men cracked their nuts, and he wisely understood that a girl from Winnipeg would not know enough to withdraw on her own. I drank more that night than I had in all my life.

For some reason, Maurice Bowra begun to reminisce about Yeats, whom he had known. He had even known Maud Gonne, with whom Yeats had been madly in love. My husband, the legal scholar, knew little of Yeats and had never heard of Maud Gonne. I, however, had spent a month or so in my half-year at university reading Yeats, his biography and poetry, and I knew about Maud Gonne. I begged Sir Maurice to tell more and more stories about Yeats and Maud, adding the three anecdotes I had read about her. He was too polite to let me know if they were well-worn chestnuts. Sir Maurice, one of the greatest, if not the greatest, non-stop talkers of his generation, actually believed that he had a knowledgeable listener, and let the word spread throughout the college that Allan had married well. Invitations to dinners from Oxford dons and their wives soon poured in. Sir Maurice had a kind heart and great sympathy for the young, even from the colonies. For my part, I was stunned by Sir Maurice that evening, by the food and especially by the wine, and promptly went to sleep for forty-eight hours.

I was not used to the cold in our unheated flat and I took to sleeping from the early evening until noon the following day. I could not bear to get out from under the covers. Marriage, Oxford, Sir Maurice and Oxford dons, so unlike the world I had known before, had an exhausting effect on me. I spent my year at Oxford like a sleeping princess, rising only to eat, cook, travel occasionally to London and go to dinner parties. But I did entertain. The first night at dinner at Sir Maurice Bowra's, I knew I had to have him back. My mother taught me that invitations had to be returned. So I would rouse myself from bed long enough to shop in the Cornmarket and try to teach myself how to cook.

Good cooks, such as my mother, like to cook alone. My mother had no desire to teach me how to cook nor did I have any desire to learn from her. I did not want to hang around the kitchen except to grab some griven, unborn chicken eggs, fried onions or to cut myself a piece of jellied whitefish. This is the way my mother wanted it; in the kitchen children get in the way. Later on in my marriage, when I called her long distance for a recipe, she was flattered—all that money spent just to get her recipe for honey cake. In Oxford, I had no idea how to cook. My husband was no help because he felt sick at the sight of a raw chicken leg lying on the counter. A bowl of flour and butter mixed for pastry made him feel queasy. The kitchen was not then, or now, a place where he felt at home.

At the professor's flat where we lived there was a gas oven and burner that had none of the safety devices now available. Flames would leap into the air the moment I lit the burners. Every fourth or fifth time I would light the oven, I would set myself on fire. Allan was usually around. We were actually falling in love and he was spending as little time as possible at college. Hearing my screams, he soon learned what to do. Rush in, roll me over on the kitchen floor and pound me with wet towels. A couple of times it was almost an *auto-da-fé*. On a few occasions, I lost my usual cover of four thick sweaters. Allan always succeeded in putting out the fire before it crossed the brassiere line.

I had a few cookbooks by Elizabeth David and the *Gourmet's Cookbook* (put out by the *New York Times*), which were given to us as wedding presents. I would study the books and then make my way to the vendors in the Cornmarket and try timidly to relate what was in the recipe to what was in the market stalls. That would take up virtually every afternoon. I would stand a long time before daring to talk to the purveyors of fish, meat and vegetables because I never knew how much I needed or wanted. I decided to stay away from the fish since I didn't recognize what they were. The only fish I knew in Winnipeg were salmon, Lake Winnipeg whitefish and pickerel. I found it easy to recognize lamb chops and roasting chicken, so that is what we ate for dinner every day for a month when Allan was not dining at high table.

Eating at high table at least three times a week was an obligation of all Oxford dons. The dons' wives stayed at home and ate sardines out of cans. A few of the kinder dons' wives at Wadham, knowing I was young and alone, would ask me to join them for a sardine meal. Aside from two motherly types (only one of whom one was English), they were an austere lot, very status-conscious and knowledgeable about who-was-who in Oxford. I, on the other hand, only wanted to talk about recipes. I asked what they really cooked when their husbands were home. "Burnt peas," one of them said. I wanted to impress my husband with my cooking prowess, but these women were certainly no help.

Anna Bamborough, who was Scandinavian, was the exception and made delicious desserts such as Mont Blanc, a puree of chestnut covered with a mountain of thick cream. Mostly, the dons' wives would brag about making do with a joint of ham for two weeks. This was partly revenge against their husbands for their lavish college dinners and partly because, being English, they disliked fussing around and spending money on food. The so-called food revolution in England, started at the time by Elizabeth David, had not yet reached the Woodstock and Banbury Roads where the married dons lived in their Victorian brick houses.

However, I was beginning to learn a lot about food. Allan had a bachelor friend at Wadham who entertained lavishly in his luxurious college quarters. In fact, the second party I attended at Oxford after the Warden's welcoming dinner for us *à trois*, was a rather grand lunch at this don's suite when he invited a half-dozen fellow dons and their wives to inspect Allan's wife. We ate gougon of sole with tartar sauce to start, followed by a saddle of lamb with pommes Anna, then coffee pudding and aged Stilton. These were accompanied, in sequence, by a sweet German hock—an Oxford favourite—a fine Bordeaux and then a heavy Sauternes—one of Oxford's standard liquids for resisting the cold. They were preceded by whisky for the men and sherry for the ladies.

Nobody told me that it was permissible to say no to a refill of one's empty glass. The scouts kept pouring and I kept drinking. You might say that it was the Sauternes that brought me down. I vaguely remember my host, Peter Carter, helping Allan take me down the narrow stairs of the college and somehow get me across the quad into Allan's rooms where I could discreetly pass out, which I did. I did not, however, worry about what the other women thought of my behaviour. I just assumed they were all passing out. The English do drink a lot. The Queen Mother, for that reason alone, became my icon.

Allan was anxious for me to take advantage of my presence in the university and urged me to study law or literature or whatever I wanted. After all, we were in the greatest centre of learning in the world. The idea absolutely repelled me. I had not gotten married to write exams again. I got married to be a housewife, not a prissy female academic like the bluestockings in Oxford. In fact, I was terrified that an English or law don would discover how incompetent I was and unsuited for serious matters. One kind don at Wadham College, John Bamborough (with the Scandinavian wife who knew how to cook), seemed to understand my reluctance to take up a serious course of study and volunteered to discuss English literature with me once a week. No exams, no essays. I also occasionally went to hear lectures by Neville Coghill, David Cecil, W.H. Auden, and some other illustrious names, but this was the limit. What I did most of all was sleep. Once or twice a week I stirred myself to have lunch with Allan in his rooms at Wadham, served on college silver by his scout Bustin in white gloves. These lunches were delicious and fattening. I managed to gain forty pounds in one year. Luckily, I didn't know it because the scales in Oxford were all in "stones" not pounds and Allan, who now loved me, didn't seem to notice my expansion.

Since I wasn't conscious of my new shape, I was not unhappy. There is nothing like avoiding a scale to maintain one's self-esteem. Nor was I intimidated by female dons. In fact, I couldn't understand why anyone would want to be a female don. Academia wasn't going to put a scratch on me. My goal at that time was simple: it was to bring Winnipeg to Oxford. I was still suffering from acute homesickness. From the moment we moved into our Oxford flat, I wanted my mother to come and live with us and stay as long as possible. My vision of paradise was Allan, myself and my mother going hand-in-hand together in life. Shortly before we were married, when Allan came along on a couple of shopping trips with my mother and me, he was taken for the father, my mother for the mother and I for the daughter. What could be better than that? In Winnipeg, my mother was lying sleepless with anxiety, worrying about having let her daughter marry too young to a virtual stranger, while I slept in Oxford, dreaming of my *mariage à trois*. It was no longer a *mariage blanc*.

Before Allan married me, he used to take out Ruth, the daughter of Sir Barnett (later Lord) Janner, who represented a largely working-class and Jewish constituency in Leistershire. While Allan was courting me by mail, he asked Ruth to his Wadham Gaudy (big fancy formal ball), where she met Sir Maurice Bowra. Sir Maurice liked her so much ("splendid girl, splendid girl") that he instructed Allan to marry "the jolly Ruth." Allan swears that marriage to Ruth was never in his mind. But Ruth's mother, Elsie, whom Allan truly loved, thought it was a done deal. (Nobody paid any heed in such matters to Sir Barnett.) Elsie, or Lady Janner as she was called, owned a huge, cavernous, gloomy flat in Albert Hall Mansions and when Allan visited London he stayed with the Janners. A room was always ready for him just as if he were Elsie's son. During his six years in Oxford, Albert Hall Mansions was his London home. Elsie, a small dark energetic woman who was a magistrate, ran her husband's prosperous solicitors' firm. Until well into her eighties, Elsie would park her Jaguar in London, using a measuring tape to make sure she could fit it into the space, while Barney, a large, heavy man, always in striped trousers, winged collar and morning coat, stood and watched.

When Elsie received a wedding invitation from my mother in Winnipeg, only six weeks after Ruth had gone to the Gaudy with Allan, she was not pleased. The connection between the Janners and the Gotliebs had been made by my mother-in-law—both Elsie and Sally were early supporters of Zionism. Their relationship was deep, respectful, each praising the other to the skies. Except when it came to carnal matters. "Why do you think Elsie takes those long trips without Barney on the Queen Elizabeth to New York?" my mother-in-law would ask. "To pick up men." Allan was horrified. But once Elsie got used to my presence, after many months, she implied that my mother-in-law used to take long boat trips to Israel, without my father-in-law, for reasons I dared not repeat to my husband. Elsie also told me that my mother-in-law had an eye for Barney. This talk was too fantastic—Sally and Elsie were old ladies to me—but, certainly, Sally and Elsie, unlike my mother, were worldly women in their ways.

When we arrived in Oxford, Allan talked of Elsie as his second mother and mentor. He eagerly called Elsie as soon as we arrived, and she invited us for dinner as well as a stay there overnight. I was totally ignorant of anything other than what my husband chose to tell me. Albert Hall Mansions was cold, Elsie was cold (although she couldn't help flirting with Allan), and Ruth barely spoke. The food was execrable, Anglo-Jewish warmed-overs, i.e., classic Anglo-Jewish cuisine. All I can remember of that evening was Elsie ordering her son Greville, engaged to Myra, daughter of the Chief Rabbi of England, to stop necking with his fiancée in her presence because it disgusted her beyond belief.

I found Allan's fascination with the Janner family mysterious. I had sort of hoped Ruth would become my buddy, like Carol from Winnipeg, but Ruth didn't even look in my direction.

Three weeks later, the gentle elderly du Maurier couple, Mr. and Mrs. Wix from the *Christoforo Colombo*, asked us to supper at the Savoy and to go with them to the theatre afterwards. We were to drive to London from Oxford and return the same night. To the dismay of the Wixes, I fainted at the Savoy, falling flat on my face in the Grill. My honeymoon cystitis had returned and my temperature was 103 degrees. The Wixes, who lived in a grand establishment, offered to take me in and care for me in any way they could. Allan had to leave that night because he had to give one of his rare lectures (very important, he said) in Oxford the next morning. While the waiters at the Savoy were fanning their napkins over me, he refused the Wixes' invitation. "I have a landlady in London," he explained, "where I have rooms." The concerned Wixes were worried about leaving me alone with some scrub landlady, but Allan insisted. I had no idea what he was talking about but, at this point, I didn't care. (I realized later that Allan, under the sway of Marcel Proust, whom he was reading at the time, thought it was chic to compartmentalize his life, in the manner of Charles Swann.) Allan even insisted on taking me to the

Janners in a taxi, although the Wixes' Rolls-Royce was ready
and waiting. He arrived at the Albert Hall Mansions, dragging
me behind him, and instructed Elsie and Ruth to take care of
me. Then he drove off. I felt as if I'd been left alone with two
witches from *Macbeth*. But both women were highly responsible. They tucked me between cold sheets and said a doctor
would arrive in the morning. When I awoke, there was no
sign of Elsie, but Ruth poked her head in the bedroom and
asked, "What can I get you, a hard-boiled egg? Perhaps you'd
like me to make you tea?" I hid under the covers and asked
after my husband. Ruth closed her eyes. "Forget about him.
He has designated me to look after you. But I'm a solicitor
and have to get to my office." I declined her egg and her aid.
She left. A doctor came by soon afterwards, wrote out a prescription and asked for a guinea. I didn't have a guinea. I
didn't even know what a guinea was, except that it was
money. He replied he would get it from Elsie. I was horribly
embarrassed.

When I was pretty sure no one was in the huge apartment
(Barney might have been hanging around somewhere, but he
didn't count), I called Allan and ordered him to get me out of jail.
His foot was on the pedal because he had already received two
outraged phone calls, one from Mrs. Wix, the other from Elsie.

Early in the morning, Mrs. Wix called the number of the
"landlady" she had wrested from Allan, and Elsie answered.
They had, of course, heard of each other, but were not friends.
Mrs.Wix asked if this was Allan Gotlieb's landlady, saying she
had been with poor Sondra when she fainted. "This is not Allan
Gotlieb's landlady; you are speaking to Lady Janner." Elsie was
amused. From that time forward, she good-naturedly referred
to herself as "The Landlady" when in our company. "Don't call
me Lady Janner, don't call me Elsie. I'm just your poor old

landlady." Mrs. Wix was so embarrassed she refused to speak to Allan for many months. Allan was humiliated because his romantic notion of living his London life in compartments, à la Swann, was foiled.

The subtleties of the episode were beyond me. I avoided the undercurrents and concentrated on my new obsession, food. I left London desolate about missing my meal at the famous Savoy Grill, and looking forward to accepting the Wixes' invitation on our next visit to dine with them at Mirabelle, the best restaurant in London at the time.

6
_

Sir Maurice Comes to Dinner

M Y FATHER, who had crossed the Atlantic only once and that was when he fled the Tsar and the Bolsheviks in 1917, was absolutely determined never to return to Europe. His only trips were to Toronto where he reluctantly went twice a year on malting business. He loathed being away from my mother. Less occasionally, and always at Mother's prodding, he would drive us to Grand Forks or Fargo, North Dakota, for shopping. My greatest fear was that he would not allow my mother to come and see me in Oxford. But he too was worried about the state of his daughter, living in the continent of decadence, and moreover, he couldn't bear listening to my mother cry. My mother's regrets about my marriage were destroying his peace of mind. For the first time in his life since their marriage, he told my mother to take a trip alone. He also wanted to find out what was happening to his daughter. "If you stay for six weeks," he told her, "the fare is cheaper." That's how my mother was able to take the longest vacation, before or after, in her life of eighty-seven years—a month and a half with her daughter in Oxford, including side trips to London and Paris, and even to Deauville for gambling.

Allan was fond of my mother because she never treated him as less than perfect, and I needed a chef. I was determined to give a big dinner party for twelve people in our flat, my reciprocation dinner in honour of Sir Maurice Bowra. I knew I had to return the Warden's hospitality and I wanted my mother to meet the most unusual man I had encountered in my life.

I knew mother was worried about our marriage, but by this time Allan and I were pretty friendly. He would spend about three hours a day in his rooms in college, tutoring his students, and the rest of the time he was either crawling under the covers with me or holding me on his lap or tasting the recipes that I was preparing for my newly beloved husband or dousing me when I was on fire. Until I found the perfect egg recipe that would please my husband, I prepared eggs poached, eggs scrambled, eggs Florentine, eggs in a wine sauce (la Laperouse) and soufflés of all kinds from chestnut to Grand Marnier. These experiments in pleasing my husband through feeding him the perfect egg were accompanied by regular gastronomic outings, lunches in Allan's rooms served up by his scout Bustin, high teas at the Randolph Hotel (sandwiches, scones, jams, clotted cream, pink cakes) and the occasional fork dinner offered by chilly dons' wives.

"What's a fork dinner?" I asked Allan when we were invited to the first such event, given by a fellow don, a brilliant historian who had been the sole don to oppose Allan's appointment as a fellow of Wadham College. Allan told me he didn't have a clue what a fork dinner was and didn't want to go. But I had met our host, Lawrence Stone, and he was a charmer. At a dinner at college, Lawrence sat at my side, and flirted with me—unlike the other dons. I adored him. I was determined to go to the Stones' fork dinner. As soon as we arrived, I realized I had been going to fork dinners all my life. In Winnipeg we called them buffets. A fork dinner invitation told the guests that everyone would need to stand up while eating and thus could only employ one instrument—the fork. I rather enjoyed myself at the dinner—cold joint, chutney, trifle, Stilton, sherry and hock for the ladies, whisky for the men after dinner. Allan, however, would not let me write the compulsory thank-you note to Mrs. Stone because he was still angry about her husband's opposition to his appointment, and moreover, disliked standing up during dinner. Mrs. Stone never forgave me for my lack of courtesy, never asked us back, nor did we return the hospitality. Not long after, Lawrence Stone moved to Princeton in the United States and became quite a famous historian. Every time he wrote something that increased his fame, I made sure to point it out to Allan.

Before my mother arrived, I had reached the letter "L" in my cookbooks. So I cooked lamb every conceivable way—curried lamb, lamb chops, lamb stew, roast lamb, braised lamb, lamb shanks, chump chops, lamb cutlets, lamb kidneys, shish kebabs and stuffed breast of lamb (very hard to explain to the butchers in the market). I also complemented my main courses with desserts, the recipes for which I took, not in alphabetical order, from other cookbooks. My desserts were making Allan queasy—he had been diagnosed with a gall-bladder condition well before we were married—and he left them untouched. So I went to "C" for custards, which he claimed eased his condition. Notwithstanding my growing culinary obsession and all these experiments, I didn't feel up to cooking a Maurice Bowra dinner alone. Never mind. Mother would be arriving soon and in time for the event.

When she arrived, my mother's après-wedding fears disappeared and she soon began to show annoyance (like Elsie) because I used Allan's lap as a chair all the time. There's nothing like a smooching couple to put mature people off. When Sir Maurice heard that my mother had arrived, he invited the three of us to an elaborate dinner for twelve in his lodgings at Wadham. I warned her that the women would have to get up from the table after the dessert and go to another room, leaving the men to drink their port and crack their nuts. Sir Maurice had put my mother on his right-hand side and they appeared to be enjoying each other's company. But I knew she had one foot on the gas pedal, so to speak, waiting for the other women to get up and leave the room.

For my mother, there was good reason for her nervousness. At home, she never sat at the dinner table. She was either in the kitchen or running back and forth cooking and serving her family and friends. She never sat through a meal. About once a year, on very formal occasions when my father had a visitor from the malting plant where he worked, she would hire a cleaning lady to do the dishes in the evening. But this woman never entered the dining room (she claimed my father gave her the evil eye), so the only means of transport for the dishes was my mother, who carried them to the kitchen herself. The only time she sat down was over cakes and coffee when the uncles and friends began to exchange funny stories at the end of the meal. Amazingly, she got through the Warden's dinner, although I half-expected her to pop up during the meal to fetch the green butter from the college kitchen. But I was stunned by my mother's behaviour. You would think she had been living all her life amidst the four-hundred-year-old college silver.

On her other side, my mother sat next to the hated (by my husband) Lawrence Stone and seemed to keep both him and the Warden amused, even though she was worried about the women leaving the men at the end of the meal and missing her cue. She kept glancing at me to get the warning signal. It was no good her depending on me because I never knew when we were supposed to go or whose role it was to make the first move. I was usually the last to scuttle out. She made her way out before me, as if she'd been doing this all her life.

My mother's task in the next six weeks was to organize the return hospitality for Sir Maurice. She was a good cook, but she had one fault. She put too many things on a plate. Oxford may have had its traditions, but North Winnipeg had its traditions too. At the beginning of each meal, there would be many fish dishes—chopped herring, pickled herring, gefilte fish, jellied whitefish, jellied salmon and smoked sturgeon. Most of the fishes were served cold, but the gefilte fish, on occasion, could be served hot, depending on my mother's knowledge of the guest's preference. Then came the soups. There was always a choice—some beet borsht, some spinach borsht, chicken broth with dumplings, and/or beef and barley soup. No one had two different kinds of soup but everyone had a choice. In the winter, which lasted from October until May in Winnipeg, the soups were always hot. You could look down the dining-room table and see ten people eating three different kinds of soup, like in a restaurant.

There was no such thing as one main course. If roast

chicken was to be the main course, she would serve some short ribs of beef as well, because somebody might not like chicken. The rule was there had to be at least two kinds of meat. With my mother, it was usually three. There was always boiled tongue (not pickled because my father disliked it) just in case.

Another rule was that there had to be a flow out of the kitchen of side dishes coming at various intervals during the meal. Basically, it was like having a smorgasbord or buffet, but served at the table by the hostess while the guests were eating. Most side dishes were served up with the meats—chicken or meat blintzes, carrot pudding, noodle pudding, a Russian concoction that my father called *zharkoya* (a sort of meat and vegetable stew), and my mother's specialty, potato knishes. Her knishes were different from everyone else's. She would take little meatballs and dip them in a mashed egg and flour mixture, and then she deep-fried them and put them into a warming oven. And then, of course, there were her much-admired dill pickles.

At dessert, depending on the formality of the occasion, there would be a pie as centrepiece—deep apple or fresh fruit in season—and a variety of keeper cookies (able to last five weeks in the cookie tin)—poppy seed, nothings made with egg yolks, knishbroit, crushed almond cookies or melting moments, my children's favourite), and something called *taiglach*, a form of tiny creampuff smothered in honey, nuts and ginger. (I tried to make this once as a Passover dish and it took me an entire day.) Of course, wines were never offered or desired, although schnapps—rye whisky or vodka—were drunk by some of the men at the very beginning of the meal.

My mother realized after she attended Sir Maurice's meal that she would have to tone down the exuberant gastronomic style of North Winnipeg. "Mama," I said, "I don't want four brown things on a plate."

Mother and I were in a frenzy about what to serve to the Warden and the other dons and their wives. "Don't make it too Winnipeg," I told her, but it was hard for my mother to get out of her old habits. Happily, my mother agreed to start off with only one soup—chicken. To make a good chicken soup with the right rich flavour, my mother used an eight-pound hen. Her philosophy being "waste not, want not," she then needed to figure out what to do with all that poultry meat. We had selected standing rib of beef as our main course. I had canvassed some of the dons' wives and it seemed that ye olde roast beef of merry England was not served that often in the homes of Oxford dons because it was too pricey, and the chef at Wadham, for some reason, only went in for filet of beef. Our original menu called for serving kasha with the roast beef. This is because Sir Maurice had let it be known to my mother earlier that this Russian dish was one of his favourite foods and he rarely got a chance to eat it. I thought the menu was set, but my mother got a sneaky look on her face when she was making the chicken soup. "I bet Sir Maurice has never tasted chicken blintzes," she said, thinking of the leftover hen meat. I was dubious. I had heard my mother discussing with Sir Maurice his other favourite Russian dish, buckwheat blini, which he had eaten with caviar in Russia before the war. My grandmother in Winnipeg used to make large blini, which she served with sour cream and melted butter and no caviar. "Blini and blintzes are two different things, Mother," I would say. "I know your blintzes are wonderful, but they are not made from yeast and buckwheat." My mother was firm. "Kasha and roast beef will not be enough," she replied. Her old bad habit of having two main courses was starting to surface. She managed to tangle me in her Winnipeg web. She convinced me it would be safer to have chicken and minced onion blintzes along with the roast beef and kasha. I had forgotten that Allan had already asked her to make his favourite, potato knishes. The day before the dinner my mother told me to get out of the kitchen, having mastered the art of cooking on our primitive stove.

At the outset of the meal, all went well. Sir Maurice, in particular, smacked his lips on the chicken soup. In the kitchen, my mother and I arranged the individual plates for the main course. In the Russian-Winnipeg style, guests would not help themselves to portions; the hostess mounts everything on the plate at the table and passes it down. Having no help, we were both cook and maid. My mother carved large slices of roast beef in the kitchen (Allan refused to carve at the table, unlike his father who did it with joy and expertise), while I arranged the kasha, the blintzes and the knishes around the meat as best I could, striving hard to keep the food from rolling off the plate. I put Sir Maurice's plate in front of him and sensed at once that something was wrong. I should have served the ladies first. My mother should have been sitting down in the dining room beside him. Sir Maurice, of course, was polite. "Kasha, kasha, delicious, delicious," he roared. But he stared suspiciously at the large rolled-up chicken blintzes. "What's inside?" he asked gently. "Chopped chicken and onion," I replied. "Chicken and roast beef?" he asked bemused, and then realized he was being unkind. It was too late. I knew we had made that fatal Winnipeg error—there were four brown things on a plate. And my mother and I were running around like crazy babushkas.

It was a heavy meal. Dessert was my only contribution and it was very rich—a chocolate rum cake, made at Allan's request. When the ladies withdrew to the living room, leaving the men to their port and nuts, no mention was made of the food, except by one bitchy don's wife who said to my mother, "You must be exhausted, I've never seen so much food." My mother and I knew we had failed our Oxford culinary exam. We had never heard of the motto, less is more.

Although I was living in one of the most beautiful cities in the world, with Christopher Wren's classical architecture, Gothic revival buildings and renowned gardens in each college, I was blind to it all. I was a visual idiot. I might as well have been in North Winnipeg. The dry wit, irony and odd mannerisms of the dons did, however, appeal to me. I was fascinated by only two things in my time at Oxford: the dons and what they ate—the eccentricity of the one and the mysteries of the other.

I could never resist an invitation to dine at a don's house. A minor figure in Oxford and certainly off the social map, the distinguished Jewish historian Cecil Roth, and his good-natured wife Irene, befriended Allan and me and asked us and my mother to dinner one night during Passover week. The gaunt Cecil Roth spoke with an effeminate lisp and in the manner of Maurice Bowra and Isaiah Berlin—non-stop and rapid-fire—and was exceedingly difficult to understand. Irene, a foot taller than him and usually flamboyantly decked with silver ropes, huge amber necklaces and long oriental earrings, could possibly be described as the worst cook in Oxford, which was saying a lot. My mother nearly retched when Irene brought out jars of what she called "water eggs." She said she had preserved them six months before. "We did this during the war," she said proudly, "and such a good idea it was, I continue the custom." The meal consisted of cold fried plaice, which she'd made the day before, accompanied by cold potatoes, also made the day before. And that was it. I wondered if this was in the old Anglo-Jewish tradition.

Although my mother was appalled by the meal and by some other not quite as bad experiences at dons' houses, I was more and more intrigued by the gossip and culture of the Oxford dons. I was even beginning to feel at home and looking forward to being a don's wife for the next forty years. I was shocked when Allan announced, a year after we arrived, that he did not want to stay in Oxford but planned to go back to Canada. "I want to be a diplomat," he said, "and that means going to Ottawa to be trained (brainwashed?) by the Department of External Affairs." Ottawa seemed as strange to me as Oxford and I did not want to go. But I was a dutiful wife whose ambition it was to be a housewife and stay home and cook. Even though Allan had encouraged me to become a lawyer or get a degree in English literature (he noticed that I read a lot of novels), I demurred. I wanted to be ordinary, just like my mother. I hated to stand out in a crowd. I wanted to be a nice person and a good cook. I did become a good cook, for a time, but was never nice like my mother. I inherited my father's temperament, quick to anger and pessimistic, and I suffered all my life from free-floating anxiety (a phrase coined by Allan, a natural optimist).

So I was especially unhappy when our landlords, the German professor and his philosophy-don wife, told us on our departure at New Year's that we had failed to provide Christmas boxes for the cleaning lady, the postman and other purveyors. Moreover, our drawers were dusty. Allan was completely unmoved, but being my parents' daughter I was deeply wounded by the criticism. Nobody had told me about Christmas boxes. Although Sir Maurice gave us a farewell dinner, as did several of Allan's colleagues, my departure from Oxford was not a happy event. I had no interest in going to Ottawa, no desire to be a diplomat's wife, and did not look forward to being seasick crossing the North Atlantic in the dead of winter.

7

No Sty in the Eye

WE SPENT FOUR YEARS IN OTTAWA, the capital of Canada. Allan practised becoming a foreign service officer while I tried to get over the shock of leaving Oxford. There were no Sir Maurice Bowras or eccentric dons in my new life. We lived in bland, unremarkable apartments, moving ever time I had a child. Not that I wanted children. Fear of pregnancy still remained one of my strongest emotions. The few married couples we made friends with used to say, "Sondra, what do you do all day?" The wives all had jobs. Since I had stopped sleeping all day I couldn't use that as an excuse. "I'm a housewife," I said. They laughed. "I have you over for dinner. I cook." They admitted that I cooked. "But what else do you do?" They knew

I didn't iron Allan's shirts, or make beds. "I read." Wasn't that sufficient? I was totally without ambition.

Why were people always pushing me to do something? Even Allan, the traitor, suggested I might attempt to go to the local university. He didn't care whether I had a job or not, because neither his mother nor mine worked after marriage. But my mother (not my mother-in-law) did housework. She hung the sheets out to dry in forty-below weather. She and her cleaning lady whacked out the ice before hauling them in like sails on a ship. My mother also had a mangler that she used to press out the sheets and my father's shirts. She ironed standing up. She ironed sitting down. That's what you call a housewife. I never ironed anything in my life. I was no housewife.

Our parents believed that a working wife was a sty in the eye of her husband. It was a sign that the husband was incapable of making a decent living, a shiftless type, unable to support his family. My mother always felt sorry for our next-door neighbour who went bankrupt, "Poor Bella has to go out and work as a secretary because Chic went belly up."

I knew some women who had careers and worked for reasons other than supplementing their husbands' incomes. But in my view, the husbands were poor things, unable to assert themselves and without he-man goals. A man who let his wife work seemed weak to me and lacking purpose. Money was not a factor in our lives. Happily, Allan's father at that time was able to supplement our tiny civil service income. So there was no push for me to put bread on the table except to bake it—as a hobby.

I was about twenty-one when I began to have painful menstrual periods. (The honeymoon cystitis had disappeared but there were always problems down there.) A gynecologist told me that I had the beginnings of endometritis. I didn't quite understand his explanation, something about bits of ovaries floating around inside the pelvis. "What's the cure?" I asked. "Get pregnant," he answered, laconically. I dutifully became pregnant the following month. Now when someone asked me what I did with myself all day I used the minor nuisances of pregnancy as an excuse for my inaction.

Even Allan's superiors criticized his wife's laziness. Especially the women. Allan had a habit of leaving his desk at 10 a.m. to go down to the canteen for coffee and a jelly buster (a big sugary doughnut filled with raspberry jam). His boss, the formidable Agnes Ireland with whom he shared a room, caught him at it. "Why are you eating that junk?" she asked. "It's my breakfast," he replied. "I like it." "You mean your wife doesn't give you bacon and eggs before you go to work?" she asked. "She likes to sleep in," Allan said. Miss Ireland replied, "That may be, but I fear your habits are the symptom of a disorganized mind. The brain cannot function without a proper breakfast in the morning." Allan was outraged. He was an Oxford don and had easily passed the External Affairs exam. Miss Ireland was, in his eyes, little more than a jumped-up secretary without provenance. She had no degree or prizes from Harvard or Oxford. (In fact, she was one of the first women to be admitted into the Canadian Foreign Service.) But Allan began to fear that she would not recommend him for promotion because of his bad breakfast habits. Feeling guilty, I asked Allan if it would help if I got up early and gave him a morning meal. "It's got nothing to do with you, I like my coffee and jelly buster at 10 a.m. and damned if she's going to stop me." He hated all bossy women except his mother. I always thought the reason he married me is that I never told him what to do. If I didn't like something, I practised passive resistance or let my temper fly. I never initiated anything.

Allan was also chastised by another superior in External Affairs for his crumpled suits and unshined shoes. Looking down at Allan's wrinkled attire and dirty shoes as they walked together on Parliament Hill, he said, "If you won't shine your shoes, at least your wife could take an iron to your suits." (He didn't think that shining shoes was woman's work.) Allan made things worse by sloughing off the criticism and telling his boss that in Oxford it was not considered chic to have shiny shoes. Before this encounter, I had met the superior at an office party and perhaps I had not been suitably deferential. For Allan this was serious business because, at that time, on the annual rating form evaluating the young foreign service officers for their performance, there was a section on the suitability and contributions of the officer's wife. I was only aware of this because one of the wives warned me. Allan told me to put that stupid rule right out of my mind. I didn't.

I spent a lot of time visiting Winnipeg until our daughter was born. This was the era of the baby boom and they lined up the women in the halls of the hospital's maternity wards until a nurse decided when we were ready to pop. There were no sedatives or spinal taps. My baby was stuck sideways and the labour lasted thirty-six hours, so I was conscious during the entire period. Husbands were not allowed in the hospital, let alone the delivery room. There were just too many women having babies, and husband congestion could result in a strange male holding the hand of an embarrassed woman pushing out a baby who didn't belong to him. Allan spent the time pacing in the hospital parking lot. Giving birth was a painful, hateful and lonely experience. I was left alone such a long time that I may as well have been having a baby in an empty field. Moments before Rebecca was born, the doctor, whom I loathed, came in and ordered me to push and something was then placed over my head so I had the pain but not the gain—I didn't see her until I woke up twelve hours later.

Actually, I didn't really want to name her Rebecca, but Allan's mother insisted because it was her dead mother's name. Allan had no warm recollection of his grandmother, who had lived in the same house as his parents. When she would catch him cutting out paper animals on the Sabbath, she would whack him on the hand with the scissors. His father disliked her too, but like all responsible Jewish sons-in-law, he took her into his house. She took over the housekeeping chores, so my mother-in-law was left free to travel and do charity work for her great passion, Hadassah. (She did *not* whack ice from the sheets drying on the line.) Grandmother Rebecca died when Allan was seven, so his own memory of her was weak as well as unpleasant. But my mother-in-law insisted, and so after seven days of resistance from me, Rebecca was named. If Rebecca, who now has her own child, wants to blame me for being a bad mother, she can always use her painful birth as an excuse and my failure to prevail over her grandmother in the fight over her name.

After the birth, I lost all the weight I had gained in Oxford, plus twenty more pounds. I had never been so thin in my life. Unfortunately, after giving birth, my bum was so painful that I had to sit on a rubber tube, which I carried around with me everywhere for four months. I felt shy about telling everyone about my hemorrhoids and the various tears down there. After all, I was only twenty-one. After Rebecca's birth and my naming concession, my mother-in-law sent me an extravagant assortment of flowers. They knocked me over with delight and nothing made me happier, until I saw my mother. What a glamorous sight. She appeared at my hospital door in a beautiful navy blue suit with a white collar, weeping with delight over her granddaughter. I had never seen anyone look so radiantly happy. She should have been the mother and in fact replaced me for a while. Because I was weak and uncomfortable after the birth, she stayed in Ottawa for more than a month, caring for me and the baby.

Shortly after, Allan was told that he had to attend a meeting of the United Nations General Assembly in New York for several months. My dream of living again with my mother in Winnipeg, with no exams or responsibilities, was coming true. But the longer I stayed in Winnipeg, the more objections I heard from Allan in New York. Finally, my mother and my father (who adored Rebecca—she didn't talk back to him like I did) decided that the proper place for their daughter was to be with her husband in New York, so they kept Rebecca for three months and I joined Allan at the United Nations.

At first I had a marvellous time resuming the style of life I had been accustomed to in Oxford—doing nothing. Only now I did not have to worry about returning hospitality for Oxford dons and their supercilious wives. All I had to do was to select restaurants where Allan and I could dine each night. Nor did I have any Ottawa wives criticizing my laziness or superiors hinting that I should be ironing Allan's suits or feeding him bacon and eggs for breakfast. If we didn't dine out in restaurants, we ordered room service in our small suite at the Beekman Towers, and I decided I wanted to live in a hotel forever.

But there was a thing looming over my head that I was trying to avoid thinking about. I had missed a couple of menstrual periods, although we were practising the most advanced birth control methods of the day. I used a diaphragm that was supposed to be the latest thing—no need to apply that horrible spermicidal jelly that was widely used at the time. Rubber condoms were a no-no because they gave me cystitis. I tried to forget the fact that I was missing periods, but I was sufficiently worried to drop into the pharmacy across from the Beekman to buy a primitive do-it-yourself pregnancy kit. To my joy, the results were negative.

When I returned to Winnipeg to pick up Rebecca, who was now some five months old and drinking from a glass thanks to my mother's training, Mummy told me I was looking pale. "I don't know what's wrong with me," I said. "Maybe it's all that rich food in New York, dining out all the time or living off room service. I know I'm not pregnant." My mother cast a doubtful eye and made an appointment for me with a gynecologist, this time a lady doctor, not the barking-mad Catholic I had seen before my marriage. The doctor pronounced me three months' pregnant. "It's impossible," I said. "What about this special diaphragm?" I asked. "You should have used spermicidal foam," she said.

Some months later, we were back in Winnipeg again to visit the family, with my twelve-month daughter in tow. I had just finished making a strawberry pie (crème anglaise as a filler and my mother's special recipe for piecrust). I was getting to be a nice little cook and my mother made me feel so good when she praised my culinary feats to her sisters over the phone. Even my mother-in-law was impressed. As I was putting a redcurrant glaze over the strawberries I felt some labour pains. I knew about childbirth. You aren't supposed to eat when you feel the pains coming on. I decided that I was not missing that family dinner, labour pains or not. Rebecca was sitting in a high chair gnawing on a turkey bone beside my mother and my labour pains seemed fairly infrequent. I proceeded to eat an enormous turkey dinner and my strawberry cream pie before I announced to Allan and my doctor-brother Barry that they had better take me to the hospital. My brother and Allan, startled, rushed me to the hospital and called my physician. Three hours later, and without much distress, I gave birth to a boy, almost twelve months to the day that I gave birth to Rebecca. For someone who didn't want to get pregnant, I could now look forward to two babies in diapers. In a way it was worse than twins because they ate different things and one cried at night while the other cried during the day. I wanted to name this child Accident, but with all my family around me I knew this joke would not be appreciated, all the more so because I had given birth to a boy.

Instead of the flowers I received on the birth of Rebecca, my mother-in-law gave me a magnificent antique amethyst necklace. "Now," she said, "the Gotlieb name will be carried on." (Both my daughters kept the Gotlieb name when they married but how was Grandma Sally supposed to foresee the crazy things women do today?) Since the name Accident was hardly going to be considered by my family, I was determined to name my son after my recently dead grandmother, whom I loved dearly. Her Russian name was Masha, and my son became Marc.

In this period of my life, the words "garden, flower, weed" were not part of my vocabulary. The dwellings we chose to live in were yardless, porchless, lacking balconies and even the cedar decks that were *de rigueur* in the backyards of Ottawa's civil servants. We were renters with children. I focused on playpens, cribs, high chairs, bridge tables to dine on and early Canadian Arborite (circa 1950s) for the kitchen. As our family enlarged, we moved from one rented premise to another.

Our friends in the foreign service and in our little group of junior diplomats amused themselves by giving tiny and very informal dinner parties. The usual menus were spaghetti, coq au vin, blanquette de veau, and cheese or melted fondue—the chic dishes of our time. One of our friends who had an English wife served a traditional joint. She would cook a lamb, beef or pork roast for Sunday lunch and when we were invited for dinner towards the end of the week, we inevitably got the cold scraps, served up with horseradish and relishes. A few of us would whisper about her parsimony behind her back. None of the young couples had as yet bought a dining-room table and chairs, so we usually ate sitting on the floor.

The only time we dined out was on Sunday mornings. We went to a popular Ontario chain called Murrays in a downtown hotel. The restaurant would supply two high chairs for our children; Allan would buy the Sunday *New York Times*, which he graciously shared with me; and we would order pancakes, feeding bits of them to the children, who would throw them on the floor. Our children were happy in their high chairs because they could throw their food overboard. We would linger over coffee for a couple of hours and leave the employees to clean up the mess. This was the highlight of our week.

Ottawa had very few restaurants other than the usual Chinese-Canadian ones that all served the standard sweet and sour chicken balls with pink gunk and spareribs smothered in a black garlic goo. When Allan's parents came to visit, they took us to the one restaurant in the National Capital Region that was supposed to serve haute cuisine. Allan's superiors, who had travelled everywhere in the world, said that Madame Burgers across the river in Hull was as good as the best French restaurants. Madame Burger herself sat imperially in the front hall of the old house where the restaurant was located and greeted everyone in a severe manner. She was never known to have smiled. My husband likes to brag to anyone who will listen about my remarkable culinary memory. "She is a true idiot savant," he likes to say. "She can remember every good meal she has had since she was four years old." Of Madame Burger's cuisine, I can remember absolutely nothing. Only her sour reception was memorable. I found that no one in Ottawa agreed with me, so I kept quiet about this grand institution in the nation's capital. I was learning that in the culture of Ottawa, you agree or you shut up.

After my second child was born, my mother-in-law wrote me a cheque for live-in help. We hired Emily whose basic job was to look after Marc. She came from Newfoundland with a boyfriend in tow and lasted precisely six months.

Emily had trouble understanding my shy requests. When I asked her to do something that did not appeal to her much, she would get a bewildered look on the face and say to me, "You know, Mrs. Gorlib, when I rises up, I get's confused." This was her way of telling me she didn't much like the pressures in her life. I sympathized with her. There would be too many times in my life that I felt the same way. When I experience a little stress coming on me or too much pressure, I too rises up and gets confused.

Emily's boyfriend did not exactly sleep in our house, since we had only one bed for grown-ups, and we used this for ourselves. But he appeared to have nowhere to stay. When we were out, he and Emily spent a good amount of time in our bedroom doing whatever. She would make sure Marc was okay by keeping him in the bedroom. This was her way of showing responsibility.

Emily disliked store-bought bread and every day baked her own, which she shared with us. Her other favourite was "mash"—turnips and mashed potatoes, which we all ate every day. She was a laconic girl who mentioned casually that she had had a child by a Mountie when she was about thirteen, and whom she gave to her grandmother to raise. Like many poor Newfoundlanders, Emily had bad teeth. She would stay in bed a day or two a week (without her boyfriend) moaning, "My gums are rising."

Allan was unhappy about the boyfriend stealing into our

bedroom when we were out, so he put his foot down. "No more boyfriend in the house," he announced one day. (I was too afraid to give Emily orders.) So whenever we were home at night, she moved into her boyfriend's old truck, which he parked in front of our house in our quiet neighbourhood. Because of the cold Ottawa winter, he kept the engine of the truck idling so Emily and he could stay warm. We became accustomed to the noise but our neighbours were not happy. They got together and told us the truck had to go. During the Second World War, it was suggested to Queen Elizabeth that she leave London with the princesses to avoid the blitz. "My duty is with my husband," she said (or words to that effect), "and he won't go, and if he won't go, I won't go, and my daughters won't go without me." Emily's speech was the reverse of the Queen's. "If the truck goes, he goes. And if he goes, I go." She went.

This was my first experience dealing with domestic staff. Actually, the timing of her departure was good. Allan informed me the next day that he was being appointed second secretary at the Canadian Mission to the United Nations in Geneva. I had felt sadness at leaving Oxford, but I couldn't wait to get out of Ottawa. My only regret was the long distance between Geneva and Winnipeg.

8
—

In Search of the Perfect Quenelle

GENEVA WAS OUR SECOND HONEYMOON, this time without tears and with two children in diapers. During the four years we were there in the early 1960s, a Canadian dollar bought four and a half Swiss francs. Today it buys not much more than one. So our Genevois style of life was luxurious compared to our dingy routine in Ottawa. We had a large apartment with especially grand living and dining rooms, where we were supposed to entertain whomever Allan said the government told us to entertain. I never knew what he thought of these people. But if he considered them important, so did I. For the most part we partied with rather solemn, kindly socialists who were working for the ILO or the WHO or the UN, or delegates from Eastern Europe or the Third World accredited to these organizations. I lost my taste for them after a while. They were all so earnest. The cleverer ones, who were witty and made me laugh, were KGB spies or other intelligence types. Unfortunately, many of them were shot or disappeared when they were recalled back home to Bulgaria, Czechoslovakia or Poland.

Our apartment had three small bedrooms and a tiny kitchen, and I had a live-in nanny as well as a laundress who came twice a week. No paper diapers or nappy pick-ups in those years. My children wore the finest cloth diapers, held in place by old-fashioned safety pins. Unfortunately, we had no garden and/or dog, but our balconies overlooked Mont Blanc and Lake Geneva and I decorated them with red geraniums in the tradition of my father. My father's taste was Swiss taste. Everybody's balcony in our building—and it was one of the best in Geneva—had window boxes with red geraniums. Even if I had wished otherwise, I don't think the regis responsible for the building would have allowed me to plant trailing plumbago, petunias or even pansies. The Swiss regulate everything.

Besides being neat and beautiful, Switzerland is a country where everything works. The amenities of life that North Americans are used to are even better. Not only do the toilets flush efficiently, they are constructed in such a manner that your stools fall in a little depression above the water in the bowl, so you are able to examine your excreta minutely for blood and other unwanted detritus before flushing. The first question Swiss doctors asked me was how my stools looked. But I also discovered that this country, so easy on the eye, so comfy to live in, was run like a police state. A Swiss citizen cannot move within his own country without notifying the authorities.

About 5 a.m. Christmas morning we heard pounding at the front door. My husband answered and three grey-clad Swiss policemen pushed him inside and belligerently asked about the whereabouts of our German-Swiss nanny, Alice. Alice had returned to her family farm for about three weeks, for the harvest and the holidays. Allan thought something dreadful had happened to Alice. He asked, "Is she alive?" The police became nastier and answered with questions, "She is supposed to be here with you under your roof. Is she here or not? And if she's not here, why didn't you notify us?" Allan was dumbfounded. "She went home for Christmas." The police became even angrier. "The girl is not supposed to move without her employer notifying us." Alice was as innocent as Heidi, and Allan couldn't fathom why he had to inform the police about her movements. "Has she committed a crime?" he then asked. "No, Monsieur," they shouted, "you committed a crime. *C'est une contravention*. You didn't fill out the proper papers about her movements in this country." Furious, Allan pulled out all the stops. "You can't talk to me like that. I don't fill out forms, I'm a diplomat."

The Swiss have rules. And one rule is that diplomats have carte blanche. The moment they heard the word "diplomat," and examined Allan's passport, they apologized profusely. They even apologized for waking us up so early on Christmas Day. Like the lackeys they were, they backed out the door wishing us a Merry Christmas. When we repeated this story to a friend who had been living in the country for most of his life, he told Allan that invoking his diplomatic status saved him from spending a good part of Christmas Day filling out forms and paying a fine. The Swiss love rules and hate anyone who breaks the least of their laws. It is rumoured that every Swiss carries a piece of chalk in his pocket in case of a car accident, whether he owns a car or not. If two cars become involved in a minor accident, passersby, as well as the car owners, highlight the tread marks of the tires with their chalk to help the police if they don't come to the scene of the accident on time. Each Swiss is a vigilante at heart.

Allan's office was housed in a nondescript but very desirable building called Chateau Banquet, which rented out to individuals as well as foreign missions. The building was owned by an Arab sheik who lived in Monte Carlo. The parking spots were separated by inconvenient iron poles, instead of innocuous white lines. One day, as Allan backed into his spot, he dented the iron pole. Knowing the Swiss mentality, he immediately called the regis of the building and admitted to the terrible deed.

"We know about it all ready," the woman said smugly. "Four people living in the building saw you bump the pole and rang us up *tout de suite*. It's a good thing you called. Otherwise, Monsieur, it would have been a contravention and you would have spent a good part of the day filling out forms at the gendarmerie and paying a fine."

Our apartment was furnished by the owner of the unit and he had unique taste. All fabrics had to be furry, but not made of real fur, of course. He was a pioneer in the art of faux-fur decoration. The colours were strong—wine and lime were preferred. The shape of the furniture was late 1950s angles and fins, like the American cars of the period. We christened the style "Mode Soutine" after our landlord. I never saw such furniture anywhere before or since. We thought that he had it manufactured to his peculiar taste for the various units he owned scattered around Geneva.

We were nevertheless fortunate to get the apartment for there were few to be had in Geneva at that time. One had to put down substantial amounts of key money to obtain any place at all. There was a large park across the street where the nanny took the children to play every day. Rebecca stood on the rail of the *poussette* while Marc, not yet walking, occupied the seat. Since it was a Swiss park, there was no children's equipment and you could not, of course, step on the grass. But no one seemed to mind because that's where the nannies and children congregated. There were no complaints from the children, nannies or parents—especially from the Gotliebs.

I was the chef. The world of French cuisine opened up to me in Geneva and the surrounding French countryside. Instead of chopped liver, there was *terrine de la maison*. Instead of green butter, there was *pâté de foie gras*. Instead of Lake Winnipeg goldeye, there was *filet de perche* from Lake Geneva, and the best fish I ever ate, *omble chevalier*, a delicious cousin of Arctic char found only in Lake Geneva and Lake Annecy in France. I learned how to cook *truite au bleu*. You buy a live trout, bang it over the head with a cleaver and poach it in wine and bay leaf until it curls up and turns blue.

I could have gone to the University of Geneva if I wished, but it never crossed my mind. Study? Be a swat when I could go to a different restaurant in France for lunch or dinner almost every day? Or make an elaborate paella for dour delegates from Canadian labour unions attending conferences at the ILO? I did manage to learn the language quicker than Allan. He went to the office to send telegrams back home in English, while I shopped every day like a good Swiss housewife for everything from toys and crayons to beefsteak and tomatoes. This meant a couple of hours every morning struggling to communicate in French.

I fell in love with the butcher shops in Geneva. I never saw before in Canada, let alone Oxford, such elegant and clean butcher shops, with vases of fresh flowers on the counter, beautiful tiled floors (no sawdust), and cuts of meat exquisitely curled, rolled and dressed by the master craftsman's hand. When I saw these shops I at first had no idea what I was looking at. The Genevois display their meats like they display their jewellery. Visiting a butcher shop was for me like visiting Piaget or Vacherin-Constantin.

One of the butcher shops near our apartment had a lovely old tapestry in the window. The design was that of a prancing pony and the shop's sign said "Boucherie Chevaline." I did not know what that meant—I thought it was owned by Monsieur Chevaline. When I took home some inexpensive but very tender-looking filets, our Swiss nanny Alice congratulated me on being a frugal shopper. "Oh," I said, "Monsieur Chevaline's prices are lower than all the others." "Of course his meat is cheaper," Alice said. "It's horsemeat. It's very good. But don't call him Monsieur Chevaline, the word means 'pony.' The butcher's name is Monsieur Berner." I never went again nor could I bring myself to eat what I had bought, although I'm sure I ate horsemeat unknowingly in the restaurants of Geneva and even at the homes of some of my Geneva pals.

I was also fascinated by the hundreds of shops in Geneva selling marzipan in all shapes and sizes—as dolls, cars, animals and jewellery. I did not like or dislike marzipan. I could take it or leave it. But there was something about the idea of turning ground almonds into fantastic shapes and forms that obsessed me. I couldn't resist buying new shapes or designs every time I went shopping, although no one in our family, including Alice, would eat marzipan, nor would the dinner guests. Our living room began to look like a marzipan shop. I often wondered who in Switzerland bought the marzipan, other than me. (Even though I had two children, it was taking some time for me to grow up.)

When I wasn't cooking dinner at our apartment for visiting delegations, we indulged in my new, overwhelming passion for eating in the modest country restaurants in the areas of France surrounding Geneva—restaurants that had a style of cuisine that does not exist today. Some of these small establishments carried a star in the *Guide Michelin* and occasionally even two. In recent years of dining in France, I have never found their like again. They were in villages or outside small towns in the Haute Savoie and Jura and occasionally inside the Swiss border, or in places like St. Jean de Gonville, Belley, Crepy, Annecy and Messery, tucked away in remote corners of the districts of Bugey, Ain and Bresse, and often near a river or stream or surrounded by a farm. They were always family owned and run. Sunday lunch was, of course, the major gastronomic event of the week. This is when the farmers of the region and the local bourgeoisie gathered in their Sunday clothes, accompanied by their children. (French children are justly renowned throughout the world for their inexplicable ability to sit through five-course meals without fidgeting, fighting, whining or running around.)

The closest country restaurant that we frequented in France with our children was in St. Jean de Gonville, some twenty kilometres north of Geneva, snuggled up in the shadow of the mountains. The restaurant was part of a small farm, family owned and located in a medium-sized barn. As you drove up to the restaurant to park your car, you needed to be alert to avoid the ducks, geese and chickens blundering about in front of the entrance. The wooden tables had vases containing small bouquets of freshly picked wildflowers. In the French country restaurant tradition, there was no other attempt at decor. The menu usually offered a choice of only two or three items, but we usually selected the same thing whenever we went. We started with *terrine de la maison*, then *quenelles de brochet* (in plain English, pike fish balls), *sauce Nantua* (crayfish sauce), *poulet de ferme rôti*, *gratin de pommes à la dauphinoise*, followed by ripe oozy *reblochon* or *tomme de Savoie*, ending up with a *vacherin glacé aux cassis* or *île flottante*. All this would be washed down with local wines, Crepy or Fendant, followed by a Brouilly or other Burgundy. We usually managed to consume a Marc de Bourgogne as a digestif at the end of the meal. In today's currency we would pay four or five dollars apiece, with wine and service included. The efficiency of the middle-aged, harassed and tired-looking women who were the waitresses was without peer. They had a way of preparing the salad which I had never seen before or have not seen since. A waitress poured the vinaigrette over the fresh green seasonal ingredients (harvested from the garden in the back) and then flipped the leaves with deft flicks of the fork and spoon so that each leaf was covered with a delicious sheen. Notwithstanding the number of Sunday diners, the service, if not *soignée*, was faultless in that it was conducted with great speed from the kitchen so as to ensure the freshness of the food, but without customers feeling rushed.

Sunday after Sunday we would go *en famille* to eat and nothing changed. Never an off day. The calibrated dance of the waitresses, the perfection of the simple dishes cooked according to the same recipes, gave me a deceptive assurance that I could return forever and it would always be the same. Of course St. Jean de Gonville is long gone and I have not since been in any restaurant in France or elsewhere to match its simplicity, consistency and authenticity.

Every restaurant in the region had its own recipes for its terrines and p t s, *quenelle de brochet sauce Nantua* and *pommes à la dauphinoise*. Although St. Jean de Gonville was our favourite, we would often go farther afield in search of the perfect quenelle.

The most difficult to find and the ultimate in taste was the *quenelle de brochet "en soufflé" sauce Nantua*. This was a puffier, airier, lighter version of the usual *quenelle de brochet* of the region. Sometimes the restaurant that would serve it did not even rate a star in the *Guide Michelin* and would be in such a remote part of the Jura or Haute Savoie that it would be difficult for us to find again. At a tiny remote establishment called Reygroballet at St. Germain-de-Joux where we made an unplanned stop, I tasted the finest *quenelles de brochet en soufflé* that I ever experienced. When I swallowed the first bite of the quenelles, I knew immediately that it would be a once-in-a-lifetime event. They were torpedo-like in shape but virtually weightless. The combination of fresh ground pike and crayfish in frothing cream, almost swelling in front of my eyes, was one of these gastronomic experiences that live on forever in one's mind. I never found the restaurant again and I doubt that any chef could reproduce such a dish.

One of the few eating experiences that equalled the quenelles was at another simple family-owned restaurant halfway between Geneva and Lyons, which in subsequent years earned two stars in the *Guide Michelin*. Its signature dish was *omble chevalier* served fresh from the lake in a sizzling *beurre blanc* sauce that came straight from the oven to your plate in a huge copper pan. You could hear the sizzle through the whole restaurant. I had many an *omble chevalier en beurre blanc* at several times the price at upscale restaurants in France and Switzerland, but nothing matched this experience. The closest place to this simple culinary heaven was a large popular lakeside outdoor caf called the Creux de Genthod between Geneva and Lausanne. There were swings for the children scattered among long wooden tables, from which you could see Mont Blanc on a sunny day. Among the hundreds of lakeside restaurants serving *filet de perche* fresh from the lake, this was the only one that we would dine in. The tiny little fish were fresher, crisper, juicier and more plentiful than anywhere else. Waitresses would fan out among the long tables carrying huge platters of perch crackling in the butter in which they were fried. The platters were placed on copper warmers heated by candles for the second and third servings. The perch were accompanied by mountains of *pommes frites* and garlicky salad. The main course was usually preceded by a *"pâté riche"*—a selection of terrines—and Russian salad and followed by a *glacé* saturated in cassis. Never before or since have I eaten in such quantities and never before or since have I been so thin. When I see pictures of myself in Geneva, knowing what I ate and drank without exercising, I stand in awe of the miracle of my ex-slender self. At that time of my life, nothing was more meaningless to me than the notion of diet.

There were other regional dishes that I craved. Across the street from the Canadian disarmament offices in the suburb of Chambesy where Allan worked, there was a small *relais* with tables under and surrounding an enormous spreading plane tree. The specialty of the *relais* was *jambon à l'os*. A huge ham on the bone would be slowly basted in its juice, from which the waitress would carve moist thick portions at your table, serving them along with unsurpassed delicious french fries or *pommes à la dauphinoise*. It was served with a young effervescent Swiss wine (the kind that doesn't travel) to wash it all down. When Allan completed his work at the morning disarmament sessions at the Palais de Nations, we would meet under the tree at the *relais*, devour great slabs of ham and drain carafes of young wine.

On special occasions, birthdays or anniversaries, we would dine at P re Bise, then regarded as the greatest restaurant in France. Facing Lake Annecy in Talloires, it was about a two-hour drive from Geneva. Of all the grand three-star restaurants I ate in in those years, including Laperouse, Grand Vefour, Lasserre and Le Pyramid, P re Bise was easily the most memorable. We used to go about three times a year, usually at Sunday lunch, which was when it was busiest and not always the best time for the most careful service. Ideally, we should have slept over in the beautiful inn and had lunch or dinner there the next day. But the hotel was extremely expensive, even more so than the restaurant. We couldn't afford to stay over so we would endure the long, winding, and nauseating ride back.

Still, we tried to follow careful preparations because of the quantities of the food and wine offered—and never refused. I made Allan leave early in the morning so I could take a swim around the lake before eating. Otherwise my appetite would flag when the cheese trolley would wheel by. At that time there was a set menu, and all the desserts—fresh raspberry napoleons lighter than a dragonfly's wing and flavoured with Grand Marnier, *fraise de bois* with *glace maison* and *crème fraîche*, hazelnut confections, and chocolate bombes—were thrown in for nothing, so to speak.

At P re Bise, all was for the eating. If you liked one dessert, the rest would be wheeled to your table by the waiters eager to please you. But the desserts, as delicious as they were, were not the true specialties of P re Bise. There was a remarkable entree called *"pâté chaud."* Every cuisine in the world has its own *pâté chaud*—dough wrapped around meat. Call them Welsh pasties, knishes, dim sum, empanadas, spring rolls, flautas, tortillas, pelmeny—I've never tasted anything that could compare to the rich concoction devised by P re Bise. The dough, so buttery and flaky, would have been enough to make it unique. The rich wine and truffle sauce inside this oval ball would also have been sufficient even if eaten with a piece of toast. But combine these with the mystery and deliciousness of the p t 's innards, sweetbreads, tongue, bits of beef, veal, onions—I'm just guessing the ingredients (I would have been too shy to ask)—and I would say that the *pâté chaud* at P re Bise was the single best thing I've ever eaten, anywhere. Rich? Of course it was rich. And it was only the second course. The set menu at P re Bise at that time consisted of five courses, not counting all the little extra tidbits that came with the kir, or the cognac.

Once we dined with some state department officials, including Tom Pickering, a disarmament colleague of Allan's who eventually became US ambassador to the UN. Tom was a big tall guy with a fine appetite who was nevertheless experiencing a certain fade-out just before the cheese. He said, "I can't let the cheese go by. I'm doing this the Roman way," and trotted off to the vomitorium. Refreshed, he managed seven different cheeses. The cognac was served at little tables at the edge of the lake. The ma tre d'hotel would pour the 1904 brew into the balon, almost to the brim, his eyes turned away from the glass as he nonchalantly performed the ritual. The men drank the cognac, while the ladies withdrew to the chaise longues, breathing heavily.

Homard, sauce diable, was a close runner up to the *pâté chaud*, and a lighter dish. If it were springtime, we would start with white asparagus, with blue tips, big as totem poles, accompanied by *sauce mousseline*. When we sighed over the asparagus, the waiter would bring all of us second helpings. Allan was particularly fond of the *poulet de Bresse, sauce morille à la crème*, which came after the *homard* or the *pâté chaud*. The *poulet* would give him his usual gall-bladder attack. Later his choice became the more austere, but certainly the finest, rack of lamb anywhere. (Allan's gall-bladder condition lasted twenty years. He refused surgery even though he was laid low every three months. I had no say in the matter.)

This copiousness, for better or worse, has disappeared from the French countryside and from P re Bise. I regret the lack of the generous hand, the eye that doesn't measure. With the excess went a certain gaiety and warmth that was also peculiar to the P re Bise and the other less-starred establishments. They had none of the pretensions of the celebrated restaurants of today with their publicity-hounding chefs. *Soignée*, yes; solemn, never.

During the gastronomic excursions, picnics and skiing holidays with or without children, we were usually not alone. Two other couples, with children approximately the same age as ours, were often with us. The husbands worked with Allan in the Canadian Mission or UN while the wives, like me, stayed home. For two and a half years, the six of us planned parties, went to casinos, took art lessons and dined out or in each other's homes. One couple, the Belknaps, had three children and the Mercouris had two. Giselle Mercouri, younger than me, was a beautiful Franco-Ontarian married to a Canadian economist of Greek origin. Giselle married very young, like me. She would describe to me the glamorous balls at Government House in Ottawa that she used to attend when single. Giselle was a stunner and very sure of herself. Her husband kept her on a short string financially and she complained to me from time to time about his stinginess.

Giselle and I decided to make a short trip together to Florence. We were both in our early twenties and wanted some adventure. We left our children with our nannies and our husbands behind and for five days went to Florence ostensibly to see the museums, but we spent all the time beating off the men. Giselle's Italian was a little better than mine. She knew three words, one of them being *basta*—go away—which she screamed when too many men followed us down the street. Because

Giselle was on short rations, she only wanted to eat at the cheapest trattoria, but I was dying to eat real Florentine beefsteak. Actually, we never paid for anything in Florence except our hotel rooms. This phenomenon started on our train trip, once we had passed the Italian border. We were travelling third-class with working men and women and their chickens and baskets. During the short stops along the way, the workers bought hot cannelloni and lasagna from the swarms of vendors on the platform. The cannelloni and lasagna went in the window and the lira came out. We caught on immediately. We would thrust out our lira and ask for cannelloni, but longer, hairier arms than ours, belonging to the workers, would pass over lira and pay for our pasta. The men refused to be reimbursed. They didn't squeeze us or bother us. They just seemed pleased to have us in their company and this is how it was to continue for two proper young Canadian married women alone in Florence.

The first night we ate at the cheapest trattoria we could find and our tab was picked up by whom we did not know. After this happened at three cheap trattoria, I suggested to Giselle that we move up the ladder and let the richer men pay. I knew that, like me, she was also slathering for the famous Florentine beefsteak. We sought out an expensive-looking establishment that grilled beefsteak on an open fire, and the two of us, with our three words of Italian, were seated at a prominent table. There was no way we could figure out how many thousands of lira were in a Canadian dollar so we had no idea what the prices were. We picked out the house wine and ordered the beefsteak with the most zeroes after it on the menu. Although there were some girls dining with the men at the restaurant, we were the only women dining alone and two-thirds of the tables were taken up by groups of men dining without women. The beefsteaks were huge and we ate them nervously, wondering what we would soon have to pay in real money, but things began to look up. Glasses of grappa began to appear from the direction of one of the tables, then champagne from another, then vintage Barolo from a third. We acknowledged all gifts, including a variety of desserts, with shy smiles. One waiter spoke a little English. "Don't worry," he said, as he brought us a platter of sweets, "you don't pay, the men pay."

When we rose to leave, a number of the kindly men rose with us, asking in halting English if they could show us Florence at night. I was tempted, but Giselle came out with her usual "*basta, basta,*" which I thought was a tad unappreciative given that she had eaten and drunk so well and so willingly. "You can at least smile and thank them," I said. "You can't," she replied. "They'll swarm all over you like hornets. Just walk out and whatever you do, don't look back." I was feeling guilty and also thought that an after-dinner drink might be in order but Giselle was puritanical and trotted me back to our *pensione.* Younger than me, Giselle was the one to keep me on the narrow path.

From all the money she saved on the meals, Giselle had enough to buy herself a pretty pair of violet velvet shoes. "Whatever you do, please don't tell my husband about all the men following us," she said. "He's awfully jealous." Allan laughed when I told him how much money we saved from our meals. He thought Giselle's husband was petty-minded for being jealous. "He should know what Italian men are like," he said. "What's wrong with taking advantage of them?" I had an open-minded husband, lucky me.

9

Innocent and Blind

O**UR OTHER FRIENDS IN** G**ENEVA,** the Belknaps, were very different from the Mercouris. I liked Stephen Belknap much more than I did Giselle's husband. Stephen Belknap was fair, handsome, widely read, an aesthete, a Greek and German scholar, an accomplished violinist and, above all, an amusing raconteur. I could forgive a man almost anything if he made me laugh. Stephen did not make his wife laugh. He and Marcia had a difficult marriage. She had a tendency to belittle her talented husband and contradict him relentlessly. She even told me, *sotto voce*, that she tricked her husband into having a third child. Nevertheless, she had gumption, an appetite for life and enjoyed her food as much as I did. Witnessing the money

strains between the Mercouris and the destructive competitive-
ness of the Belknaps, I decided ours was the perfect marriage.
But if the Mercouris and the Belknaps had their problems, they
didn't rise to the surface then, and I assumed they were enjoying their second honeymoon in Geneva as much as we were.
For a couple of years, I must have seen a Mercouri or a Belknap
at least three times a week behind a fork or on a slope or in a car
on an excursion. Whatever problems the Mercouris and
Belknaps had, I thought the six of us represented the happy
bourgeois couples of the Eisenhower years that are now so
mocked and even despised.

The Mercouris returned to Ottawa and we stayed on in
Geneva with the Belknaps. Shortly after their return, the
Mercouris' marriage broke up. I was shocked. It was the first
divorce among my friends and there had been none in my
family. At that time, divorce seemed to me the most wretched
business on earth. When I went back to Ottawa after Allan's
assignment was completed, I visited poor pretty Giselle, recovering from hepatitis all alone, among still unpacked boxes in
sad disarray. I had to ask her why she broke up with her husband. "He was despicable," she said. "I left him. He didn't leave
me. He never gave me any money or helped with the children.
He couldn't stand the fact that Stephen Belknap and I were
having an affair." "What?" I exclaimed. "An affair? You were
having an affair?" "Oh Sondra," Giselle replied, "you're such
an innocent." Giselle Mercouri, my puritanical young chaper-
one in Florence, was having a torrid affair with Stephen
Belknap the whole time they were in Geneva together and I
hadn't noticed a thing. "The only time Stephen and I weren't
together," Giselle told me, with some disdain, "was when you
and Allan were there with us. You two made everything look so
normal and middle class. You were the perfect beards."

Innocent and blind—the best ingredients for an extended honeymoon. When I told Allan, with his superior sophistication, worldliness and experience, he downright refused to believe me. "It's impossible," he pronounced, "I worked with the guy every day. He's my best friend. He tells me everything. He didn't tell me about Giselle Mercouri." "Well, it's true," I replied. "The marriage is finished. She threw out her husband and she threw out Stephen Belknap when he refused to leave his wife. Anyway, she said she never loved him."

Innocence and blindness—they affected me even closer to home. On the top landing in the apartment where we lived, there were two apartments, one occupied by us and the other, a very grand affair, rented by an American of Russian origin named Michael Josselson. He lived with his wife, Diana, two maids and a daughter who played with Rebecca, my eldest. The Josselsons, in my eyes, seemed to be the complete cosmopolites, in the best sense of the term. Going in and out of their apartment, we would see a parade of European and American intellectuals including Isaiah Berlin, Raymond Aron, Stephen Spender, Nicolas Nabakov, Denis de Rougement and Melvin Lasky, then editor of the influential magazine *Encounter*. Josselson explained to us that he was secretary or something of the Congress for Cultural Freedom and also head of a couple of large American foundations, which, he explained, funded the Congress and *Encounter* magazine. We never had any idea what the Congress for Cultural Freedom actually did other than give dinner parties for the cultural elite of the world. In the tiny elevator leading up to our landing, we would often share space with illustrious writers, but also with gorgeously robed Africans, Indian ladies with exquisite saris and horned-rimmed glasses, and Arab princes in flowing Bedouin robes.

Michael Josselson was a very sick man who was one of the

first people to have a heart by-pass operation. This pioneering and very risky surgery had been done in Holland where he was required to be kept under ice for ten or twelve hours. It did not seem very successful as he breathed and walked with great difficulty and rarely left his apartment. A Russian Jew himself, his wife was a Boston blueblood and bluestocking. The Josselsons were very kind to the young Gotliebs. One New Year's Eve, they asked us over by ourselves to celebrate. We were surprised and flattered that with all their famous intellectual friends they just wanted us in their company that night. From the point of view of how to spend New Years' Eve, it was one of the best in our lives. It had all the essential ingredients: vintage champagne, fresh Russian and Iranian beluga malassol caviar scooped out of two great cans—one with large and limpid grey eggs and the other with equally large and limpid black eggs (Michael explained that he liked to compare them), fresh foie gras with truffles, and a brilliant, mysterious conversationalist as host.

A few weeks after our New Year's Eve get together, Diana Josselson called and apologetically asked if I could come to dinner the next night. They were having eight dinner guests at their apartment, including Raymond Aron, Denis de Rougement and Stephen Spender, and there were too many men. "We need you—your French is so much better than your husband's," she said, "and besides, we need a woman—especially, she said slyly, someone young and pretty." I jumped for joy. I didn't know I was young and pretty. My trip to Italy was long forgotten. In any case Italian men didn't count. They went after any English-speaking hags on the loose, as Giselle said.

Airily, I mentioned my dinner engagement to Allan and suddenly my beloved husband transformed himself into a Taliban mullah. "I think you should decline the invitation." "Why?" I asked. "Because they didn't invite me. It's not proper for you to go alone. It's a deliberate insult to me." It didn't occur to me to remind him how often he went out to dinners when the wives were not invited. Obedient wife that I was, I told Diana that I didn't think that it was proper for me to attend without my husband. She was dumbfounded by Allan's lower-middle-class mentality. "Winnipeg roots," "jealous," were some of the words I heard. Innocent and blind. That's what I was. She insulted my husband and I resented it. But I also deeply regretted not being at that dinner with Raymond Aron and Denis de Rougement. More than forty years later, about every third week, I remind Allan about his mean-spirited response. Then he doubly irritates me by agreeing. "Diana was right. I was wrong. Forgive and forget," he says smugly.

Some years later, when we were in Ottawa, I picked up the *New York Times* and saw Michael Josselson's face on the front page. It reported that the CIA secretly funded the Congress for Cultural Freedom, its sponsoring foundations and *Encounter* magazine. They were all portrayed as CIA fronts. Poor Michael Josselson was characterized as the evil genius behind it all. The press in the United States and Europe railed about treachery, trickery and deception, while former friends and colleagues outdid themselves in complaining about being used as innocent dupes. But today many regard Michael as a hero of the Cold War. A decent liberal thinker, he helped expose, at a time when it was not fashionable to do so, the fraudulence of the Soviet system, its front organizations and its useful idiots (in Lenin's phrase). We saw Michael Josselson only once more after the disclosure occurred, when we visited Geneva. He was dying and deeply saddened by his Judas-like friends. But I do thank the CIA for the caviar.

10

Swiss Comforts

IN GENEVA, all was in place for family expansion. I had just found the most delightful of nanny-maids, an exuberant, beautiful, titian-haired Spanish girl with blue eyes and exquisite skin named Amelia, who had previously taken care of a family of seven Spanish children in one family. She told me the family in Madrid had treated her badly and so she decided to come to Geneva as a guest worker. Her Spanish boyfriend in Geneva marched in Communist parades and participated in demonstrations. She described to me in her heavily Hispanicized lisping French how Manolo, the boyfriend, took her to a Communist rally one day where Stalin's name was mentioned every few minutes. Everyone had to rise and shout "Yo Stalin!" "What do

I care about Stalin?" she asked me. "Why should I cheer him? So I sit and knit for your baby. I am the only one sitting down in the hall. They're so funny," she giggled. And she'd raise her arm, imitating the crowd. "Yo Stalin. Yo Stalin. I tell Manolo he looks like a fool." (Amelia was basically apolitical. Her father had fought on Franco's side, which resulted in a small pension for her mother.) "You know," she said, "I'm sure the Swiss take pictures of Manolo waving his arms around like a crazy person." We both were afraid that soon Manolo would be shipped back to Spain in a train, along with so many other Spanish guest workers at that time, even if they never even yelled "Yo Stalin!" If a watch company went bankrupt, the Spanish workers who might have been at that factory for a decade were told they were being taken by train to another factory with their families where new housing awaited them. Of course they found themselves on the wrong side of the Spanish border.

Amelia's first job in Geneva was working at a boarding house for residents where she was the only maid and she had to change linen for twenty beds. Soon after, she became a member of our family. She was a marvellous cook and had such a happy disposition that she became the first and only nanny who ate meals with us. In fact, Amelia was our only real nanny ever. In order to improve our French, the three of us would watch television together, while Allan ceremoniously poured out little glasses of green chartreuse. Amelia loved children and kept asking, "Why only two? Why not more?" So, heeding her advice, I immediately got pregnant.

Geneva, at that time, was filled with Northern Italians and Spaniards who were craftsmen of the first order. I never bought clothes. Saturnia, the sister of Donetella, my laundress (what wonderful names), made me lace dresses and silk velvet evening gowns. She used to make a canvas of my figure and knew how each material would hang. To this day, I have never worn such pretty clothes; Swiss cottons, soft tweeds—there was nothing Saturnia couldn't make. Everyone I knew had a "special Italian dressmaker" who copied *Boda* and other thick German and French magazines exposing couture clothes, backwards, forwards and sideways. Nobody looked at *Vogue* with its distorted photos of contorted models. The nannies, maids, seamstresses and laundresses in Geneva during those years had been taught every skill and knew how to turn their hand to whatever was needed. They lived precarious lives in Switzerland, never knowing when they would be thrown back over the borders. It's hard to believe in the Europe of today that Northern Italians and Spaniards were treated as badly as the Turkish guest workers were treated in Germany in later years. Now the Spaniards stay in Spain and the Northern Italians are one of the richest groups of people in the world.

Having a baby in Geneva was very different from having one in Canada. The ladies of the diplomatic core in Geneva all advised me that Dr. de Watteville was the gynecologist I had to use. He was famous for somehow fertilizing Sophia Loren with her first child after many years of disappointment. His office was grand high baroque, filled with Bouille furniture and ormulu ornamentation. He was the coldest man I ever met and I immediately regretted my decision to use him. Happily, I only had to see him once a month. He never bothered to attend the birth of Rachel. He sent me to a Lamaze teacher who instructed pregnant women how to breathe during childbirth and showed us a variety of exercises—all useless. Pregnant women had to attend Lamaze classes. I think Swiss law required it. Our teacher was an old spinster who told us stories of women peeing in the doctor's face during childbirth and even worse. Husbands did not have to attend the Lamaze breathing lessons but were required to be present during the birth of the child. This did not sit well with my husband.

After rushing three times to the hospital in response to false alarms, Allan was not shocked when the fourth call came. I was lying on the back seat of our car having spasms every five minutes when Allan, who had never picked up a hitchhiker in his life, decided to give a ride to a drunken hobo (the first and last I ever saw in Geneva). I screamed at the two men in the front seat, "I'm having a baby!" I yelled at Allan to kick the man out. He was giving Allan some complicated instructions about where he wanted to go. Finally I became so abusive (Allan's words) that he dropped the drunk off without taking him all the way to his destination. Till this day I can't fathom Allan's motivation, but he seemed quite dazed. Well, it was the fourth trip to the hospital.

It was natural birth all right. No time for sedatives. I could hear the doctors and nurses yelling, "*Il ne faut pas vanouir. Monsieur, il ne faut pas évanouir.*" My husband, it seems, had turned dead white and was swaying heavily, trying not to faint. A nurse turned around and told him to look at the wall and not at me. It was the first time I had been awake at a birth but I felt little pain. The handsome doctor explained, "Your birth canal is used to travel by now, Madame."

The clinic where I gave birth was exclusively for maternity cases. The routine for the new mothers was three bottles of black beer a day "to increase the flow of milk," a lot of beef with marrow and other food rich in protein. A pichet of Swiss red wine at meals was included in the price of the stay. Allan often came to eat dinner with me and would carefully study the wine list, which he pronounced excellent. All the mothers in the clinic had private rooms and the babies were brought to us to suckle by the young assistant nurses. The maternity clinic was keen on mothers nursing their babies, but Amelia was not. When I returned after a boozy seven-day holiday in the clinic, I told Amelia I was going to nurse Rachel. This led to the only argument I ever had with her. She thoroughly disapproved of a high-born lady like me suckling her child. "This is what peasants do," she declared. She explained to me about bottles and sterilization and formulas, as if I didn't know, and sulked while I nursed Rachel. Amelia's disgust wore me down and I handed Rachel over to her and the nursing paraphernalia that she had already bought. For the next two years, she became Rachel's mother.

I was heartbroken leaving Geneva when Allan's assignment ended. I was even more heartbroken to leave Amelia. She accompanied us and our three children when we went by train to Genoa to board the *Christoforo Colombo* (again) to take us back to Canada. I kept in touch with her for many years. She married the lovesick Manolo and eventually they returned to Spain and purchased a small bar near Barcelona where we visited her and her husband, her aging mother and in-laws. She and Manolo lived upstairs above the bar with their small children. We both agreed that those days in Geneva were the best in our lives.

11

The Return from Paradise

ALTHOUGH I RELUCTANTLY RETURNED to Ottawa, I was keenly looking forward to our passage on the *Christoforo Colombo*. I felt that I would now be better able to appreciate its luxuries and cuisine than I was when I was a naive teenager. I was twenty-seven years old, a sybarite after four years in Geneva, and I had acquired a modicum of sophistication. Alas, first class on the *Christoforo Colombo* was not the same as it had been a decade earlier. Gone was the lady's maid who laid out my nightgown each night with such panache, gone was the unlimited supply of caviar and gone also was the "we-will-make-whatever-your-heart-desires" menu. The waiters were still friendly and Italian and adored children, but I had no Amelia to look after mine.

I spent most of my days on board chasing after three children aged five and younger with the aid of the good-natured Italian stewards and officers. One day the weather was rough and they tied down the furniture. Rachel, who was two, flew out of my arms and sailed across the huge drawing-room floor, only to be caught like a football by one of the ship's officers. My children's slaughter was prevented when two other stewards threw themselves over the bodies of my other two as poorly tied heavy furniture broke loose and careened towards them. And where was Allan during all this? He was talking to Gore Vidal. But he didn't know it was Gore Vidal.

Allan had heard from some people in the first-class lounge that there was an interesting man on board called, as he understood the name, Gorvey Dahl. They thought that Allan, being a worldly diplomat, should meet him. Of course, there was no logic in the suggestion, but somehow an acquaintanceship was struck up. Allan's favourite movie actress at the time (along with Hedy Lamar) was Arlene Dahl, the red-haired beauty whose specialty was bodice-ripping historical dramas, one of Allan's favourite movie genres. He figured that Gorvy must be her brother, so he engaged him in conversation on several occasions. Allan told me he was too shy to ask about Arlene but he was sure he was her brother because he was tremendously knowledgeable about Hollywood.

One afternoon at teatime I was listening in on one of their conversations when a stranger whispered to me that Allan was talking to Gore Vidal, not Gorvey Dahl. I knew Gore Vidal was famous but I didn't know why. As I heard him talk with boundless self-confidence about everyone and everything, I realized he was an extraordinarily well-connected man of luxurious taste, the real embodiment of the words "sophisticate" and "sybarite." But I couldn't stand it any longer; I needed to know why he was famous. "What exactly do you do, Mr. Vidal?" I asked. I was cut short by an angry grimace from Allan. He thought I had mispronounced his name. I had also committed another faux pas. According to Allan's Oxford training, one never asked another what he or she did for a living. Receiving the dirty look and no answer, I bolted after my youngest child, Rachel, who was toddling towards the waiters standing at the sweet table prepared for afternoon tea. But as I withdrew, I was able to catch a left-handed compliment from Mr. Vidal. He had learned that Allan was a diplomat and deduced that he was Jewish (not difficult). "You've got it made," he said to Allan, teasingly. "You're a diplomat and you're Jewish. You have a wife that looks like a young Ingrid Bergman. You saddle her with three children. You leave it to her to run around looking after your children and you spend your time sitting and talking to me."

I was puzzled by that remark. At this time I had no knowledge of what Gore Vidal did, but I knew that he was a homosexual. According to both my father and father-in-law in Winnipeg, homosexuals did not exist and I believed them, but in my year at Oxford I learned differently. Like my baby daughter, Gore Vidal would toddle towards the young waiters at the sweet table during teatime every day. I wouldn't have grasped the situation except that I could see that both he and Rachel (age eighteen months) were drawn to the same handsome young waiter. Gore Vidal always seemed to be whispering in the waiter's ear. I assumed he was asking for some delicacy that was not on the sweet table—he loved food. One afternoon, Rachel was pestering the waiter as Gore Vidal was putting in his order (as I thought). There was an explosive exchange, just as I was dragging Rachel away. In the midst of the contretemps, I received another compliment. "You don't understand, Mr.

Vidal," the waiter said. "I like the ladies. I like the young mother with the curly-haired baby girl. I would like to sleep with her, not you." I thought it was very brave of the waiter to say that, as Gore Vidal was known on the ship as a big tipper. And for a nanosecond, I wondered whether it would ever be possible for me to sleep with that waiter on board the ship. But no, too many children to take care of.

I believe that this was the first time in my life that I really understood that men could be attracted to other men. But how could a homosexual compare me to Ingrid Bergman? I felt that Gore Vidal's compliment to me was negated by his homosexuality. I didn't grasp that there were men who liked to look at women but didn't like to touch them.

12

The Squalid Brown Patch

W E ARRIVED IN OTTAWA not long after Lester Pearson became prime minister and a year before Pierre Elliott Trudeau slipped into the National Capital and changed everything. I was not interested in politics or the workings of the bureaucracy or the backstabbing gossip of Allan's colleagues in the foreign service. It was a good thing that I did not realize that I was going to be spending the next seventeen years in a government town located in a snowbelt in winter and a dank swamp in summer.

At that time in Ottawa, there was no skating on the canals, no National Arts Centre (or any theatre) and few decent restaurants, but as everyone told me, it was a wonderful place to raise children. As it turned out, the next decade was to prove to be one of the most fascinating periods in the history of Canada, and Ottawa was the place to be. All thanks to the colourful and enigmatic personality of Pierre Trudeau, the brazenness of Charles de Gaulle and the spymasters of the   lys es and Quai d'Orsay, the rise of the separatist movement and the appearance of our own home-grown terrorists in Quebec.

When I arrived in Ottawa, I had only one concern. I wanted to buy a house. We had been married eight years and moved eight times, not counting our extended stays in hotels and in my mother's house in Winnipeg. For six months we looked all over Ottawa, as there was a housing shortage in the rapidly growing city at that time. I decided the only place I wanted to live was Rockcliffe Park, or the Village of Rockcliffe Park, as it was pretentiously called by its inhabitants. It also happened to be the most expensive place to buy a house. During our long search, I began to realize that I was not looking for the house at all. I was looking at the space surrounding it. Houses that were too big for their grounds bothered my still feeble sense of aesthetics, but then most houses were like that in Ottawa. Unconsciously, I think I was responding to a latent gardening gene, inherited from my uncle Lord Rex Winograd in Winnipeg, that had never emerged in my more than four years in Geneva.

Switzerland, horticulturally, was famous for large clocks made out of flowers that were unavoidable in its public parks, and for baskets of geraniums that seemed to hang from every lamp post in the land. While the clocks fascinated my children, I thought they were absurd. (Now I'm not sure.) Every time we went with our children to stroll on the Quai de Mont Blanc on Lake Geneva, I would see guest workers deadheading the flowers, cleaning out the leaves one by one, and endlessly clipping and trimming in order to keep the borders of one row of flowers from invading another. As far as I was concerned, gardening in Switzerland was just another way to keep it tidy. What the Swiss were engaging in, with their harmonious displays of geranium baskets, was more akin to municipal management than to gardening. But there were exceptions.

Once we went for a mountain walk when the gentians and profusions of wildflowers were blooming. My heart knocked the same way as when I saw my first delphinium in a park in Manitoba. It was one of my first moments of true excitement in Switzerland—something I could never feel by looking at a mountain. In early spring, farm women would pick wild mountain narcissus and sell them on the street corners of Geneva, beside Piaget, Boucheron and other expensive jewellery emporiums with their bulbous chunks of precious stones in heavy gold and platinum settings. The delicacy of the flowers was a startling rebuke to the vulgar style of the jewellery on display. Do they still sell wild narcissus near the Quai de Mont Blanc in the springtime? Or have the environmentalists and the Swiss police laws abolished that tradition?

Geneva, of course, had many rich foreign nationals living there, as well as Swiss families who could trace their presence back through the centuries. The diplomats and the UN people did not mix with the invisible Swiss nor with the reclusive tax-avoiding expatriates and exiles who lived furtively behind ten-foot hedges on the northern shores of Lake Geneva and on the Route de Lausanne. The Swiss were to me a mysterious race, and judging from the few I had met, I did not crave to enter into their society—not that they would ever have let me in. Even if I had then known, which I did not learn until many years later, that the famous English landscape designer Russell Page had created some magnificent gardens for the rich Swiss and expatriates, I would not have had the slightest interest. I had no idea that gardening was something other than what my father or uncle did in Winnipeg, which was planting flowers and trees. I had never heard of garden design or landscape gardening, Gertrude Jekyll or Vita Sackville-West, or the expression "the bones of the garden" so beloved by garden designers. But even then, certain flowers lifted my heart, the way Villon prints and drawings lifted the heart of my husband.

In Ottawa, there was one house I kept coming back to during our long search. I didn't particularly like its kitchen, or its dining or living rooms or its bedrooms. The whole interior was ordinary, as was its clapboard exterior. It was one of those poorly built, put-them-up-quick postwar houses that happened to sit on an ample lot at the end of a dead-end street in Rockcliffe. What drew me to it, aside from the spacious side and back lots, was a hedge of wild roses blossoming in the springtime when I first saw the house. I knew nothing of roses or hedges in those years, but I was drawn back to the house again and again.

Allan was much more interested in the architecture of houses and their interiors than in their surroundings. In Europe he had begun to collect pictures and was looking for wall space. He liked turn-of-the-century brick houses and particularly disliked postwar construction. But the price was right for the house that I liked. His father was lending him the money and would go no higher for the grander places Allan wanted, so we bought the house with the rose hedge on Ellesmere Place, where we were to remain for the next nine years. I was especially happy because I thought that a dead-end street would be safe for my children, and the neighbouring streets seemed to be teeming with kids the same ages as mine.

My experience house hunting taught me a few things about

myself. I discovered I was a city girl who wanted a house with a large lot, but not in the suburbs or country. I discovered that I never wanted to live in an apartment again. I also began to have some sense, even if I really did not yet know it, that I was a gardener at heart.

The house on Ellesmere Place proved to be a disaster. A friend of Allan's introduced him to an architect, an amateur thespian who would rather have been on the stage than struggling with blueprints. Allan hired him to design a garage and a breakfast nook and to refurbish our kitchen. I asked Allan, "Why do you need an architect for this? You can't do much with this house. Can't a contractor do it?" "The architect," he explained impatiently, "is necessary to supervise the contractor, in case he makes mistakes." Both architect and contractor were delightful people and we spent many (far too many) happy hours in their company. Unfortunately, when Allan tried to drive his second-hand Chevy (it had belonged to his father) into our newly constructed garage, he couldn't get it in. The opening was too narrow. The architect had measured two inches short and the contractor faithfully followed his specifications. During the next decade, Allan spent every winter shovelling snow off the car, removing chunks of ice and scraping the car windows, in the nation's worst snowbelt. The unheated garage remained in pristine condition.

The breakfast nook was to be designed to seat a table and chairs for a family of five, and a nanny or domestic, if I ever got one. It was to be a happy family nook, where everyone had their pancakes and maple syrup and conversation together before Daddy went off to work, the kids trotted off to school and Mommy—well, Mommy wasn't too sure what she was supposed to do. The architect thought of putting in an elegant glass sliding-door cupboard on the wall of the nook above where the breakfast table was placed. The glass doors of the cupboard were so heavy they could not slide, so we took them out. So much for non-dusty dishes. (Not that I cared.) Unless you were a child, you could not get in or out of the nook without hitting your head on the cupboard shelf. The architect had designed the nook for five midgets, and the contractor, again, followed his specifications.

Although Allan regarded the house as undistinguished, he dreamed of a front hall and kitchen floor covered with black-and-white squares, as in the paintings of Vermeer. The architect and contractor duly researched the project and laid out the floors in large black-and-white squares made of some mysterious state-of-the-art substance. For three months, the hall and kitchen floors looked stunning. Then one by one, the squares started to rise, loosen, shrink, wrinkle and expire.

Our house on Ellesmere Place sat adjacent to a path leading to Juliana Street, which led in turn to the neighbourhood school. Juliana was a joyful street, always full of little children playing, all of an age similar to that of my own. For my children, the path to the street might as well have been the Ho Chi Minh Trail. In order to avoid the Viet Cong, Rebecca, Marc and Rachel followed a roundabout path to school that managed to avoid streets with kids on them.

As far as the rose hedge was concerned, once we moved in, it never bloomed again. I had no idea how to cultivate roses or maintain a hedge. I did not know you were supposed to cut out deadwood, remove suckers and slash away in order to rejuvenate. I didn't know what was wrong and never thought of buying a book about how to garden. I thought I had a black thumb for gardening. The solution for maintaining a hedge was so easy to find out. Yet, at that time it was as far from my mind as decoding the human genome.

The next summer, I wanted to grow some flowers in the back garden. The previous owner had left some sort of squalid brown patch, turd-ish and disgusting-looking, behind the house where they planted a few flowers. Grass and weeds had already invaded this so-called flower bed—nothing planted survived when we moved in. A friend said I needed topsoil. So I sent Allan to the outdoor farmers' market in downtown Ottawa to buy three large bags of topsoil. Allan, the children and I all tossed the soil on top of the weeds and nettles growing out of the brown patch. That's how I made my first garden. I didn't understand that to make a garden, there had to be some sort of division between the flowerbed and the grass. I didn't even know there was an instrument called an edger. I didn't know how to enrich or dig in the soil. I didn't know that worms were good. I didn't know the difference between an annual and a perennial. A professional garden designer would have been helpful but I had never heard of such a person, or if they even existed in Ottawa at the time.

But Ottawa did have something that began to educate me about gardening—a rather splendid experimental farm only a fifteen-minute drive from our house. Preston hybrid lilacs were bred there and a sample display of perennial plants and shrubs showed the locals which plants could be maintained in Ottawa's horticultural zone. The experimental farm was also the site of a much- admired rock garden (by those who like rock gardens) and many varieties of hedges that the civil servants could plant around their yards, safe from the cold. Unfortunately for me, there were no rose hedges. I used to spend a lot of time at the farm with my children, sometimes returning three times a week to see what might be coming up next. I noticed for the first time that there was such a thing as perennials. The problem was that I didn't know where to buy them. One could, I knew, buy annuals, vegetables and trees in the farmers' market in the centre of the city, but there was only one perennial nursery that I was aware of. It was run by a German lady, Mrs. Knippel, assisted by a few mentally challenged teenage girls.

When I saw my first columbines at the experimental farm, I had no idea where I could buy them (the hybrid Mckana giants) but I decided to try Mrs. Knippel. She indeed had the same columbines but she never wanted to pull them out of the ground. "When can you take them out?" I asked.

"Come back in three weeks, in early May," she told me, "we're going to put some flowers in front of the store for sale." She seemed to be the only one at the nursery who knew anything. (This is a tradition in garden nurseries—only one person knows the stock.) She added, "When you come back, bring a list of the different flowers you want, so we can dig everything up at once."

This sounded promising. I went to the experimental farm to see what appealed to me. I then discovered an unusual flower (to me at the time), the tall bearded iris that was growing in a large display garden. I assumed (wrongly) that it bloomed all summer long. I was ignorant of the most basic gardening facts, including that annuals bloom for a longer period than perennials but don't come up again the following year. At the farm, there was also a great display of peonies, singles and doubles—a flower familiar to me from Winnipeg—as well as some odd flowers in the rockeries that I liked and recorded, if the name tag wasn't stolen.

A few weeks later I returned with my list of about five flowers. Mrs. Knippel looked at it dubiously. As far as I could see there were no flowers for sale in front of the store. Knowing she had a real dummy on her hands, she took me back to where there were a lot of green shoots growing, but no flowers and nothing in bloom. "I have roses," she said, "but I don't want to sell them until next year. But I have peonies and evening primroses."

I had no idea what a primrose was but was pleased she was willing to sell me some. "What about delphiniums?" I asked, remembering these from Manitoba. "Maybe I have a couple to sell," she said grudgingly. After an hour and a half of grunting and sweating, one of her dim assistants dug up a peony bush, the colour and form of which she could not describe, plus a lot of green things that she said were evening primroses, and two scraggly things that she told me were delphiniums. I planted them all that evening in higgledy-piggledy fashion in the brown patch where we had heaved the topsoil. I soon realized why the nursery had so many evening primroses. The flowers didn't open until four o'clock in the afternoon and then they soon demonstrated that they were a master race by taking over the whole patch and smothering the delphiniums. The peonies did survive but it took four years for them to bloom.

There was another kind of gardening that I discovered in Ottawa but about which I had no previous idea—digging bulbs into the ground. Queen Juliana and her family of The Netherlands lived in exile in Ottawa during World War II. After the war, a grateful Dutch government made an annual gift of thousands of tulip bulbs to the National Capital for planting along the canals and parkways of the city. Ottawa in spring is a mass of tulips, thanks to the government of Holland. The result is huge gawking crowds creating the only traffic jams ever seen in Ottawa. In the market, I came across a kind of farm implement and garden-tool shop called Ritchies Seed and Feed, which not only sold bulbs but offered lots of bulb catalogues for sale—something, again, I did not know existed. I bought the catalogues, which had pictures of tulips, and chose what I considered the prettiest shape, lily-flowered tulips with pointy petals. My first combination was White Triumphator (tall blooms), China Pink (a little smaller) and Captain Fryatt (beautiful dark-pink colour). I planted them around the peonies and miraculously they flowered in the spring, turning out to be a happy combination. Over the next thirty-five years, in each garden I have owned, I have tried without success to keep this combination. The only one of the three bulbs that I have been able to find on a steady basis is White Triumphator. China Pink turned up later in one of my catalogues as "a new find" while poor Captain Fryatt (beautiful wine colour) disappeared in some foreign war. But my affection for lily-flowered tulips and my gratitude to Queen Juliana have always remained.

Allan had no interest in flowers but liked trees. He decided to plant some in the front of the house, next to the Ho Chi Minh Trail. He went to the Byward Market (where the preponderance of trees for sale, it was widely believed, were dug up illegally from the Gatineau Hills) and bought several birch, his favourite tree at the time. With the help of slave assistants (the children) and a friend that knew a little about gardening, he planted them in awkward spots in front of the house. Then he went through a crazed period. He stole some large smooth round rocks from somewhere in the Gatineau and to my astonishment, placed them on the edges of our front lawn and began to paint them white. My children were so embarrassed they refused his command to help—one of their few acts of rebellion. "Why is your husband painting those rocks white?" our neighbour Mr. Pick asked me. I told him it was a mystery. Allan's only explanation to me was that he liked it that way. "They look clean," he added. I thought they made the house look like a gas station but he was stubborn and persistent. Later, much later, he confessed to me that he had experienced a calamitous lapse of taste.

Like other Ottawa bureaucrats, we filled our yard with trilliums that we stole from the Gatineau Hills (actually from the property of a friend). We had red, pink and white specimens and then I discovered wild columbines, also in the Gatineau, which I scattered round and about the trilliums. So much for the hybrid columbines that Mrs. Knibbel wanted to keep for herself. Within a few months I had fine array of wildflowers, given to me by friends with cottages in the Hills, mixed with my lily-flowered tulips. Although the garden had no shape or design—or bones—it was a pretty patch of spring flowers. Trilliums from the woods seemed to have a special affinity for my Ottawa garden and I miss them to this day.

Special to our garden on Ellesmere Place was an old plum tree that flowered very early in the spring. Because of its beauty, we asked our contractor to put a large sliding-glass door in the room that overlooked it—we'd be able to walk out and see the blossoms in spring and look at the tulips in the brown patch. Unfortunately, the sliding-glass door, like the sliding-glass panel in the breakfast nook, refused to slide. So there was no door to the garden as long as we lived there.

In the autumn, the tree produced tiny yellow plums in amazing profusion from which I made the most intensely tart jelly. When we sold the house, the only thing I really regretted was leaving the plum tree. I have never been able to find that variety of tree again. I never knew its name but I did know that it was the first tree to flower in the Ottawa spring.

13

The Northern Plantation

WHILE LIVING ON ELLESMERE PLACE in Ottawa, my culinary skills far exceeded my horticultural ones. I had all Julia Child's books on my shelf, but not one on gardening. The desire to garden was not the reason for our move out of Ellesmere Place. In fact, we had no reason at all except that my husband hated the house, his collection of prints by André Masson was expanding and he needed more wall space and less sunlight because the direct light threatened to cause his prints to fade. I loved bright houses but only gloom would preserve his pictures.

The family didn't know he was looking for a new house. When I found out about his furtive search, I told him it was a preposterous idea to be moving to a larger house at the height of sky-high oil prices caused by the OPEC embargo (this was in 1973). Ignoring my pleas, he managed to find an old monstrosity in Rockcliffe, facing the park and the Ottawa River. Because it was so large, difficult to heat and in such terrible condition, it was going cheap. He took me through his find. It had the air of a fading plantation manor house, with a two-storey wraparound porch that looked as if it had been kept standing to use as a horse barn while the Northern armies ravished Georgia. If it was a wreck from the outside, the interior was worse. The house was owned by an aged aunt and her RCMP nephew, who had divided it into two units. Nothing had been touched since it was split after World War I.

The house sat on Embassy Row, with the Soviet and American embassies as near neighbours. I asked Allan how he could even consider buying it. "I already bought it," he said. "It was a steal. Look at the location—facing the park. I've put the house in your name in case I die." This dying theme has been a favourite of his during our marriage. Once I found little notes to me in my underwear drawers, written by Allan. "I owe Sondra Gotlieb $4,000." "What's this?" I asked. "It's so you won't pay inheritance tax in case I die."

Houses were not selling well because of the oil crisis and recession, so thanks to Allan's folly, we found ourselves with two houses on our hands. To pay for the increased cost of our new house on Lisgar Road, he decided to auction off his precious collection of rare Canadian postage stamps. I began, for the first time, to take an interest in the stamps he sold. I noticed that, after he sold them, they soared in price while we spent vast sums to reclaim the Lisgar Road monster. I harassed him constantly about his foolishness but this did not deter him. I learned long ago that I could only deal with his stubbornness by a doleful passivity, increasing to nagging, then weeping. But because the house had large grounds and faced a park, I decided not to resort to my usual weapons. Eventually, we sold Ellesmere Place at a deeply discounted price, a fact that only further increased my financial anxiety.

I suppose I could have stopped him, but I liked the space around the house. That secret gardening gene was beginning to assert a certain dominance. Although the house itself was large, the yard was far larger. It covered about a third of an acre—the largest amount of land I owned before or since. And it was right smack in the centre of the city. Never mind the rats in the basement, nor the bats in the huge spruce trees out front (they flew into our house at night as long as we lived there). Despite enormous efforts by pest-control squads, we were never able to get rid of the vermin.

I tried not to think about the rats and the bats and what to do with the inside of the house. I left these tasks to Allan. This time he promised me no architect to supervise construction. Instead he hired an aging, crusty Ottawa Valley contractor. Mr. Bowen and his sons were recommended to him by an old Oxford chum, John Turner, then minister of justice. Mr. Bowen turned out to be the most honest contractor we ever dealt with. He took a look at the house, shook his head and said, "If I give you a set price now, you're going to lose money. As I don't know what I'm up against, I will have to charge you an arm and a leg. If you trust me, and we deal with each mess as it comes along, it will come off cheaper for you."

Mr. Bowen and his sons and their various subcontractors lived in our house for the next two years. Many sessions were spent over a bottle of what Mr. Bowen called "corgnac," discussing the sad state of the electricals or the "killer asbestos" in the walls and on the pipes (which he and sons removed without masks). And what to do with the enormous antique furnace in the basement? "Leave the furnace alone," Mr. Bowen said, "Why replace it? It's been working for seventy-five years. It will cost you a fortune to get a new one and it won't keep you any warmer."

Unfortunately, a huge pipe from the furnace extended from the basement into the centre of the master bedroom on the second floor, so we could never fit more than a three-quarters bed into the room. "The only thing you can do," Mr. Bowen said when I complained about its appearance, "is to tie a bow around it." After that, I gave up on the inside of the house, including the turn-of-the-century kitchen and butler's pantry.

The kitchen had a very high ceiling criss-crossed by a number of fat heating pipes that today would be considered retro-chic. But at that time they were regarded as eyesores. I bought a small grapevine and attached it to one of the pipes. It was a good marriage. The ceiling of my kitchen turned into a glossy green arbour—lovely, especially during the long winters. Cooking in a jungle, for me, made up for the lack of built-in ovens, marble counters and state-of-the-art cupboards that people were beginning to clamour for. Unlike at Ellesmere Place, there wasn't a nook problem. A large convent table in the centre of the cavernous kitchen served as my cooking counter (I was writing cookbooks by this time) and the family dining table.

When Mr. Bowen tore down the walls separating the two units of the house, it created a vast open space in the centre. He asked Allan, "Now what are we going to do? You can build a bowling alley or an indoor skating rink." That's when Allan said, "Where am I going to put my books?"

Since his days at Oxford, Allan had collected books, but he didn't care at all what was inside them. He only cared about the

covers. He wasn't into particular authors or subjects or first edi-
tions. Content was irrelevant. Since his sorties into Marcel
Proust when he was courting me, he had read no fiction
(although he did have a weakness for Sir Walter Scott, forcing
me to listen to passages that he read out while the children
fled). He had a pile of elegant leather books with India paper,
some of which were eminently readable—Anthony Trollope,
Jane Austen, Charles Dickens, Wilkie Collins, George Eliot
and William Thackeray—my favourite writers. But I was not
allowed to touch them. "These books are not for reading," he
explained. "They're for collecting. It's the bindings that count.
If you insist on reading Collins or Thackeray or whoever, buy
them in paperback." This was his reaction when he found me
reading one of his precious books with onion-skin paper in the
bathtub.

Allan asked Mr. Bowen to build a shelf or two that would
measure up to the quality of his collection. "You can't build a
few shelves for all those books," Mr. Bowen said. "I'll make
your shelf into a wall of bookcases. That way you'll have a front
hall." He found a carpenter, a guy from the Gatineau Hills,
who, for a year, sat on a ladder building Allan's wall. Michel was
not a carpenter, he was an artist, whose skill and devotion could
not be equalled. He built the most beautiful mahogany bookcases—sawing, sizing, planing, filing, cutting, shaping. For a
year, Michel became the person closest to me. He was there
before the kids got up in the morning and left just before Allan
came home in the evening. Tap, tap, tap, knock, knock, knock I
would hear all day. A cigarette always in his mouth, he never
spoke a word. When I offered him coffee, he would refuse. He
didn't want to take time off from his bookcases. In the end, I
believe we had the finest wall of bookshelves in Canada. "It will
cost a mint," Allan kept muttering, "but it's worth it for my

books." Mr. Bowen never itemized his bills. When everything in the house was all completed, Allan was surprised at the total. "That's not including the bookcases," he said to Mr. Bowen. "Yes it is," he replied. "I told you to do it my way." (The people who finally bought Lisgar Road from us tore down the mahogany bookcase wall, first thing.)

After the renovations in our house were completed, my mother-in-law, Grandma Sally, would stay with us from time to time. She liked her comforts. Her idea of roughing it was playing the occasional game of golf after she reached the age of fifty. She moved immediately to an apartment when her husband died. She had no interest in keeping up the "grounds" as she called the front- and backyard of her substantial house (for Winnipeg) in the old South End. Grandma Sally was horrified by Allan's Lisgar Road purchase, and even after our improvements, she stayed with us only with great reluctance. "Third-class hotel," she muttered, when I told her she had to share her bathroom with the girls. Our own "master bathroom" was located behind the six-foot furnace pipe in the bedroom, and you had to squeeze to get in the door. But Allan was her only and adored son and in principle, she never harped on something she disapproved of once the deed was done (unlike me). She disliked the idea of him becoming a civil servant, she disliked Ottawa and she loathed the house on Lisgar Road. But as the real estate agents say, location, location, location. She liked the fact our house was close to the Governor General's residence, the prime minister's residence and the embassies. But we knew she would make Allan sell the house if she found out about the bats.

When it got dark, the bats would often escape from the attic and fly around the house. After dinner, my mother-in-law would sit in front of the TV in the small downstairs den on the other side of the bookcase wall. This was the tensest time in the evening. Rachel, Rebecca, and I feared and hated the creatures. When we heard their terrifying whoosh, we would whisper hysterically to the men, "Bat bats," and they would grab tennis racquets while the three females sat taut and watched *Ed Sullivan* with Grandma Sally. Neither Allan nor Marc played tennis. The racquets were there for bat swatting. Often Allan and Marc would swat the bats away from the area of the little sitting room, trying to manoeuvre them into the front hall and living room, while Rachel, Rebecca or I would run back and forth, doing spot checks in the living room to see how the men were doing.

The most critical moments were when Grandma was thinking of heading to the bathroom. She usually took her time because she had to climb the stairs, which she hated. We expected a bat or two to swoop down on her. Equally terrifying was when she would rise to see "what the fellows were doing." But she was amazed and pleased to see Marc and Allan practising their swings and leaping and lunging up and down in the hall or living room. "I never could get Allan to play tennis when he was little," she said. "His father even got him a private coach." She even congratulated me for making Allan into a tennis player. The truth was that the only time Allan picked up a tennis racquet was to kill a bat. I too tried to get Marc to play tennis, private coach and all, but he was a chip off the old block. Tennis racquets, for the men in my family, were there for scaring away the critters.

Spring arrived not long after we moved into our renovated house. I walked around our huge back garden to see what was growing. The first thing I noticed was that there were no bulbs of any kind peeping from the ground. I soon discovered that my back garden presented two major difficulties.

The first was that, as the spring progressed, half the yard was soon covered with a weed that a neighbour identified as Queen Anne's lace. As far as I was concerned, this plant was no different from poison ivy. Whatever I tried to grow in the back garden—basil, black-eyed Susans, peonies—would be strangled or smothered by the expanding white web of this giant carrotlike plant. I never dreamed there would be a time in my life when I would see Queen Anne's lace selling for four dollars a stem in the best flower shops in Washington, or that rich and famous ladies would be touched by the gift of a bouquet of "wildflowers." (This was another thing I was to learn about gardening: anything you don't want is a weed, anything you can't grow is a rare plant.) Among the grand hostesses of Washington, Queen Anne's lace was a rare and coveted wildflower. And on Embassy Row, their majestic bouquets brightened the darkest terraces. On Lisgar Road, I never once thought of cutting a stem of Queen Anne's lace, let alone making a whole bouquet of them to bring into my house.

There was a second problem in the backyard. Allan became very interested in cedar hedges. The cedar became to Allan what the apple seed was to Johnny. Both at Ellesmere Place and Lisgar Road, Allan planted cedars with abandon. He would never let anything or anybody interfere with his cedars. The first thing he did when he bought the house on Lisgar Road was to plant a cedar hedge in the backyard, using his children as forced labour. Within a couple of years, the overfed, heavily nourished, never-trimmed cedars had achieved their intended purpose—separating our property completely from our neighbour's house behind us. Allan considered this new structure so esthetically unpleasant that he had to protect his family from having a view of it.

One morning—after the cedars had exhibited exceptionally

gratifying growth—Allan opened the back door and saw that his beloved hedge had been cut in half by the neighbour. The young blond Central European woman who was the owner of the eyesore that Allan wanted to hide from the children confirmed to him that she had cut and levelled the hedge because it didn't look tidy. "It is very important for me to have things neat," she said. "If they are not neat, I get upset. Your hedge was very untidy." "My hedge, precisely," Allan replied. "Not yours to cut. You never planted one tree. You ruined my hedge. Now I have to look at your ugly house." There were murmurings about lawsuits, reprisals and other unpleasantries.

The castrating neighbour-lady and the Queen Anne's lace were two good reasons for me to keep out of the backyard. However, there was something behind the house that intrigued me—a vine on the garage that didn't bloom. A friend who knew something about vines told me that it was called clematis. The trailing plant was a tangle of vines but during the following summer it produced one exquisite flower. To cut or not to cut, that was my question. In an act of desperation, and despite the beautiful flower, I took some shears and cut the thing right back to its roots. But there was no way I could get the roots out. They had probably been there for fifty years. That desperate act was my first garden triumph—the happy accident that all gardeners need. The following year a profusion of magnificent mauve-blue flowers covered the whole garage wall. My shears had wakened a sleeping beauty—Ramona. She was the one thing that flourished in my backyard, aside from the Queen Anne's lace.

After a few years, I did make an attempt to assert my mastery over the Queen's Anne lace. With the loss of our remarkably productive plum tree on Ellesmere Place, I made no fruit jams until Allan suggested one day that perhaps we could try to grow raspberries in the midst of our Queen Anne's lace jungle. There was nothing he liked better than raspberry jam, unless it was wild cherry preserve, and the climate did not allow for cherry trees.

I planted two dozen raspberry bushes among the Queen Anne's lace, hoping that the raspberries would smother the latter and produce enough fruit for jam for the family. I found an older couple, the Meynards, who had a little perennial farm and actually were delighted to sell their plants. As long as I called in advance they would usually dig them out and have them ready for me. They told me that raspberries were indestructible and all I needed was space and sun. The first-year plants bore little fruit the following year, so I decided to hurry up the process and bought three dozen more. The third year my patch of raspberries had skipped over the Queen's Anne's lace and increased so much we couldn't get easily out of the back door. Every member of the family had their eyeballs scratched by the raspberry thorns—and once Allan had to wear a patch over one eye for a month. Despite the manure and leavings from my compost heap (my first and last because it attracted vermin so that my kids and Allan refused to turn it), the raspberry canes bore little fruit. Every morning, during raspberry season, I made the dangerous way between the thorns and only found sufficient raspberries to cover one bowl of cereal. By the fourth year I had more raspberry bushes than the Meynards, but little fruit. Now my backyard was overrun with both fruitless raspberry bushes and unconquerable Queen Anne's lace. "It's the revenge of the raspberries," Allan said, after he had been scratched in the eye. But as with the Queen Anne's lace, there was no way of getting rid of them. He hated them as much as he hated the neighbour woman who still kept cutting our hedge. Except to harvest a highly successful return from my basil seeds, no one went into the backyard apart from me. I made enormous amounts of pesto, which I froze for the long winters. Instead of jam, we ate spaghetti with pesto sauce until Marc and a couple of his friends threw all the jars out of the freezer.

I wasn't demoralized by the state of our backyard because, in the front of the house and facing the park with its huge stand of mature white pines, there was a deep and wide yard with very sunny areas in which to plant a garden. The front lawn led up to our great wraparound two-storey porch and because of the park, there were no neighbours around that it was necessary to block from view. I still had no idea about garden design and such things, but I did know that I liked to look at flowers close up. What better idea than to put in garden beds that aligned with the walk leading to the front door and porch and from which you could see everything growing at once. No surprises around the corner. A visitor could walk up to ring the front bell and see every flower I planted. (I learned only later that this is not considered good gardening design.)

By this time I began to take an interest in garden books. I liked them simply written for simple minds. I didn't know or worry about whether they left out important information. The Time-Life gardening books with their big pictures and not-too-inspiring texts were good enough for me. Thanks to the Time-Life logo, their books were like chapters of the Bible. I became a Time-Life fundamentalist. I read that a flowerbed didn't have to be set out in straight lines. I was amazed because my father and Uncle Rex in Winnipeg had built rectangular gardens with right angles and straight edges. "Take a garden hose," one of the books said, "and fling it about. Let it fall where it may. See what shape it makes. If it pleases you, cut the bed to that shape. Or, if you prefer, arrange the hose to the shape of your desired design. And then cut out your garden bed." How bohemian, I thought. I didn't have to have straight rectangular gardens laid out along my sidewalk. They could be kidney-shaped in the manner of Hollywood pools, or formed like a spider web.

On one side of the walk, I had the children form the garden hose into a shape that pleased me. It was large, long and thin but bulbous and fat at the top end. As long as I lived on Lisgar Road, everyone who noticed the shape of the bed said the same thing—"it's very phallic." How annoying. On the other side of the walk, I decided not to fling the hose, although I wasn't sure why. In the Ottawa Experimental Farm, I had seen a circular garden for rose bushes. I thought that perhaps I would like that in my garden. I realized that if I threw the hose on the other side of the path with a view to forming a spider-shaped garden, I might have no room for a circular rose bed. The grass was in such terrible shape that we had to lease a Rototiller to tear up the soil. This made it quite easy to form a circular bed. The children drew up a large rather clumsy circle. I knew (thanks to Time-Life) that this time I would need more than a flimsy layer of potting soil to plant the flowers. A farmer from the Byward Market dropped off a massive load of horse manure in front of the house and Allan forked the stuff into the newly made beds (and dropped the Patek Philippe gold wristwatch his father gave him into the horseshit, never to be seen again). It was early spring and as yet there were no perennial plants to buy at the nurseries, so I decided to fill the beds with annuals for the first year.

That first summer, I went with Allan to England where he was attending a conference for a few weeks. I had recently read an autobiography by Harold Nicholson in which he described the making of Sissinghurst by himself and his wife Vita

Sackville-West (the couple were not yet made notorious by their son). I decided I would go to Sissinghurst to pick up a few gardening tips. I arrived on an extraordinarily hot day early in July and all the Old Roses were in full bloom—Cardinal de Richelieu, Belle de Crecy, Reines de Violette, Madame Lauriol du Barry, the gallicas, damasks and the bourbons from Josephine's famous Malmaison garden. The shape of the flowers, the form of the petals, the tiny green discs in the middle of the centifolia and gallica roses, the range of colours, especially the deep purples and reds with silvery edges, and, above all, the fragrances were unlike anything I had ever seen before in a rose. In the Experimental Farm, I had seen only modern hybrid teas, grandifloras and floribundas, so popular at that time in North America. The Old Roses, by and large, had not yet been rediscovered on our side of the Atlantic.

The first thing I did when I left Sissinghurst was to go to a bookshop in London and hit the gardening section. I bought a book titled *Old Shrub Roses* by Graham Stewart Thomas, a famous English gardening writer whom, of course, I had never heard of. I had no idea whether I could grow those roses in Canada, but I was determined to try.

When I got back to Ottawa, I managed to track down two catalogues on Old Roses, one from a nursery in Northern California, and the other, to my astonishment, from a nursery in Ontario called Pickering. I decided to fill up both my beds, the circular one and the phallic one, with the roses that Graham Stewart Thomas seemed to especially like. Foolishly, I had not written down the names of the Old Roses in Sissinghurst that had appealed to me. I cross-checked the references between Thomas and the two North American catalogues as best I could. Ordering from the United States was particularly difficult because you needed a special permit to do so. Luckily, Allan the civil servant knew another civil servant in the Department of Agriculture and the roses came early and soon.

Foolishly, I did not take into account the size of the shrubs when they matured. My main criteria for selection were the description of the flower, the perfume and, to a certain extent, whether the rose was hardy. I discovered that what was hardy in England and California was not necessarily hardy in Ottawa. But for the most part I was lucky. When all the precious sticks arrived in the fall, I was so worried whether they would remain alive that I planted and buried them in the horse manure. I realized later that I need not have worried that much because most of them were hardier than the new and spindly hybrid teas and that moreover, I was living in the midst of a snowbelt, which offered tremendous protection from the cold. Within two years some of the roses had grown six to eight feet tall, but lacking anything to climb they flopped all over the beds. Almost every plant I bought bloomed and the flowers were all strikingly beautiful. But what I didn't realize was that Old Roses bloom only once a year and many needed somebody to lean on, as the song goes.

I was terrified of cutting the roses back because I thought that would destroy them, so my beds looked like an assembly of thorny green fingers growing every which way but up. In fact, within all the manure and snow piled up on the rose beds, I could see roses blooming in March under the plastic, which was not exactly the time of the year I wanted them to grow. Nevertheless, I kept adding more roses, mostly hardy, still paying no attention to their height or spread. I never planted a hybrid tea.

By this time I was also growing seeds under Gro-lites in the basement (in the midst of the rats). There were only three kinds of seeds that grew for me under these lacklustre lights—

nasturtiums, basil and morning glories. These are the easy seeds one gives to children if they wish to grow flowers. I planted into the ground, among the rose stems, large pots of nasturtiums and morning glories, in order to give the beds colour after the roses bloomed. The nasturtiums and morning glories spread like ground cover.

So basically my garden at Lisgar Road was a mixture of rare Old Roses that bloomed only once a year and a profusion of nasturtiums and morning glories. But I was bothered by the fact that the morning glories bloomed only in sun. Then I remembered my evening primroses on Ellesmere Place. I realized they would open as the morning glories closed. As much as I hated those primroses at Ellesmere Place, I realized their value on Lisgar Road and planted them in profusion among the morning glories.

I spent every afternoon in spring and summer fooling around in the front garden. When my neighbours walked by, including Margaret Trudeau, then married to the prime minister, they would tease me. I never knew if anyone really liked my garden. My husband could never figure out what I was doing and my children resented being conscripted help. One thing I knew. I was never happier than during those long afternoons in Ottawa when I was trying to get those rose bushes to grow upright, a frustrating task as I had no pillars, arbours, pergolas or walls—nothing but bamboo sticks. Eventually I graduated from Time-Life to Vita Sackville-West's own writings (not of great practical use but interesting to read) and even discovered a couple of rather dull but informative Canadian writers who helped me find out which Old Roses really flourished in Canada and how high they grew.

14

The Beast

THE ONLY THING MISSING from our ideal house and garden on Ellesmere Place was a dog. Our best friend Stephen Belknap, a family man still married to his first wife even after his mad affair in Geneva with Giselle, said to me, "You can't be a real family without a dog." Marc was seven, Rebecca was eight and Rachel was four. Rebecca overheard the dog conversation and began to cry. "Why are we the only family without a dog?" Our friend who gave the advice had three daughters but he didn't have a dog. He had an angry wife instead. "Dog, dog, dog," the children screamed and jumped up and down, listening to the conversation.

"You see," Stephen said, "they're missing something essential in their lives." I was convinced. "What kind of dog should we get?" "Not a Scottie," I said, remembering my trauma with the bad-tempered animal named Sport who was dispatched to his death by an Eaton's horse. "And not a cocker spaniel," I added, remembering my heartache when my parents put Timmy down for no good reason. "I know a farmer north of Ottawa who raises dogs," Stephen said. "Airedales, they're beautiful dogs, perfect for children. And the farmer's Dutch," Stephen pointed out, "and keeps a very clean kennel." This was good. I'd never buy a dog from a dirty kennel. Did I do any research about Airedales or seek out other breeders? Of course not. I do things spontaneously whether it is gardening or getting married. Even having Marc was not thought through. Clean kennels was all the information I needed about choosing dogs. "How big is an Airedale?" I asked. Stephen shrugged. "Could Rachel take him for a walk?" "Absolutely," he said.

We made an appointment with the breeder and drove north to pick up a pup. The kennels were clean, the farmer raved about his heroic strain of Airedales, and they looked small—not surprising since they were only eight weeks old. I didn't see the mother. Rebecca burst into tears when one of them nuzzled her. We paid for him on the spot, named him Hector and he sat in her lap during the whole trip back, while she elbowed out the younger children.

Before we bought Hector, I thought I had better mention the matter to our only neighbour, Mr. Pick. "Airedale, eh," he said, "very scrappy dog. A terrier. They love to dig. Watch out for your bulbs. Very, very scrappy." Mr. Pick's remarks made me uneasy, and I repeated them to Allan. "He just doesn't want a dog on our little street," Allan said.

Hector the Protector, as we named him, adored us, the children, our friends, the contractors and the cleaning ladies, but disliked all strangers whether they were cats or joggers. He killed the cats and would have killed the joggers too, if Allan hadn't kept an eye on them while he sat on the front porch in the evening. At that time, Rockcliffe Park was still a separate jurisdiction in Ottawa, and dogs were allowed to run free without a leash as long as they behaved. Neither Allan nor I knew how to train dogs. We assumed Hector would learn things in a natural way. I was much stricter with my children than I was with my dog. Dog training was not my number one priority. In a desultory fashion, I was beginning to write about food as well as continue to cook obsessively. Moreover, Allan had nagged me relentlessly to go back to university and take some courses for a BA. Why, I'll never know. I did know from my Oxford days that I only liked being at university if I was wife of a professor. I enrolled in a few English and art history courses at Carleton College and hated being the oldest person in the class. This was well before the idea of adult education. Hector just grew up. We figured that if there were problems, the kids would train him, since they liked him so much, or at least did at first.

Hector had his quirks. While the family called him Hector the Protector, our neighbours called him the Beast of Rockcliffe Park. Because he was often in attack mode, his name began to come up regularly at meetings of the Council of Rockcliffe Village. Notwithstanding the council's no-leash-is-necessary ordinance, the councillors wanted us to put Hector on a leash. Fortunately, a number of council members were our friends. As Hector was always well behaved at home, we would entertain the members to show them how sweet, pliant and lovable Hector was. As a result of our continual lobbying, the restraining order was never issued, although the threat was always over our (or rather, Hector's) head.

When I went shopping in the market downtown, I would sometimes see Hector harassing some woman walking her Yorkie on a leash. I would hear people yelling, "Whose dog is that?" I could usually slip away before Hector caught my scent. While keeping a respectful distance, sometimes I would join in the small crowds surrounding him and agree how terrible it was that the dog's owner allowed it to wander around downtown without a leash. I was not interested in where he went on his daily wanderings. He would always get home before the children arrived from school.

Matters became worse when, a couple of years after we bought Hector, the National Capital Commission foolishly built a jogging path right in front of our house, completely ignoring Allan's protests. He hated the idea of people running in front of his property. Hector shared his distaste for joggers. He would sit on the front porch early in the morning and at dusk, waiting for the familiar sound of a loping jogger. No human could outrun Hector. In the evenings Allan would often sit on the front porch beside Hector, but would try to slip away into the house when an attack was about to take place. There were many joggers not from Rockcliffe on the path and they didn't know that Allan was the owner. In this way he was able to reduce the number of times he had to accompany the wounded to the hospital. He would listen for the jogger's scream inside the house. The tone of the scream was sufficient for Allan to know if the jogger was hospital material. If so, he would emerge from the house. Here I have to say that Hector never seriously hurt a human. He'd just take the odd rip off a stranger.

Eventually, a number of Hector's victims, led by a young bearded doctor terrified of rabies (of course Hector was inoculated), formed into a group of vigilantes. Most of them had felt Hector's teeth on their posterior—the dog's favourite target.

The doctor threatened legal action, unless Hector was leashed. Allan refused to give ground. He would argue with the joggers. "Dogs are territorial," he told them. "Go jog somewhere else."

Unfortunately, our problems with Hector worsened as he grew older. Allan detested cats but Hector grew to hate then even more. In time, skunks, raccoons and squirrels all became his natural prey. Then he developed an aversion to other dogs, particularly the small, overbred and expensive kind. Hector had by now grown large and powerful. (This came as a surprise to us because we thought Airedales were a more modest size.) He was an extremely handsome animal with a large head and a thick wiry brown coat. If they were feeling better disposed, the Villagers would refer to him not as the Beast of Rockcliffe Park but as the Lion of Lisgar Road.

While refusing to bow to the growing demand of the Villagers not to let Hector run free, Allan occasionally thought it politic to leash Hector and take him for a stroll through Rockcliffe. This was designed to show his neighbours that he was a good citizen, but in truth Allan was proud of Hector's magnificent leonine appearance and loved to show him off. Allan had a collection of hickory walking sticks with ivory handles acquired during his Oxford days. He would take one of the sticks with him when he went for walks through the Village— "for disciplinary reasons" he would explain. Inevitably, Hector would get into fights with other animals. Allan would use the stick to beat him over the head. The dog's head could have been made out of stone. In time, Allan broke all his canes. "Cruelty to animals?" "Nonsense," Allan would say. "Hector feels my blows less than he does a mosquito's bite. He grabs my stick with his mouth and thinks he's playing games with me."

Our children's affection for Hector diminished as they got older and as Hector's character deteriorated. They were afraid to take him for a walk on a leash because he was so much stronger than they were. If he didn't manage to break loose on the walks, he would drag them along on the ground as he lunged to attack an unsuspecting enemy. But he was fond of the children and would accompany them to school in the morning and wait for them at the bus stop after school. Unfortunately, for a strong dog, he had a weak constitution. Sitting in the back seat of our Chevrolet with the three children when we went on frequent outings into the Gatineau to visit friends at their cottages, Hector would become nauseated, slobber and then vomit all over them. They soon learned to pile up on each other at the corners of the back seat and let Hector sprawl out in the middle. Even in the dead of winter, the children would keep the rear-window wide open so Hector could have plenty of air and presumably avoid nausea. Sometimes, one of the children would ask, "Why don't you take Hector in the front seat?" But Allan would refuse, alleging that this would interfere with his driving.

In desperation, we would let Hector out of the car, but we learned that it was exceptionally difficult to get him back in. We would drive off in a mock effort to abandon him but to no avail. He would run after the car as we drove away but could never be coached back into it. He would sometimes chase after the car over a dozen miles of back country roads. But we still loved Hector enough not to want to lose him. So Allan would reduce our speed to about ten miles per hour, but the result was always the same—Hector could not be lured into the car. A twenty-minute drive would take three hours. The long slow rides over back roads would make my children car sick. They would vomit in the car all the way home, but Hector would return to Lisgar Road lively and refreshed, his endomorphins having kicked in during his work-out.

As Hector's temper and behaviour worsened, he became a menace to everyone except the members of our family. It was like having Frankenstein's monster living in the house. Calm and peaceful within the family, Hector was hated and feared by the Villagers outside the gates. I expected them to come with torches and horsewhips in the middle of the night.

One morning when Hector was about seven years old and Allan was away, the front doorbell rang at 7 a.m. I opened the door to a small posse of Villagers, workers and crying children carrying wounded pets. It seems that the monster had been on one of his early morning prowls while we slept, and had a particularly productive walk. I couldn't take it anymore. Rebecca and Rachel were still asleep in their bedrooms. I woke them up and, in a state of hysteria, explained the situation to the three children. A family decision had to be made, even in the absence of the patriarch. The two girls pulled the blankets over their heads and opted out of the decision-making. But Marc, now fifteen, was fed up with our habitual crises with Hector. He got dressed and said, "I'm taking him to the pound." "What are you going to do there?" I asked, trembling. He didn't answer. He drove off to the pound with Hector and returned without him. The Villagers rejoiced. I forgot that Marc only had a learner's licence.

15

The Food Critic

*I*T WAS AT ELLESMERE PLACE that I realized that I achieved more or less everything that my parents and I wanted. I was happily married, had a reliable husband and three children, and as everyone told me, I was a talented cook. I liked to entertain and would often have cocktail parties for sixty people or more, buffets for thirty, and smaller sit-down dinners—sometimes attended by Pierre Elliott Trudeau, who was then prime minister—as well as members of his inner circle. Trudeau may have been eccentric in his politics and personal relationships, but unlike some in his inner circle he had style. Trudeau symbolized, whether he was aware of it or not, the ancient English motto of Winchester public school: "Manners maykth the man."

I was planning a dinner for twelve (I could only sit that number in my tiny dining room) and the prime minister had accepted. The morning of the dinner party, the phone rang. "Sondra, I'm so sorry to disturb you, it's Pierre." How many prime ministers, CEOs or self-important slobinskies would make a direct call to the wife of a civil servant in order to sort out a minor social difficulty? He's going to cancel I thought and being a gentleman, refused to pass the task on to an aide. "Sondra," he said, in his whispery tone, "I don't quite know how to put this. I have a house guest, so I'm afraid I will have to stay home and entertain her. But of course that means I will miss your party." I didn't know whether he wanted to stay home and entertain the house guest or wanted me to entertain both of them. I told him I'd be happy to invite his house guest as well. What was in his head? Maybe he wanted to sneak away to Harrington Lake with a Miss Scandinavia. But his tone brightened immediately when I extended the invitation. Whoever she was, he didn't want to be alone with her. "She's the sister of the King of the Belgians, and entertained me when I was in her country." "Bring the Princess along," I said, giving him my North Winnipeg welcome. "Well," he said, pausing, "there's another problem. She's brought her lady-in-waiting." "The lady-in-waiting is not a problem," I responded, mentally moving the dinner to the living room. He sounded so relieved that whatever difficulties he was having with Quebec were probably nothing compared to what he was having with the Belgian Princess and her entourage. For reasons unexplained to me, the lady-in-waiting turned out to be a Canadian socialite, Catherine Nugent. When I met her twenty years later in Toronto, I asked about the Princess. "She was very neurotic," Catherine said. "She eventually ran off with a piano player and died."

Pierre added on the telephone, "Don't cook anything extra. The Princess doesn't eat much. She's very thin." Trudeau was very much part of the Ottawa social scene, such as it was, and was aware that civil servants' wives never used caterers. He occasionally flattered me on my cooking. My reputation as daughter of Fanny the Feeder had reached the hallowed halls of Parliament.

Yet, I told Allan that being a perfect wife, a good cook, and a pretty good if absent-minded mother was not enough. I also told him that I didn't intend to live the rest of my life in Ottawa. Although I had enrolled in some of the easiest courses at university, I still panicked when exam time came around. The last time I had cured my panic attacks by getting married, but now that I was married and had children I had no similar recourse. I was at least fifteen years older than the other students and I was the only one in my art history and psychology classes who constantly failed exams.

My ego was at its nadir. As my husband rose in the civil service, becoming what was called a mandarin, I felt I was becoming more and more invisible. I was the perfect example of the feminists' unfulfilled and unhappy housewife, even though I doggedly and unwillingly went to college. I was becoming a feminist cliché. Betty Friedan or Gloria Steinem or Germaine Greer would have wagged a finger at me and said: this is what happens when you fulfill your parents' dreams. But I refused to jump on their bandwagon because being true zealots they claimed to know all the answers, and zealotry always troubled me. When I was fifteen, I had joined an extreme Zionist youth movement because the milkman's son, whom I loved, was a member. Instead of meeting for coffee with the boys and talking about planting trees in Israel, the leaders of the group went into inexplicable anti-American tirades. What had this to do with romance? What had this to do with my agenda? What did this have to do with meeting boys? Their words upset me, and I never returned. I had nothing against the States. The shopping was better in Minneapolis than Winnipeg and our dollar was worth more. Much later, someone told me that the organization was a Communist front under the guise of Zionism. Not that that would have meant much to me then. When I was fifteen, I didn't know the difference between Communism and Rosicrucianism, except that my father didn't approve of the former.

Although I couldn't get excited about the women's movement, I knew family and children were not enough. Allan meant well when he thought a university degree would be a useful step towards a career, but I was reading Freud's *Interpetation of Dreams* in my psychology course and it made me weep every night. I wasn't weeping over Dora's dreams. I was weeping because I couldn't understand the text. What was Dora or Hannah talking about anyhow? I couldn't fathom Freud's interpretation. I was certain that the feminists and intellectuals would have some sort of answer. But as far as I was concerned, I could have been reading the *Interpretation of Dreams* in the original German. It was all gibberish to me.

At Ellesmere Place our back-hedge neighbours suddenly played the role of *deus ex machina* in my life. The back-hedge family on Ellesmere Place ran a cottage publishing business from the basement of their home. At this address they published, edited and printed (as far as I could tell) their books and received grants from the government. A married neighbour in her mid-thirties was their only assistant other than the two young sons of the husband and wife. The family was very close-knit and kept strictly to themselves until one day they came into my life and changed everything.

They told me that they were thinking of doing something never done before in Canada—publishing a Canada-wide guidebook to the best restaurants in the country. The wife, who was both writer and editor, knew that I was deeply interested in cooking and restaurants and asked my advice about a couple of her reviews. They read as if the restaurants had paid for them. I told her they were puff pieces. Her husband feared, she confided, that if they criticized the restaurants they could be sued. I explained to her that in the United States, Britain and France there were many critical restaurant guides and they managed to prosper. We agreed that I would provide critical reviews and shortly thereafter we also decided that I would be co-editor of the restaurant guide.

Allan, the children and I dined out as often as possible, and during the summer months we drove through the different regions of Canada, sampling restaurant fare. This was the beginning of my career as a food writer. *Where to Eat in Canada* became quite a successful publication but the back-hedge publisher decided, after the first edition, that they didn't need Sondra Gotlieb as co-editor anymore and turned down my book suggestion—*The Gourmet's Canada*, which had little to do with restaurants. Happily, the proposal was picked up by another publisher who knew my name as co-editor of *Where to Eat in Canada*. Maybe the back-hedge publisher rejected the idea because he was having family troubles. The neighbour lady—the only non-family member who worked for him—left her husband and ran off with the best worker, the eldest son. The father was a demanding man and I could easily understand how the two labourers needed to liberate themselves from this cloistered arrangement. Although the lady was twenty years older than the son they fled to England to, as far as I know, live happily together.

The Gourmet's Canada was not a restaurant guidebook; it was a survey of the best food in Canada from coast to coast. With a five-hundred-dollar advance, I managed to travel from Vancouver Island to Newfoundland, testing the best places to eat, the best ingredients, the best recipes, bakeries, butcher shops, fish and chip stands, take-outs and the best of everything else imaginable that had anything to do with food. Staying at the homes mostly of strangers, I tasted everything from seal-flipper pie in Newfoundland and *poutine râpée* in New Brunswick to white salmon in British Columbia. Amazingly enough, *The Gourmet's Canada* did very well.

In Vancouver, investigating pastry shops, Freud and Dora ceased to disturb my dreams. When exam time came round at Carleton College, I didn't set foot inside the university. I happily gave up my academic career to pursue my new vocation as a food writer. I wrote about imaginary thanksgiving dinners for *Chatelaine*. *Maclean's* sent me cross-country to all the major cities to see what it was like for a single woman in her mid-thirties to dine alone on Saturday evening—a daring thing to do in Canada at that time. A few places, mainly in the West, treated me with courtesy, with curiosity and with some admiration. They were the exceptions. In one sophisticated restaurant, the Three Small Rooms in Canada's most urbane city— Toronto, of course—the m itre d'hotel refused to seat me although I had a long-standing reservation. "We do not allow young women to dine alone at night in our restaurant," he explained. "They attract the wrong elements." Since I was staying in the hotel where the restaurant was located, the Windsor Arms, I asked where I was supposed to eat. The m itre d'hotel kept me standing for fifteen minutes while he investigated what kind of a working woman I was. Then he begrudgingly offered me a table behind a door. I squawked until I got a centre table.

This experience did not deter me from becoming a restaurant spy for Cara Foods, a company that was concerned about the quality of the cooking in some of its restaurants. The senior executive who hired me was worried about quality but, as I discovered later, the other top executive in the firm was concerned about cost. The food was uniformly expensive and bad in all restaurants. When I discussed the so-called lobster soufflé with one of the chefs, he said, "How can you make a lobster soufflé with one egg white? We follow recipes for robots made by an accountant at headquarters." The cost-conscious executive ousted the quality-conscious one and I was told not to bother making a report. All the restaurants I visited disappeared not long after.

I then agreed to write a cookbook for the department of the federal government responsible for multiculturalism. It was to be a celebration of ethnic cooking in Canada and of the people who did the cooking. From beginning to end, this project was a misadventure. I wrote *Cross Canada Cooking* for a minimum amount of money and no royalties. Although the book was well received, the government unfortunately selected an inexperienced (affirmative action) publisher. The title on the cover of the book came out as *Gross Canada Cooking*. Its publication marked the first occasion, but not the last, when my writings and behaviour were discussed in the House of Commons. A rising Opposition member, Joe Clark, for reasons unknown to me but presumably not to himself, questioned the payment I received for the book and for my magazine articles on cooking. He seemed to imply that maybe I had been paid twice and maybe improper influence was brought to bear (by my husband, of course) in my obtaining the assignment. I consulted a libel lawyer of high repute who told me I had an excellent basis for a lawsuit. I was keen to sue, but Allan, figuring a lawsuit against Joe Clark wouldn't advance his career very much, was less enthusiastic. I let the matter drop. I learned from this that in Canada at that time anything I did as a writer risked affecting my husband's career, whether it was a recipe book or the humorous non-political newspaper columns that I was beginning to write for the *Ottawa Journal*.

Perhaps I would have had fewer problems if I had from the outset of my career used a pseudonym or my father's name instead of my husband's. But these were early days for women using their own names and Allan was not thrilled when I told him I might use my father's name. He asked rather huffily, "Who have you lived with longer, me or your father?"

While writing the cookbook, I was also the recipe-lady for CBC-Radio in Ottawa. This ended when a listener claimed that she faithfully followed my recipe for dill pickles and the bottle blew up in her face.

Then, the late editor of the *Toronto Star*, Martin Goodman, invited me to become food editor of the newspaper. The *Star* had its own test kitchen and a huge food section. This was a major job and a major challenge but it would have meant spending five days a week in Toronto, which neither my husband nor I wanted. And I didn't want to leave my children, all in their early teens. I turned it down. But there were other reasons why I didn't accept. While writing the restaurant guide, *The Gourmet's Canada*, *Cross Canada Cooking* and a growing number of articles on eating and cooking, I realized that writing interested me more than food.

I also began to hate the gushy way I was expected to write about cooking and cooks and everything that was gastronomically in vogue at the time. Editors expected food to be written about reverently in moral terms—whether it was good or bad for your body or your teeth. Food editors were becoming like the editors of the church pages in newspapers. Food writers had to be pious, like religion writers. I knew I was not meant to be reverential about anything, and certainly not food.

Perhaps there was also an anarchistic streak in me. This made me want to make fun of professionals and pretentious experts who cooked or wrote about food in a manner too solemn for my taste. As a cook, I liked to be spontaneous, even creating as I went along. Testing the same recipe over and over before it went to print—this I found tedious. Eating bad food several times at the same bad restaurant before I could review it—this I found boring, even disagreeable. As a recipe taster, I had a further problem. Canada was going metric and I was not. I was never that comfortable with centimetres, kilograms and the like. To this day I think in inches, quarts and Fahrenheit.

Allan was very unhappy about my losing interest in food. He thought I had a career ahead of me in gastronomy, even a lucrative one. I did like the sensation of making money. But Allan was harbouring a dream. He wanted to start a family restaurant in Ottawa. When he said family, he excluded himself, because he was a mandarin, a deputy minister, an adviser to powerful men. But with what he considered my vast culinary experience, he thought a restaurant would be a cinch and a money-maker, as long as the children pitched in. My teenage son Marc was the only one of my children who appeared to be interested in food. He even worked three evenings a week as a busboy, cutting cabbages for coleslaw at a steak restaurant called the Keg and Cleaver. Every evening Allan would bring up the subject of the restaurant and my eldest, who wanted to go to Queen's University, began to weep, along with her mother. Rachel, who was still very young, liked the idea: "I'll be the hostess and show the people to the tables." Hostesses got to wear the nice dresses. Encouraged, Allan asked, "Why should Marc waste time making coleslaw at the Keg when he could train as a real chef using his mother's recipes?" "Sondra's Salon," he christened it and he wasn't joking. "Who's going to be at the cash register?" I wailed. "I can't count my change at the supermarket." He looked hopefully at Rebecca who said, "I hate math." I threw words around like "bankruptcy" and "family slavery." Allan finally realized that he could only push a dream so far.

My decision not to go to the *Star* marked the end of my gastronomic career. I had reviewed virtually every major restaurant in Canada and explored every perogy house and pastry shop in the nation. I was sick of the whole thing. I would not be a food writer anymore. But my obsession with cooking and food did not end.

I began to realize, when I looked at my food writing, that what I liked about it were the descriptions of the characters who cooked and ate and the culture in which eating was so deeply a part. This was especially true of my early years in Winnipeg. Almost everything to do with my growing up in Winnipeg seemed to have a food connection, not to the recipes, or ingredients or their preparation, but to the lives of the people in which the kitchen played so dominant a part. As I mused to Allan one day in my usual discontented way (he called me *La Malcontenta* after the unhappy woman in the castle in northern Italy) about my lot in life, my boredom with food writing and my miserable performance at university, I told him that the only thing I liked about my work were the bits and paragraphs I wrote about the characters I knew when growing up in Winnipeg. Tired of my lament, he muttered to me one day, "You sound just like your Aunt Dolly." My mother's older sister, Dolly, was the greatest lamenter in my family. Allan said, "I remember that bare patch on the carpet under the wall phone in your mother's den." This was the result of my mother's pacing up and down listening on the telephone to my Aunt Dolly moan about everything in life. Allan, disappointed by my unwillingness to pursue a career in food, said, "Sondra, each member of your family is bizarre enough to make a short story. Why don't you write stories about your family in the North End where you grew up?"

Allan had always lived in the bland and genteel South End, but he appreciated the richer flavour of Winnipeg's northern regions and he ventured there often. The North End was where the immigrants lived. If you were going north by street-car from downtown, you took the garlic line up Main Street, which led to the heart of where the Ukrainians, Jews, Poles and working-class people lived. "Short stories are in," Allan declared. "Multiculturalism is becoming fashionable. The Liberals are trying to win the ethnic vote. They're throwing money at them. Maybe if you wrote a book about ethnics in Winnipeg, you'll get a publisher."

Without a publisher, I wrote a number of short stories over the course of the next year where food was the connecting theme. The first chapter, "Fanny the Feeder," was about my mother's food obsessions and those of her friends and relatives. Another described the North End caterers, including the one who served five hundred people at a sit-down banquet at my wedding "four brown things on a plate" as a main course, followed by sculptured sponge cake swans for dessert. Because I wanted to describe the caterers and their foibles, I had to give them a context—my marriage. I showed my short stories to a few friends. One said, "Sondra, these are not short stories. You have an autobiographical novel." "About what?" I asked. "About your marriage," she replied. "You married a man you didn't know. You had an arranged marriage. That's the story, not the food." I had never thought there was anything strange about my marriage until she spoke those words. Growing up in Winnipeg and the events that led to my wedding were the themes of my tale and I entitled it *True Confections*. After a dozen rejections, I found a publisher.

From this point in my life, I knew I wanted to be a writer. After *True Confections* won the Leacock Prize for humour, I immediately started on a detective novel situated in Ottawa and Geneva. But, although I was writing every day—the novel was subsequently published as *First Lady, Last Lady*—I still loved to entertain. In the next few years of our life in Ottawa, we entertained as never before.

16

The Salonista

S HORTLY AFTER I WROTE *True Confections*, Allan was promoted to be undersecretary of state by Pierre Trudeau. We
began to go out constantly to embassy parties, dinners and
receptions at Government House, and occasionally to
24 Sussex Drive, when Pierre and later Margaret Trudeau felt
like entertaining. If there was such a thing as a social life in
Ottawa, we were a part of it.

Our house on Lisgar Road became a gathering point for
politicians, civil servants, writers, diplomats and anyone interesting in the National Capital that we could find. I did all the
cooking all the time for all our parties. This continued until
we finally left Ottawa to go to Washington when Allan took

up his assignment as ambassador to the United States.

I used to ask myself why I always wanted to entertain. And why did Allan aid and abet me? Were we social climbers? The ladder in Ottawa had very few rungs. I was in a way following in my mother's path. You could hardly call my mother a social climber. In the social world of North Winnipeg where she lived there was no ladder at all. Yet she was in her own way a "salonista."

Yet, my mother believed that having a stranger in the house for dinner was "pushy." The nearest she came to entertaining a celebrity was when she asked my high school principal for dinner. The evening made my father so uneasy, he couldn't sleep afterwards. "I don't need this kind of excitement," he said.

Still, she had open house almost every night. Streaming through our living room were my girlfriends, my brother's medical student friends (possible marriage material for me), uncles, aunts, cousins, in-laws, neighbours and friends who all had to be fed. No one in our house, or in many other Jewish houses in Winnipeg, went to bed without a second supper. About 8:30 p.m., two hours after the first supper was concluded, I would hear the Mixmaster whining. My mother would be preparing a fresh coffee cake or scones or putting together a cheese and noodle casserole. She would have everything ready for the second supper at ten o'clock, around the kitchen table.

My desire to have people over and entertain them, for whatever purpose, was genetic. With Allan, it was different. His mother, living in the South End, had political ambitions. She aspired to a leading role in world Zionist circles. No important Jewish leader or personality who ventured west of Montreal (and there were not many in those prewar days), could come to Western Canada without dining in her home at 121 Elm Street. This included notable Jewish historians, American and

Palestinian political leaders, including Golda Meier, and eminent polysyllabic American rabbis. (I never met a rabbi who couldn't make ten paragraphs out of three sentences. Is there such a thing as a taciturn rabbi?) Allan's mother would set out her best china and silver, always invite a Bronfman or two (they originated in Brandon, Manitoba), dress her maid in cap and frilly apron, to whom her husband would hand a plate with roast beef (always roast beef) which he carved from a huge joint on the sideboard in the spacious dining room. The maid would walk the plate of roast beef towards my mother-in-law, who would delicately lift the covers of Minton tureens filled with Manitoba wild rice, brussels sprouts and other green vegetables. All the Jews at the table thought they were eating kosher meat, but Allan's father, who liked his meats, worked out a deal with the city's leading kosher butcher that enabled him to buy delicious non-kosher cuts of beef with a kosher label. Although their reasons for and style of entertainment were different, both Allan's parents and mine were Western Canadians. Open house was far more common for them than among Easterners.

With these genes and background, it was inevitable that we would have what passed for a salon in Ottawa. As I once described the Ottawa hostess role, "Put wine on the kitchen counter, ham on the dining-room table, mail out a few postcards, preferably bought at the National Gallery and, presto, you're a hostess in Ottawa." We would give a big party three or four times a year, sans chef, sans waiters, sans place-cards and sometimes sans tables and chairs. These were political parties because people of every stripe would meet there. Sometimes, at least to me, they were exciting. It made me believe, as Jane Austen put it, that "everything happens at parties."

Not long after Pierre Trudeau came to power, Allan became a close adviser to him on constitutional issues relating to

Quebec and foreign affairs. Trudeau and his inner circle were often to be found at our house on Ellesmere Place, where he made the decision to run as prime minister, and later when we lived on Lisgar Road. Among the inner group was Michael Pitfield—numero uno in power and homme extrordinaire, far more powerful than the ministers—political insider Jim Coutts who took care of Liberal Party matters, strongman and confidante Marc Lalonde, and the mysterious Roy Faibish who would go around to all the pretty wives at our parties and explain to them that they were "seeking but not finding." In this manner, he unsettled many of us for months. A particularly memorable party (all the parties that Trudeau attended at our house were memorable) was to mark the occasion of Canada's first launch of a communications satellite (our sputnik, so to speak). The prime minister brought with him as his date a young woman named Margaret Sinclair. It was the first time, I believe, that he took her to a private party. She was twenty-one and the most ravishing woman I had ever seen, a black-haired Marilyn Monroe, so beautiful that even the most politically obsessed people at the party stood and gaped at her when they thought she was looking in the other direction. Dressed in a thigh-high lace minidress, she was enthralled by Leonard Cohen and spent a large part of the evening touching fingers and twining her legs around him. He was, after all, the poet-singer and icon of the sixties.

I did not see Margaret for a while after she married Trudeau. The prime minister and she then asked us to what might have been their first social evening at his residence after the marriage. It was in honour of flautist Jean-Pierre Rampal who gave a recital before dinner. Most of the guests were his old friends or a part of the inner political circle. We were all grossly overdressed. I wore, for the first time, the antique amethyst necklace that my mother-in-law gave me when my son was born. Margaret was at first nowhere to be seen but then she descended the grand staircase in her bare feet, wearing a peasant skirt and carrying a baby on her hip. She prepared most of the food herself and it was delicious.

Although Margaret had not been the prime minister's wife for long, she had already tired of official parties. So she decided that the party that night was going to be an informal neighbourly buffet. But most of the guests, not having been at the Official Residence during Margaret's regime or perhaps ever before, were expecting place-cards, prancing waiters and protocol. The guests were mollified, however, by the huge vats of caviar that the prime minister and Margaret brought back from their recent official visit to Moscow. Although Margaret seemed a little confused and unsure of herself at times, she exuded warmth, a quality that she always projected, and this caused her party—and it was her party—to be a success. The prime minister was, however, remote.

The party made a strong impression on me. I liked what Margaret had done. I admired her style of entertainment. By this time I was attending an untold number of deadly diplomatic dinners. Allan was invited, and so was I, to dinners by the more than one hundred foreign ambassadors accredited to Canada. When he took up his position as undersecretary, Allan decided that it was his solemn duty (it wasn't) to accept an invitation from each embassy in Ottawa once, but not necessarily more than once. This proved to be a much heavier burden than he thought. These dinners, except ones at the US, British, French and Israeli embassies, usually originated in the following way. The Finnish ambassador, say, would feel he had to pay off the Turkish ambassador, who had previously entertained him (the Turk probably paying off the Finn for a previous obligation and so on ad infinitum).

To make sure that their government back home would pay for the dinner, they would have to ensure that a high-ranking Canadian official (one would suffice) would attend the dinner. This would justify the expense. That's where Allan came in— and his spouse. I would find myself staring at a sea of faces that I would not find anywhere else in Ottawa except the embassies. You could never see them in a Canadian house because the diplomats entertained only each other except for the justifying official in whose honour the dinner would often be held. Conversation at table was usually about extracting money from home office to replace drapes.

Ottawa was then (still?) known in the diplomatic world as where the elephants would go to die. I began to think of the diplomats' faces as elephants' trunks. I vowed that if ever I became an ambassador's wife, I would entertain only the people of the country to which my husband was accredited. No foreign diplomat would cross my threshold unless he or she had something to offer at the dinner table, other than diplomatic status.

Although I was not then aware of it, I would soon have an opportunity to put my vows to the test.

17

The "Wife Of"

M Y LIFE IN WASHINGTON, as wife of the Canadian ambassador, could not be compared in any way to my years in
Winnipeg, Ottawa, Geneva or Oxford. It was a shock to leave
Winnipeg for Oxford at the age of eighteen with a strange man
for a husband and for the life of a wife of an Oxford don. I did it,
not the least among other reasons, because my mother promised
me we could shop for my wedding dress in Minneapolis. I never
gave a thought to the idea of marriage. Because of all the planning and preparations, the wedding was very real to me.
Marriage, the aftermath, was far too nebulous to worry about.

This time I was going as a mature woman to Washington in
an ideal situation. My children were away at university, there

were no tears, and I even told Allan I would never forgive him if he didn't take the job as ambassador to the United States. I was as desperate to get out of Ottawa as I was to leave Winnipeg.

What I didn't realize was that, for me, being wife of the Canadian ambassador would bring about an even more traumatic change in my life than getting married, even though I was grown up and following the steps of many other ambassadorial and political wives. I could have stayed in bed all day at the embassy residence and watched soap operas (as many political and diplomatic wives did, I found out later). But I was my mother's daughter and it would have been "too shaming"—to use Nancy Mitford's phrase. I was determined to do what I could to be a good ambassador's wife.

What I didn't know was that I would meet more people in one day than in a half a dozen years in Ottawa. I didn't know that if I refused to respond to the most idiotic demands on my time a nasty swipe about me would get into the newspapers. I didn't know that I would have to keep a fixed smile on my face while talking to the pompous and powerful (not all powerful people are pompous, it's just that the pompous ones always claimed to know those who made the decisions in Washington).

Pierre Eliott Trudeau, as everyone knows, described Canada's relationship with the United States as a mouse sleeping beside an elephant. It's only the mouse that has to watch out when the elephant moves. Although most Canadians are happy in their belief that we are nicer, kinder and gentler than Americans, they never like to admit their huge economic, political and military dependence on the United States. This is true whether we are talking about the things we make, the products we grow and the air we breathe—one way or another, they all depend on Uncle Sam and whether or not he is feeling benign towards us. In Canada the chattering classes can take an ostrichlike position, but on the front lines—the embassy in Washington—you know that Canadians can be blown away by the smallest fart of the elephant, even one that the elephant itself is unaware of.

Allan's job was to spend his time prowling the corridors of Congress and other halls of power sniffing out the odours emitting from various orifices in the Capitol buildings. When accused by Allan of crapulating in the direction of Canada, the senator or congressman, as often as not, would be astonished. "Who me? I wasn't aiming my wind in your direction."

To Allan, of course, sniffing out odours and warning disbelieving politicians and bureaucrats in Ottawa about what his nostrils smelled seemed a very important job. That is, until one day when he became deflated. The well-known editor of a leading German newspaper to whom he was introduced, asked him, "Do I understand correctly? You are the ambassador of Canada to the United States?" Allan proudly replied yes. "That," the German said, "is a most important job, like being Polish ambassador to the Soviet Union." Allan tried to take himself less seriously after that.

As Allan was learning how to be a beggar on Capitol Hill, I was in a state of bewilderment and exhaustion. I was also experiencing pressures I had never before felt in my life. In Oxford I experienced the same thing but I was allowed to sleep my trauma away. But that's when I was in my teens.

Canadians would sometimes ask me if I ever got together with a few buddies to go to the movies or a play, as normal people do in Cleveland or Kitchener. "Go to the movies?" "Cook gourmet dinners with friends?" These things became so foreign to me after a while in Washington, that I totally forgot what private life was like. My day would unfold in accordance with a schedule typed by my secretary or in Allan's office. My biggest challenge every day was to work a half-hour of downtime into that schedule before entertaining at home or being entertained. (I don't mean having fun.) What I found the greatest stress was "representation"—doing something or being somewhere not in my own right but because of my husband's official position. Yet these complaints are nothing. The Washington years were the most exciting time in my life and, aside from marrying Allan, the best decision I ever made.

When I began to write a column about the absurdities of the Washington scene for the *Washington Post*, in the form of semifictional letters to a friend in Canada named Beverly, I signed myself "wife of." Almost every woman who was introduced to me at the time was known by her husband's job. It didn't matter whether she was a professional in her own right or had an important job outside government. In Washington, she was still the "wife of." The only exceptions were media stars (anchorwomen or other broadcasters) or top government officials, such as Secretary of Transportation Elizabeth Dole or Supreme Court Justice Sandra Day O'Connor. Ann Jordan was always introduced as wife of Vernon Jordan. Even back in the Reagan years, his name was more important than any job he ever held.

Aside from such exceptions, we spouses were always introduced as the "wife of" an important job. Susan Baker was the "wife of" the White House chief of staff, Obie Shultz was the "wife of" the secretary of state, Alma Powell was the "wife of" the national security adviser, and Lynn Cheney was the "wife of" Congressman Bill Cheney.

I, of course, was always introduced as the "wife of" the Canadian ambassador. Nobody had the slightest need to know my name. In fact, they didn't even need to know who the Canadian ambassador was. "Mr. Ambassador" was always enough. It was a legitimate title and Washington adored titles. Not long after I arrived in the capital, I was invited to a dinner by a lesser Washington hostess and I was excited to know that she was seating me beside the secretary of the interior. I found myself sitting next to a deaf, very elderly gentleman who was fond of repeating his sentences. Short-term memory loss, as it is called in the nursing homes. I was aware that some members of the Reagan cabinet were well on in years but I knew they could not be as old as my neighbour at dinner. It turned out that "Mr. Secretary" had been in Calvin Coolidge's cabinet. Americans would as soon let go their titles as their wallets.

When my columns in the *Washington Post* were gathered together for publication a few years after they began, my publisher chose *Wife Of* as the title of the book. The phrase had become current in Washington to describe the appendage wife.

In my columns, I also wrote about the ambassador's wife as "the unpaid manager of a small hotel." This was a role I was totally unequipped to perform. The Official Residence had a staff of six—butler, chef, kitchen and downstairs maid, upstairs maid, houseman and chauffeur. In addition, there was a handyman employed by the embassy and a second chauffeur present most of the time. I found this difficult because I adored my privacy. All my life, I disliked having too many people around me. Through my married years, I never had more than one person working in the house, whether as nanny or cleaning lady. In my early months at the residence, I was very ill at ease. To make matters worse, the staff at the residence were hardly compatible or efficient. I was in the midst of a very dysfunctional group, over which I had no authority. There were factions, intrigues, conspiracies and double-crosses. "Watch out for the butler," the wife of Allan's predecessor warned me, "he's getting stranger every day." (I decided to always lock my bedroom door before I went to sleep—I wasn't sure where in the house the butler slept in the early days.) The chef spoke mostly Turkish, the butler spoke mostly Spanish, and the English of both was virtually incomprehensible. Naomi, the Spanish-speaking kitchen maid from the Dominican Republic, also spoke little English. Her contact was the Turkish chef, Ibrahim, a kindly man, who communicated with her in some sort of sign language. The only other person who could communicate with her was the butler, who refused to do so because she was pregnant and unmarried. (He told me he was a religious man.) The Filipino upstairs maid, Thelma, spoke enough English to keep me informed and off-balance with her tales of downstairs life and the ever-shifting animosities among the staff. "Don't tell me, Thelma," I used to say, "it will keep me awake all night." I didn't want to know that the butler prayed to God every day that something bad should happen to the houseman. (I didn't even know what Mario, the Portuguese houseman, actually did.) I didn't want to know that Rito lost all his wages on his days off, gambling in Atlantic City. Nothing, however, could turn off Thelma's spout.

When I eventually hired a new butler—Theodora, from the Philippines and a female—recommended to me by a Belgian countess, Thelma was not pleased. She went off to work for a sharp-tongued Washington socialite, Oatsie Charles, whose ancestors were Southern gentry. At a dinner party in Washington that both Oatsie and I attended, a visiting English Parliamentarian called Trudeau a horse's ass. When I left the table shortly after because I had a bad cold and the guest of honour was becoming increasingly obnoxious, it was interpreted by the other guests that I walked out in protest. Picking the story up, the Canadian press quoted Oatsie as saying, "He's right, of course, that Trudeau is a horse's ass, but he was wrong to say that in the presence of the Canadian ambassador's wife." I got good marks in the Canadian press—a happy accident.

Oatsie was not alone among the hostesses who had a name

ending in "ie" or "y." Most of them did, although why this was so was always a mystery to me. There was Muffie Brandon (Old Boston, President Reagan's first social secretary), Buffie Cafritz (from a family of hostesses since President Truman's time), Vangie (Evangeline) Bruce (elegant widow of the much admired US ambassador to the Court of St. James, David Bruce, who had also been Paul Mellon's son-in-law), Sally Quinn (wife of *Washington Post* editor-in-chief Ben Bradley), Polly Fritchey (prominent Democratic hostess), and Polly Kraft (wife of columnist Joe Kraft). You didn't have to have your name end in "ie" or "y" to be a hostess. There was also Susan-Mary Alsop (writer, hostess and ex-wife of columnist Joe Alsop) and Pamela Harriman and the grand panjandrum Katharine Graham. But all the cute "ie" nicknames inspired me to name the fictional socialite in my "Dear Beverly" columns Popsie Tribble. My friend the real Popsie living in Ottawa, not rich and not a socialite, was not amused.

One of the greatest differences between my life in Washington and my former life in Winnipeg, Ottawa and elsewhere was that I never went into the kitchen in our house on Rock Creek Drive. For the better part of the decade that I was in Washington, the kitchen was off-limits for me. It was the chef's domain and I never had the slightest desire to invade it. I never opened the big steel refrigerator for a midnight snack. Nor did I know or want to know how to use any of the kitchen stoves. Wherever I lived before, the kitchen was the centre of my existence. That it was not so in Washington was the most unusual change in my life. But I had no regrets because I was too tired and too busy to cook. Glenn Bullard, who was in charge of the buildings and maintenance of the various embassy properties in Washington, announced to me one day that he had received permission from headquarters in Ottawa to put in a little kitchenette upstairs near our bedroom where I could rustle up coffee and snacks. Glenn was elated with the news. I was horrified. The idea of making little toasty snacks for my husband, when we were both overfed and when I could get breakfast served in bed, was absurd. Spending twenty or thirty thousand dollars of taxpayers' money for the upstairs kitchen of the ambassador's wife was equally absurd. But then I had not yet grasped how the Ottawa bureaucracy worked. It was, it seems, the year of the kitchenette. Ambassadors' private quarters in various parts of the world were being equipped with kitchens, whether they were wanted or not.

At that time, the main Canadian Chancery or office was located in an old heritage building at 1746 Massachusetts Avenue. It was not renovated and although the ambassadors and their families used to reside there at one time, there was no place in it to entertain. Arthur Erickson's masterpiece in the shadow of the Congress, with its superb dining facilities overlooking the dome of the Capitol, did not open until just after we left Washington. We did all our entertaining in the Official Residence, a large, upper-middle-class pseudo-Georgian house built in the 1930s for a private family. The dining room could not seat more than about twenty-four people but we often gave parties for forty, fifty, eighty or even a hundred and fifty guests. It didn't matter that we couldn't put a hundred people in the dining room, as can be done today in the new embassy on Pennsylvania Avenue. By placing tables in the library, sun room and even the front hall, we attained a more at-home feeling than in a single large room. Although I greatly admired Erickson's structure, I never regretted not entertaining in it because it was, after all, an office building, a beautiful one it is true, but not a home.

I discovered in Washington that the more I had to entertain, the less interested I became in cooking. The fascination that cooking had for me all my life disappeared and I was to discover that it would never return. So far as food was concerned, my job in Washington became one of finding and training chefs. I wanted nothing to do with the actual preparation of food. After our chef Ibrahim left us to open his own restaurant, I tried for a while to rely on caterers but this was not satisfactory because of the high volume of entertainment we were providing. It soon became obvious that we needed a chef and it fell to me to hire one. This was not part of my job description for the simple reason that there was no job description for an ambassador's wife. I could let Allan take care of the household management. Perhaps this was part of his job description. But of course he was far too busy and, more important, he knew nothing about food and I would have been a rotten wife not to take on the role of manager of our new establishment. I believed, perhaps wrongly, almost from the moment of arrival, that if the Gotliebs were to entertain successfully in Washington, the most important person in the embassy was the chef.

Ibrahim was a reasonably good cook but he had a deep penchant for shish kebabs and baba ghanoush, although he was capable of making some marvellous desserts. His specialty was an extraordinary concoction of spun sugar that he fabricated in the kitchen by winding the spun strands around a broomstick. The problem was that if I wanted to change the menu to escalope de veau or a dish from Julia Child, he became mulish and responded invariably with, "I cook for five hundred people for King Hussein of Jordan. I know what's best." This was usually the end of the conversation. I was intimidated by the king. After Ibrahim left to start up his own restaurant (which proved to be unsuccessful), I placed an ad for a chef in the *Washington Post*. But no one at the embassy who ran the finances could tell me how much I could pay or what perks to offer. "Try them out,

Mrs. G," they would say "and we'll see what we can do." It was a comical business with sometimes disastrous results. I hired chefs that, as I was to discover quickly, could cook meat but not fish, or fish but not meat, or pastry but not fish or meat. There was an Egyptian amateur gourmet chef with splendid training who could not cope with more than eight people for dinner and threw up his hands at the thought of manufacturing hors d'oeuvres for large rotating receptions for visiting Canadian delegations. (He had my sympathies.) There was the chef who forgot to feed the models at a fashion show we held at the residence for which I was roundly criticized by the Canadian fashion press. When I read the criticism I wanted to scream, "But I told the chef, I told him." He walked the next day because it was too much work. "I'm only a grill chef," he said, "and I knew those skinny models wouldn't eat steak." In fact, the whole dinner was inedible.

Through a personal contact of my own, and without embassy assistance, I finally found a young, masterful Belgian chef, Christian, who we helped emigrate from Brussels along with his family. Within a short time after his taking on the job of chef at the embassy, we knew we had the best cook in the Capital and so did most of official Washington. He stayed for many years at the residence after we left Washington and then went on to shine in the Canadian embassy in Paris when Raymond Chr tien was appointed ambassador to France and Christian joined him there as embassy chef.

18

The Washington Hostesses

ALTHOUGH ALLAN AND I WERE PROUD to have one of the best chefs in Washington at the Canadian residence, I soon discovered that the nation's capital was not a town where people cared a great deal about food. The celebrated hostesses of Washington who entertained relentlessly during the Reagan years were themselves indifferent about what they served at their dinners, luncheons and Sunday brunches. This was the first time I lived in an environment (unlike Winnipeg, Oxford, Geneva and even Ottawa) where there was such disinterest in food—whether eating or just talking about it—among people that I mixed with. Politics and power, who was in and who was out were the only topics of conversation in Washington. Food talk was a distraction.

Many of the Washington hostesses, such as Kay Graham, Pamela Harriman and Jennifer Phillips (wife of Laughlin Phillips, director of the Phillips Collection established by his father), had their own chefs. What was surprising to me was that hostesses whose income was more modest, such as Polly Kraft, Kay Evans (wife of political columnist Roland Evans) and Sally Quinn, rarely did their own cooking. They always used caterers. Our first chef, Ibrahim, belonged to a group of culinary brothers and cousins. Their dishes seemed to be extraordinarily familiar to me at Georgetown parties. The Turkish chefs formed a network among the hostesses and their signature dishes, like roast lamb and fried zucchini would turn up everywhere.

When we dined out in Georgetown, I was at times pretty sure that Ibrahim was in the kitchen giving a hand to a relative. If one of the Turkish cooking clique was not present, other caterers prepared what could be described as bland, WASPy fare—what Vice-President George Bush would eat at the exclusive Alibi Club, to which only a very small number of people could belong. The informality of the club was such that if you were lucky enough to sit beside the vice-president at the long central table, he would open oysters for you and toss the shells into a large bowl in the centre of the table (a ritual informality?). The simple fare at the hostesses would often consist of well-done roast beef, well-done veal, shepherd's pie, and chocolate mousse or apple crisp for dessert. Occasionally, somebody would go quail-hunting and then tiny birds, with shot inside, would appear as a main course. Allan would complain to me about those birds, with their tied feet sticking up and no meat on the bone. "No meat, nothing to eat," he would mutter as Jacques, our chauffeur, drove us home. "Let's stop somewhere for a hamburger," he would say, to Jacques' delight. We never did.

If appreciation of fine food was not high among the politically powerful in Washington, there was even less appreciation of fine wine. Guests, usually the men, liked to start their evening with hard liquor—martinis, manhattans, scotch and bourbon. The president of the AFL-CIO, Lane Kirkland, a learned Southerner and the most powerful union leader in the land, was perhaps the only oenophile we knew in political Washington. He was much mocked by his associates for his refined taste. Only fine vintages were served if you dined with him and his wife Irena at small dinners they gave in their modest bungalow in Chevy Chase. Nevertheless, it was Lane Kirkland who applied the first fatal blow of the sledgehammer to the Soviet Union through providing financial and moral support to Solidarity in Poland when it was politically isolated. In our own home, when dinners for important guests were concluded, Allan would stare at the army of wineglasses filled to the brim with Chateau Pichon Longueville or Chateau Gruard-Larose, or fine Sauternes and flutes of champagne, barely touched by anybody's lips. The martinis and manhattans had done their job. People may have been voluble but never drunk. Depressed about the wineglasses filled with vintage wines, Allan would say, "Maybe they were flattered to read the fancy names on the menus in front of their nose." (Mrs. Charles Bronfman was kind enough to let us order wines from Seagrams' wholesale wine catalogue.)

The reality of Washington was that food and drink, no matter what the quality, never brought people to the table. Power did. But there were a few tables at the home of the private hostesses that combined excellent cuisine and the presence of the politically powerful players of the day. Katharine Graham was pre-eminent among the hostesses who could provide both. There were no people of power in Washington who would refuse to accept her invitation (unless they were previously committed and even then they would probably cancel and attend). It was a Washington rule that, if invited to Kay's, one could not not be there. Unless it was a large group, she would entertain in her red-lacquered drawing room, done by a decorator and much copied in Washington, although Mrs. Graham took little interest in decoration. A shy but dominating woman, she was in turn dominated by her French chef who loved to cook four or five courses—generally a no-no among Washington hostesses. Official Washington went to bed early and started early the next morning. It was not uncommon for officials and lobbyists to book two breakfasts, in sequence, before arriving at the office at 8 a.m. (These were not popular with our chef and staff.)

Kay told me she tried to get her chef to ease off the rich food a little, such as the sweetbreads   la crème, the pheasants stuffed with sausages and chestnuts and the creamy napoleons and buttery pastries. But he had been with her so many years, he had her cowed. Then there was always the problem of the second helpings, a tradition followed in her house but also by all the other Washington hostesses. Full platters of food were routinely passed around a second time, in the unlikely event a guest might want second portions. I tried to put a stop to that in my embassy but Christian (he was, after all, from Belgium where they are notorious for their love of seconds) told me that to omit the second offering was not *"comme il faut"* at a proper table. I often thought that the second platter, with all the garniture freshly replaced, was more for the benefit of the staff than the guests. I assumed, but of course couldn't prove, that at our residence at least, they were for the dinner of the security guards accompanying the high officials, the chauffeurs and the kitchen staff.

The formality of Kay Graham's dinners was equalled by none of the other private hostesses, except for Pamela Harriman. While her ancient husband Averell was alive, she entertained sparingly in their country home in Virginia and kept close by her husband's side, tending to him in his long decline. When he died, she launched her political career as a Democratic fundraiser but received much criticism. The *Washington Post* derided her speech-making efforts (her English accent "was an affront" someone said), and Nancy Reagan was annoyed when, on Pamela's own initiative, she entertained Raisa Gorbachev. Not beloved by the other hostesses who had been recipient of certain dark manoeuvres over many years (like stealing their husbands and lovers), she nevertheless had the most exquisite manners in public and entertained in a grand style. After Averell died and she was in her late sixties, she and the director of the National Gallery, Carter Brown, many years her junior, were said to be more than good friends. According to Joe Alsop, the English Digby family from which she was descended produced a courtesan of international standing once every century for three hundred years.

Evangeline Bruce belonged to the opposite school of gastronomy as Kay Graham. She believed that enough is as good as a feast. Although she used a caterer for her entertaining, her servings were meagre, in line with her eighteen-inch waist. But of course, she also followed the second-time-around rule at her sit-down dinners. At her Sunday brunches for which she was famous, in her exquisitely decorated home in Georgetown with yellow taffeta silk curtains and double facings flowing out over the floor and boxes of pansies and floral arrangements of great whimsy and imagination, she usually provided only a few things to eat. It was invariably finger food.

Allan would say, "To find the food you have to search behind the curtains." He would send me out into the darkest corners to look for the smoked salmon, miniscule egg-and-cucumber sandwiches and caramelized strips of bacon (a fixture with Washington hostesses). There was always an oyster bar on the landing between the lower floors where a waiter would crack open the shells for those who were not oyster-phobic, as Allan was. If I was not gathering food for him, I would take my position by the oysters along with the large-stomached Henry Mitchell, the *Washington Post* writer who was one of the greatest authorities on gardening in the United States. Washington being a political town, not a gardening one, he was usually out in the cold at these parties. But he was one of my gardening gods. I would ask him questions about gardening to which he would usually reply with a harrumph. There was no other food to be had at Evangeline's parties, except at Christmas and Easter, when silver bowls of chocolate truffles would be passed around by the waiters.

Evangeline's priorities placed clothes well ahead of food. She could often be seen on the shuttle from New York to Washington or vice-versa, carrying a large green garbage bag containing her poofy evening dresses, so popular during the eighties. Her skinny tall figure appeared constantly in *W, Vogue* and *The Tatler*. She was trained to regard it as bad manners to fuss over what she was served in a restaurant. Dining with the Kirklands and us in one of Washington's finest steak-houses, Evangeline went with the flow. Advised to do so by her host, she ordered a slab of roast beef that was so large it drooped over the edges of the plate. I knew she wanted a small salad and some grilled fish but she considered it good manners to act like a Roman in Rome. I was fascinated to see what she was going to do with the slab. She took three bites and left it alone, all the while trying not to call attention to herself. This was the old-style good manners. The Kirklands and the Gotliebs, of course, cleaned up their plates.

Evangeline Bruce, Susan-Mary Alsop and her friend Marietta Tree (who lived in New York), Kay Graham, Pamela Harriman, Polly Fritchey, Joan Braden, Buffy Cafritz and Jennifer Phillips (who hated the role) were among the star hostesses in Washington during the Reagan era. They had many things in common. Aside from Kay Graham and Pamela Harriman, great wealth was not one of them. Each had many personal connections in London, Paris, California and New York. Each also had many personal miseries—marital or family-related. Katherine Graham's husband shot his head off in their bathroom, Polly Fritchey's husband, senior in the CIA, leaped off a bridge, Evangeline Bruce's daughter was murdered (her son-in-law was a suspect), Jennifer Phillip's son committed suicide, and there was much more.

Most important, none of these women were affected by the feminist disdain for being a hostess. Today, these women could not carry on as they did. This is not because of the absence of willing guests in Washington, or money or power, but because the feminists have turned the image of the hostess into something frivolous and degrading to women. Now, if you want to play the role of the hostess in Washington, your only excuse is that you are doing it to raise money for some political party, politically correct cause or charity. As a result, the hostesses, who for so many years brought powerful political people together at small dinners where conversation was memorable and partisanship all but absent, have disappeared from the Washington scene.

Although the hostesses knew each other for many years, sometimes generations, they were jealous and competitive and malicious about their rivals. One of them, Susan-Mary Alsop, had been married to the columnist Joe Alsop during his glory days in the Kennedy era. Evangeline Bruce's late husband, who had been a diplomatic icon on two continents, had been unfaithful to her. Joan Braden, one-time mistress of Nelson Rockefeller, claimed to have been unfaithful with Evangeline's husband, and while still married to husband Tom, would fly everywhere with Robert McNamara, Kay Graham's designated beau. They all went to each other's parties and poured out gossip about each other after the events. During the Reagan years, most of the ladies were in their late sixties or seventies. They could surprise you by wearing beautiful Balenciaga silk harem pants to one party and black widows' weeds to the next. Although they seemed to like rich and vulgar people at times, none of them were vulgar themselves. They were all literate and considered themselves bluestockings. For many years, Evangeline was editing the letters between Napoleon and Josephine. (Her book was published shortly before she died by George Weidenfeld, who published many international socialites.) Susan-Mary, a blueblood as well as a bluestocking (she was descended from the Jays, signers of the Constitution), wrote many books including the acclaimed *Letters to Marietta* (about her friend Marietta Tree). She was employed by *Architectural Digest* to open the doors to great houses (Allan opened the door of Pierre Elliott Trudeau's art deco mansion to her for an article in the magazine). Susan-Mary lived in the Victorian house in Georgetown where her mother had lived until she was ninety-nine. It was decorated with eighteenth-century monkey pictures, Victorian pouffes, deep red and green walls and upholstered chintz furniture. It was a warm comfortable house with an air of proper gentle decay. She didn't mind the springs coming through the down in her sofas. Her long-time French maid cooked the same meal every time we dined there—hot cheese soufflé followed by cold jellied beef and an apple or other tart for dessert (delicious). Susan-Mary loved to make warm, gushing toasts to the guest of honour and other favourite guests, while her ex-husband, whom she always invited to her parties, glowered. Snob and social arbiter Joe Alsop considered toasts in private houses—so fashionable in Washington—to be in bad taste. This served only to egg on the loquacious Susan-Mary to make longer and more elaborate remarks.

Joe Alsop, former influential political columnist and art historian, had his own small salon in Georgetown where he had entertained everyone of consequence in Washington since the days when his cousins Franklin and Eleanor Roosevelt occupied the White House. Jack Kennedy dropped by his small house in Georgetown for a late-night drink immediately following his own Inauguration party. Joe liked to entertain a small group around his dining-room table in his basement surrounded by oil portraits of his ancestors. When Allan once admired a particular portrait, Joe said, "That's my pansy uncle." Political correctness was anathema to him and, being a homosexual himself (although half in the closet), he didn't mind the word "pansy" although he detested "gay." He once asked us to a dinner for a relative of his from Boston—"the last of the Adams family" as he described him. I thought of the two great presidents of that name and the writer who wrote the best novel ever about Washington, *Democracy*. I expected the last descendant to be an intellectual and austere Brahmin. Instead, "the last of the Adams" had a great deal of money and he and his bejewelled wife had more of a Palm Beach air than the aroma of the bean and the cod. The couple seemed rather remote from their ancestors. Joe the snob seemed more excited by their money than their pedigree.

But the Washington hostesses, and of course Joe, well knew that for a dinner party to be successful they did not need to have guests who were rich or important in the business or financial world. You rarely met such people at their table. What was essential was to mix the powerful political people of the day in Washington with good conversation. This is why the hostesses loved entertaining great English talkers. At the table of Evangeline Bruce, Susan-Mary Alsop and Kay Graham, you might meet Isaiah Berlin, the British historian A.W.L. Rowse, Lord Weidenfeld, the Duchess of Devonshire, Antonia Fraser and Howard Pinter. This also accounts for the popularity of Henry Kissinger, a regular guest at Joan Braden's and David and Susan Brinkley's dinners and at the table of other Washington ladies. Among people of influence, Kissinger was unique because he combined power, celebrity, ego and a wicked sense of humour. Larry McMurtry, the novelist, who lived in Washington, was also much sought-after by the hostesses, as was Gore Vidal. A good talker, McMurtry's interest in politics, as far as I could tell, was nil.

The formality of Kay Graham's dinners was equalled by some of the more prominent embassies in Washington. But of course, very few could attract the top officials, senators and congressmen, like Kay Graham could. The power elite disliked going to embassy parties in Washington and they had good reason to. Power seeks power and they were unlikely to meet other powerful people at an embassy party. This includes, of course, the haut media who were rarely to be seen on embassy grounds. For ambassadors and their wives, it was a dirty, low-down business getting people you needed to dine at your home. You might have to tell some whoppers about who was coming to get them to turn out. The most important requirement was to coax a guest of honour in the Washington political world to serve as bait to attract other important guests, while using the other powerful or glamorous guests to attract the guest of honour. It says something about my character that people told me that I was quite accomplished at practising this strategem.

Unlike at most embassies where social secretaries organize the dinners and even pick the guests (usually ending up with a bunch of duds locally known as embassy rats—hangers-on who can do nothing for your country), I called the "wives of" the powerful jobs myself. I learned that the best way to attract the powerful officials was if the wife wanted to come to meet someone more powerful or famous than her husband, whose name I would casually drop. Even then, the chance of getting a sought-after senator was remote. "Important senators never dine out," Joe Alsop used to say to us. Nevertheless, the mighty Jesse Helms, who, as he told us, never dined at an embassy before, did so at our own. Maybe I had a talent for this sort of thing but I found getting Powerful Jobs and Close-to-the-Presidents to come to dinner at the embassy was the most stressful and wretched part of my Washington life.

The Canadian embassy, traditionally, was never a big attraction in social and political Washington. Over the years, the only "drawing" embassies were the British, the French and, to a lesser extent, the Italian. Occasionally, another embassy would pop up on the diplomatic social screen for a while, usually a European country with a titled ambassador. The Swedes, for example, with Count Willy Wachmeister at the helm along with his artist wife Ula, were a draw at the time, as was (and still is) Prince Bandur, Ambassador of Saudi Arabia, who could attract crowds with his oily magic wand. The Geogetown set were very snobbish, as well as anglophile, and British royals, even Princess Michael, could be a powerful lure that would bring people to their embassy. Cap Weinberger, for example,

Reagan's secretary of defence and an anglophile, was a regular at the British ambassador's table. Titles were also an allure to many Reaganites. "What the Reaganites are all about," the late Joe Kraft once told me, "is social climbing." You could not count on snobs and social climbers being drawn to the Canadian embassy.

But the British embassy had a lot more to offer than social climbing. When we arrived in Washington, the British ambassador, Sir Nicholas (Nicko) Henderson, who had great charm and was very popular among the ladies of Georgetown, was at the helm, along with his Greek-born wife Mary, who also had flair. They managed to persuade the cream of British designers, architects, curators and master craftsmen, at no fee, to restore the marvellous Lutyens mansion that housed the British embassy. Mary also wrote a cookbook for ambassadors' wives. She didn't cook herself but had imaginative ideas and a deep interest in cuisine. She served one of the most delicious desserts I have ever tasted, a red-wine sherbet covered with burgundy-coloured grapes. Her magnificent meals were sometimes criticized by other Washington hostesses—illustrating again that to be a top Washington hostess you needed a penchant for wickedness and malicious gossip. Evangeline Bruce, who was a friend of Mary Henderson since their husbands served in London, once said to me, "I think her food is frightful. Every course is wrapped in dough." Her cookbook was sniffed at by many American friends, who never cared about food or went into the kitchen. Such were the ways of Washington.

Unlike the Canadian ambassador's wife, the British ambassador's wife did not manage a small hotel but a grand one. All the privileged and famous visiting Washington from London stayed in the British embassy. It helped that she had several chefs to feed them. I know. With her consent, I hired one of her sous-chefs and he ran our kitchen for a couple of years before Christian replaced him. Because he spoke French but no English and was very lonely, I sent him to a church that, I was told, was a favourite of French visitors and residents in Washington. I thought he might make friends there. He complained to me that they wanted him to sing in the choir. "What's wrong with that?" I asked. *"Je suis juif, Madame,"* he replied. Being Jewish myself, I took his point.

I'm not sure why, during our Washington years, many magazines, newspapers and social columnists called the Canadian embassy "in." From the *Wall Street Journal* and the *New York Times* to *Vanity Fair*, a stream of articles appeared about our entertainment. Did we have a formula? Perhaps. We focused a lot on inviting prominent members of the media including the leading political columnists, because we knew they attracted people in power. We avoided New York socialites. They were more of a specialty of the French and Italian embassies. Allan couldn't see how they could help promote Canadian objectives, such as our free-trade agreement with the United States. The people we needed for our embassy dinners—senators, congressmen, cabinet secretaries, White House officials—were more interested in policy than they were New York money men. Occasionally, after our embassy came to be regarded as "hot," some prominent person at a fashionable party in New York would drop her private telephone number in my bag or put it in my hand. I was flummoxed. Why did they do that? What possible interest could they have in coming to the Canadian embassy? When I would mention to Allan that perhaps we should ask this or that person from New York, he would veto all of them unless he thought they could help attract the right politicians and officials in Washington to our table. Among the New Yorkers we would regularly invite were

Marietta Tree, Barbara Walters, Peter Jennings, Henry Grunewald and Henry Kissinger. For some reason, Allan had a negative attitude towards the financial high-fliers of the time. The "Masters of the Universe" of Tom Wolfe fame were more likely found at other embassies than ours.

More than a decade after we left Washington, Kay Graham, not long before she died, attended a small dinner party in our honour during our yearly visit to the Capital. Somebody proposed a toast and made the usual kind remarks, which, of course, I didn't take too seriously. Mrs. Graham was at the table, listening. Neither a fool nor a flatterer and rather meagre with her compliments, she said to the guests, sort of thinking out loud, "Of all the embassies I have ever been to, the Gotliebs were the only one to run an intellectual salon. I was never bored at their embassy and would always have good conversation. That's why I never refused an invitation."

Looking back, I think the explanation for why Kay found our embassy interesting and others not is that we always invited people who we knew would want to see each other. When Americans came to our embassy, they knew there would be other Americans whom they wanted to, or needed to, or were trying to talk to. They knew that they could promote their own agenda with each other, which would probably have nothing to do with Canada, while Allan promoted his—which, of course, he did. But we also invited people even if they were out of power, or who never had power, because of their wit or personality. Sometimes one of my guests would say sarcastically to me, "Goodness, I haven't seen that person since he worked for Gerald Ford." A week later, I would see that neglected soul eating dinner at the lady's house.

It was always a mixed world at our embassy, Democrats and Republicans, office holders and commentators, former political

stars and future ones, but whoever they were, the most important requirement was that they could contribute to good conversation. This I learned from the hostesses.

But maybe the real reasons why the guests kept coming back
were that I never served a separate salad course, I never provided entertainment and I always allowed them to get home
and go to sleep early enough so they could make their power
breakfast shortly after dawn the next morning. This I also
learned from the hostesses.

The Tibetan Terriers

"*E*very ambassador's wife has to have dogs," Evangeline Bruce told me. "When David and I were in London, I had red setters that followed me wherever I went." This *Tatler* or *Town and Country* picture of an elegant woman, five feet ten inches tall, exquisitely attired, was for me the perfect expression of how an English or American aristocratic woman should present herself. But there was no connection between the idyllic image of Evangeline Bruce, the former ambassadrix to France, Britain and Germany, and her red setters, and my acquisition of a hysterical Tibetan terrier.

I bought a dog not to be fashionable but out of fear. At a dinner at the house of hostess Joan Braden in Chevy Chase, shortly after George Shultz was appointed secretary of state by President Reagan, Allan got into a fierce fight with Shultz about the decline of the American will. "America will never again, after Vietnam, send its troops to fight in a foreign war," Allan maintained. I thought Allan should keep his mouth shut because I never heard him talk of the decline of the Canadian fighting will. But for a while, Allan forgot he was an ambassador and thought he was in an Oxford debate. George Shultz, disagreeing completely with Allan, took on his Easter-Island-statue look and got redder and redder; the Bradens kept their mouths shut, and Joe Alsop was squarely on Shultz's side, egging him on. All other guests having cancelled their attendance due to one of those paralyzing Washington snowstorms (two inches of snow had fallen), there was no one else to intervene or smooth things over. Being always a fearful, trembling creature, I believed that the next morning George Shultz would send a wire to Pierre Trudeau and ask for Allan's recall.

When we got home that evening, Allan slept the sleep of the contented (he thought he had won the debate), and I was tormented by anxiety. I suddenly felt a tremendous urge to be comforted. My children were all away, not that they would have given me any comfort. A little after dawn and before the servants were up, I went in my slippers and picked up the snow-covered *Washington Post* outside the front door. I opened it to the dogs-for-sale section. Remembering Hector the Protector, the dead brown Airedale I owned in Ottawa, I thought I would like something similar but smaller. A lady in Virginia advertised something called a "Tibetan terrier," which I had never heard of before. She was offering terriers "of high breeding." That was the phrase I found attractive. I would become just like Evangeline Bruce.

That morning I asked Jacques, our chauffeur, to drive me to

Virginia. I was mightily impressed by the breeder's domain. She lived in a grand estate of several acres and the dogs had the run of her marble palace. She was dressed in riding boots and hunting jacket. She reminded me of Jackie Kennedy in hunting mode. There were a variety of breeds in her entourage. She pointed to a long-haired, sandy-coloured dog that looked vaguely oriental, and said, "That's the one you want. He's a bargain. His parents were show dogs and he would have been too, except for the overbite." I had no idea what she was talking about. "Overbite?" I asked. "What overbite?" The Jackie Kennedy clone was astonished at my ignorance. She closed her eyes in disapproval and said, "Since you can't show him, I will let you have him for two hundred and fifty dollars. I normally charge two thousand."

The dog was beautiful. He had long silken, golden hair, like Rapunzel, and was jumping towards me as if he were an orphan child waiting for a mother, yipping "Buy me, buy me." "You know," the breeding lady said, "Tibetan terriers don't shed." This was the clincher. The staff in the embassy would not be grumbling because of dog hair. Then she supplied me with his genealogy, which was more impressive than the Hohenzollerns', and told me he was six months old.

I returned to the residence in triumph with the dog and brought him into the drawing room to be admired by the staff. In appreciation, he peed on the white rug. "I think I'll call him Sweet Pea," I said, while a Filipino maid ran off to get a cloth. I knew I had a good thing going. As the ambassador's wife, with a large staff, I would never have to clean up after the dog. I understood immediately why Evangeline Bruce said every ambassador's wife should have a dog. She doesn't have to scoop the poop.

The breeder was right about Sweet Pea. He didn't shed. He

did something worse. He matted. Like any beautiful girl proud of her long blond thick hair, Rapunzel needed a hundred brush-strokes every morning. Even with a staff, it was impossible to devote that much time and attention to a dog's hair. So every six weeks, I sent him back to the breeder for twenty-four hours to put him on a contraption where she disentangled him. It would take her the better part of a day, she claimed. I paid more to de-mat Sweet Pea during his short stay on earth—some three years—than for a two-thousand-dollar show dog.

Ironically, the love of Sweet Pea's life was Allan, not me. Even though Sweet Pea was a male, there was something eerily hermaphrodite about him. He had a high-pitched yip and looked like Fu Man Chu, even though his genitalia were male. Tibetan terriers came from an ancient aristocratic line, not too well known in North America. They were the housedogs of the Dalai Lama. Larger than Lhasa Apsos, they were second in line in the barking command, protecting the Dalai Lama inside his palace. Sweet Pea treated Allan like the Dalai Lama. When I walked into the house, I was totally ignored by the dog. I was a low-caste wife who walked behind. Allan, on the other hand, was piped into the residence by a hysterically yipping dog walking on his hind legs. He would not drop to all fours until Allan stooped over and patted him lightly on the head. He followed him wherever he went in the house and wept bitterly when Allan left to go to the Chancery.

I can't say that anyone really trained Sweet Pea. I certainly didn't, I was far too busy. Training the dog never crossed Allan's mind. I would occasionally ask Mario, the houseman, to take him for a walk, and Jacques, the chauffeur, would volunteer from time to time. The residence had a large outdoor area smack in the middle of which was a swimming pool big enough for a public park. There was plenty of room for Sweet Pea to run around and exercise. But like many dogs, he refused to do this unless accompanied by a human being, that human being being Mr. Ambassador. Eventually we learned that if Sweet Pea stared long enough through the glass window of the side-garden door, he might go out and have a pee. But Sweet Pea was indecisive. We would open the garden door for him and he would stand with his behind inside and his head outside extending into the garden patio, trying to decide whether he would go backwards or forwards. Mario, the houseman, who never was in a big hurry, could stand there beside Sweet Pea for half an hour, letting the cold air in winter and the sickening jungle air in summer, upsetting the equilibrium of our decrepit heating and cooling system.

Sweet Pea was true to his breeding. He had a nose for detecting caste. When people came to the residence, he greeted the most powerful person first and the rest in order of importance. Once he recognized an aristocratic relative, the Aga Khan, and never left his side during the whole evening. Sweet Pea had two faults: he liked to hump the mighty (Allan dragged him off the leg of Elizabeth Dole), and he despised tradesmen. Every time the chicken man came on Friday, Sweet Pea went berserk. He once sprang at the chicken man's throat, according to the chef who thought this was very funny. (Tibetan terriers are leapers, trained to jump from crag to crag in the Himalayas.) It was probably because of Sweet Pea's snobbery that he was not beloved by the staff. No bonds of affection were formed by him with that company. It didn't help that I named him Sweet Pea; none of the personnel thought it was a good name for a dog. It also may not have helped that he was very high-strung and very vain. His favourite photographer's pose was sitting beside Allan on a silk sofa, his golden locks drooping over the cushions.

Although Sweet Pea would only go into the dog-escape-proof gardens with Allan or on a leash, he was always trying to get through unguarded exits such as the front door or the doors where the staff worked and ate. During parties, he would stand on top of the maple leaf mosaic embedded in the marble front hall, as guests arrived or said goodbye. Sometimes he was vetting the guests. Other times he was waiting for his chance to sneak out. Of course we kept a good eye on him and, if he did sneak out occasionally, there was usually a chauffeur waiting for a guest who would pick him up and bring him back in.

His snobbery led to his demise. One day Allan and I were having a quiet lunch upstairs in a small sitting room. If Allan was there, Sweet Pea was there, especially around lunchtime. That day I noticed his absence and pointed it out to Theodora, our butler, when she brought up the food. Knowing Sweet Pea preferred Mr. Ambassador to the staff, she thought he was upstairs with us. She ran downstairs to see if the dog was in the kitchen. The chauffeurs often ate there and I could understand his being with them, but I still sensed something was wrong. If there were two lunches on offer, one high caste with the ambassador, the other lower caste with the chauffeurs, you knew Sweet Pea's choice. We were having a dinner for forty guests that night and Theodora was preoccupied.

I began to hunt through the house for the dog. I went into the staff quarters. Neither the munching chauffeurs nor the chef had seen the dog. Some workmen were remodelling the back hall in the area. Not wanting to accuse any staff member of inattention, I said that one of the workmen might have accidentally left the door open that led from the staff quarters to the outside. Understandably, there was great denial all around. Jacques, a Quebecois who had little affection for our multicultural staff, immediately said he shared my concern, jumped into the embassy car and drove off looking for Sweet Pea. In the meantime I called Nina, who worked in my husband's office as a social secretary, and asked her to telephone the Humane Society to see if any lost dog was reported.

Nina called back in five minutes. A woman driving along Rock Creek Parkway, a few blocks from our house, hit a dog wildly shooting out into the two-way flow of fast-moving traffic. A dog lover, she picked him up and took him to the first veterinarian she could locate and notified the Humane Society. It was Sweet Pea and he had been badly hit. I rushed to get him at the veterinarian. He had already X-rayed Sweet Pea and advised me to take him to our own vet in Georgetown. I carried Sweet Pea in my arms in the back of the car with Jacques driving fast at the wheel. Sweet Pea was bleeding at the mouth and Jacques was crying, as was I. Mercifully, Sweet Pea had been given an anesthetic and he was sleeping when I handed him over to my vet. "Mrs. Gotlieb," he said, "I'll do my best but don't get your hopes up. If I feel he is suffering too much, do you give me permission to put him to sleep?" I said yes, of course. The vet called at 6 a.m. the next morning, just about the same time of the day, three years ago, that I spotted Sweet Pea's advertisement in the *Washington Post*. The vet told me that he died during the night and without pain. Allan and I vowed never to have another dog at the embassy, especially a Tibetan terrier.

Three months later, shortly before Christmas, Theodore asked if we would step into the drawing room for a moment. She looked solemn. I thought that her mother in the Philippines was dying and she had to return home. Then I saw Myrna, the new upstairs maid and Luce, the kitchen maid, walk into the drawing room. Then the houseman and the chef came into the room. Christian was smiling, thank God. Then Jacques the chauffeur walked in holding in his arms a brown-haired Tibetan terrier about six months old. "This is our Christmas gift," Theodora said. She was brief and solemn because she hated making speeches. Glen Bullard, the Canadian embassy maintenance boss, entered beaming. They all began to laugh and clap. Allan and I glanced at each other, trying not to betray our sinking hearts. We managed to put on a pretty good show.

Jacques and Glen begged us not to name the dog after Sweet Pea. "I always hated that name," Jacques said. "Not good for a male dog," Glen added. "But he's Sweet Pea's nephew," Theodora said, "I like the name." I stared at the dog. Although of the same bloodline as Sweet Pea, he did not have Sweet Pea's androgynous, aristocratic look. Definitely a more rustic, stumpier version of his uncle. At this time the Iran-Contra affair was gripping Washington and Colonel Ollie North's name was on everybody's lips. "Name the dog Ollie," said one of the embassy officers who had dropped by, knowing about the surprise. I was intrigued by the idea until Allan exclaimed, "Over my dead body." Fearful of Republican sensibilities, Allan said, "I'm going to call him Archie." Everyone agreed that Archie was a nice sensible name for a manly dog, but why Archie? I asked Allan. "I like the name," Allan replied, "and I hope that he will become as calm, self-controlled, faithful and obedient as Archie Roosevelt." Archie, a retired CIA bureau chief of the Roosevelt clan, was married to the chief of protocol at the State Department, Lucky Roosevelt, and a frequent visitor in our home. "Archie Roosevelt has impeccable manners," Allan said. "I hope he will pass them on to this dog."

For the next sixteen years we dealt with the most ill-mannered, disobedient, greedy and headstrong dog on this planet. But I'll say this for Archie—he was my dog, not Allan's. I had always suspected that Sweet Pea was gay. Archie loved women, particularly me. He loved them so much he went for their crotches, every time. Unlike Sweet Pea, he cared nothing for rank or protocol. Once, when George Shultz came to dinner at the embassy to watch an old Fred Astaire and Ginger Rogers movie (Ginger was his favourite movie star), he picked up Archie and put him on his lap and then sat back to watch the film in an easy chair. Archie began to cough and hork, and then vomited all over Secretary Shultz. Archie's behaviour with women was entirely different. There was the wife of a congress-man from one of the bacon-and-pork states in the Midwest who weighed in at 225 pounds and was ten years older than her husband. Every time she walked into the drawing room, Archie humped her. It would take Allan and two waiters to get Archie away from under her skirts.

Archie had another cute trick—climbing up on the buffet table and dragging the roast around in front of the guests. A terrific waiter-follower, he was always hoping to catch a flying canapé. Once he grabbed a lamb chop off the plate of the Soviet ambassador. The Swedish ambassador and dean of the diplo-matic core, Count Willi Wachmeister, true to his country's neutralist policies and negotiating skills, coaxed Archie to retreat and drop. Archie grew fat eating three breakfasts (the business breakfast with Allan and his guests, a piece of toast upstairs with me in bed, and a midmorning croissant with the chauffeur), lunch with the ladies on the terrace or by the pool and again a little pasta with the staff in the kitchen, then the usual hors d'oeuvres from six to eight o'clock, followed by dinner with Allan and me or our guests if we were entertaining. But Archie always ended up in the kitchen where the fount of all good things began.

Archie, like Sweet Pea, detested going out in the backyard, refused to swim like all members of the breed and would occasionally agree to take exercise on a leash with Allan. The hair-matting problem was the same with Archie as it was with Sweet Pea. He had to be constantly taken to his breeder in Virginia who would give me hell for not bringing him in more often for dematting.

Despite his greed and multitude of defects, Archie remained with us until we left the embassy some years later and then for a dozen more years in Toronto. Fittingly, he died from an overdose of chocolate which he stole from a locked briefcase. The vet said that if he hadn't been so greedy, he could have had a couple of more years of gourmandizing. Still, during his sixteen years, he had a good seat at the table.

19

The Embassy Garden

*I*N THE HOUSE WHERE I LIVED in Washington the garden did not belong to me. Horticulturally speaking, I felt like I was living in Ottawa before we bought our first home. I was renting. Attached to the Official Residence on Rock Creek Drive there were at least two acres of land that could have been designed, in a practical and elegant way, for an ambassador's residence. This would have been very desirable as, prior to the opening of our new embassy in the heart of the capital, all official entertainment took place at the residence.

At the British ambassador's residence, the gardens were designed for entertainment with considerable success. The architect who designed the large brick house on Massachusetts

Avenue, Sir Edward Lutyens, was very aware of gardens, as evidenced in his long collaboration with England's celebrated gardener, Gertrude Jekyll. The residence was surrounded by a large landscaped terrain with pergolas, shade trees, terraces and stairs leading to the lawn on which the ambassador and his wife could hold garden parties, without the guests protesting too much about the swelling summer heat. Theirs was one of the best lawns in Washington, something difficult to achieve because of the grass-destroying summer heat. The lawn was remarkable, if you like lawns, because the embassy used elephant dung to fertilize it, courtesy, I was told by one British ambassador, of the London Zoo. "The dung comes free," he was quoted in the press as saying. "We only pay for the transportation." The Canadian Press would have been hysterical if I had done likewise at our residence, even though the transportation costs from the nearest Canadian zoo with elephant dung would have been far lower. It was well over halfway through Allan's assignment in Washington when the tale of the British ambassador's elephant dung got me thinking about the garden of the Canadian residence—what I should do about it and whether I should be seeking out my own sources of dung.

I got my chance to procure some when the Washington Zoo asked us if we would hold a fundraising reception for them at the residence. We agreed and after the reception, the head of the zoo asked if they could provide the embassy with a gift in appreciation. I said, "Yes, elephant dung." He replied, "Tiger dung is better and we got a lot of tigers. You can have all you want." I was thrilled. Just as delivery was to take place, I told members of our staff to get ready to receive some well-rotted manure. The Canadian maintenance guys balked. Fear of the smell was the reason cited. I told them the stuff would be pretty

old and wouldn't smell much but, to quell an incipient household revolt, my husband sided with the protestors.

I found that turning our garden into an elegant and beautiful place for entertainment was an impossible task. Although
the residence was close to the centre of the city and had a
homey feeling good for entertaining, the outside space seemed
designed for a large family living in the suburbs whose owners
cared little about gardening. There were five major things
wrong with the entertaining and gardening space.

The first was the placement of the swimming pool, a huge
rectangular sky-blue affair in the suburban style of the 1950s,
suitable for Shawinigan. It was built a decade or so before our
arrival and a decade or two after the style went out of vogue. The
pool was situated in the most prominent position and dominated
the entire landscape. According to the canons of good taste, good
gardening and even good health, a utilitarian pool like ours
should have been tucked away in an obscure and shady corner of
the garden. The ideal situation for a pool is that if you didn't look
for it, you wouldn't know it was there. At the Canadian embassy
residence, the first thing greeting the visitor's eye was this enormous body of bright blue water, ideal for swimming lessons for a
class of thirty children. Meant to be a private pool, it was large
enough for a public park.

The second problem with the garden was the cement. The
pool was surrounded by large slabs of ugly stones and cement
and there were no trees and no shade around it. Beside the pool
was a squat brick house with a men's and ladies' changing room,
also designed for a public pool. During my time, nobody ever
entered into one changing room, including us (we changed in
the house). Pool parties in Embassy Row in Washington were
non-existent. Pools were as common in Washington as
Chevrolets and, after the Kennedys, pool parties were not chic.

Unfortunately, the brick house blocked out a sunny spot of land that would have been ideal for a cutting garden to grow vegetables and flowers for embassy parties. Instead there were forsythia shrubs that were so embedded in the soil that I could never get anyone to take them out. All this meant was that a substantial area of gardening space was given over to brambles.

The third problem in the garden was the design of the upper terrace next to the house and leading from the main structure to the pool and garden. It was meant to be for outdoor entertainment. The stones and concrete kept breaking up, to the despair of Glen Bullard, the chief of maintenance at the embassy. Its condition was not helped by the house and garden man at the residence. He had a passion for hosing down the terrace, which he did every day, even when it was raining, thereby further loosening the stones and cement. Moreover, there was no shade on the terrace, except for a jutting awning that took in part of it. We did give parties on the terrace in spring and fall and on the cool summer nights, but the terrace was a heat-attractor and it was useless to entertain there after the big heat started in May.

The fourth problem was my aversion to two ubiquitous plants that were grown in my front- and backyard and virtually everywhere in the capital and the surrounding areas in Maryland and Virginia. Azaleas and rhododendrons grew like kudzu, the Japanese grass that swallows everything up. The non-deciduous, large-flowered magenta- and orange-coloured azaleas were my particular *b te noire*. If I was sick of seeing them in everyone's yard in Washington, I was even sicker to see them covering most of the growing space in our own garden. There was a view among some gardeners in Washington that only white azaleas were in good taste. Although I planted some of these, my fatigue with the white azaleas equalled my distaste for the hot and deeply coloured ones. The prettiest were the deciduous kind, which didn't bloom forever.

It came as a shock to me that I disliked the azaleas as much as I did because I had them flowering in my house in Ottawa every winter. Of course, you could not grow azaleas outdoors in that climate but you didn't have to because of Mr. Peshke, the chicken, egg and azalea man. While he was respected for the chicken and eggs he delivered to your door, Mr. Peshke was renowned for the azaleas that he grew indoors and sold or rented to his favourite chicken and egg clients. They looked like no other azaleas that I had seen before or since. Although they were of the non-deciduous kind, he clipped and trimmed them so that their stems looked liked small craggy tree trunks and blooms would cascade over tables and mantels. Some of the plants were generations old, and wise clients like ourselves would, after the flowers had bloomed for several months in our houses in winter, return them to Mr. Peshke's care. I never saw azaleas in Washington, indoors or outdoors, that had the oriental originality and age of Mr. Peshke's plants.

Washington also had a love affair with rhododendrons. Large, lush mauve ones grew everywhere, reinforcing the awfulness of the purple azaleas. I hated them for being so obvious and because they were even larger than the azaleas and took up an enormous amount of garden space. I cursed the Rothschilds for introducing them into England and making them so fashionable that the Americans followed suit.

The final problem in the garden was what to plant after May when the azaleas were finished and the big, killing heat of Washington set in.

I looked for ideas for years, trying to find solutions, even feeble ones. I thought it was worthwhile doing because there were a few features of the garden that saved it from utter banality.

The best of these were the tall white flowering Florida dog-wood trees with bleeding red centres in the blossoms. A group of a half-dozen or more of these mature trees lined the edges of the garden, behind the azaleas. During the several weeks of their bloom in late spring, you could not take your eyes off them. (They are much prettier and more reliable than the famous cherry blossoms.) In addition, a former ambassador's wife had the good taste to plant some white clematis (the Miss Bateman variety), and their big blossoms covered an unattractive brick wall. This was the beginning of my love affair with clematis, an affair that grows deeper over the years. One could also detect in the garden the aroma of box and laurel trees that offered a spring reward. Southern magnolias and the purple crape myrtles also helped compensate for the bareness of our garden in late summer.

Towards the end of my stay, I heard rumblings among the embassy staff that money might be made available by headquarters in Ottawa to allow for some improvements in the garden. Until then, the only thing I did on my own was to have Yves, the carpenter, build a rather rickety rose bower by the terrace so it could be seen by embassy guests. Roses actually flourished and grew high in the bower. This modest success plus the news of money for the garden emboldened me to pursue a crazy idea that I had had for some time—to build a greenhouse. I remembered the beautiful hibiscus, oleanders, orange trees and other flowering plants that were grown in the greenhouse of the US embassy in Ottawa and that decorated the ambassador's residence in all seasons. I thought we should have a greenhouse, at least in miniature, and grow some interesting plants not available in the District or area. I don't know where the embassy staff got the greenhouse from. I believe it was made from a do-it-yourself kit, but the kit lacked the things that make a greenhouse work, such as heating and cooling units, circulation fans and louvered windows. The plants I tried to grow in the greenhouse did better outside. And the greenhouse proved to be just another ugly feature of the garden. I was very unhappy about my lack of success in improving the garden. The glare of the purple and white azaleas and rhododendrons was getting me down. Even if big colour contrast in gardens has its enthusiasts, I found the clash too strong to take every morning.

Late in Allan's Washington assignment, I still had the delusion of improving the garden, but now I was thinking along radical lines. One night TV anchorwoman Andrea Mitchell dined with us along with her future husband, Alan Greenspan, and she offered to introduce me to a friend who was a well-known English landscape gardener. The gardener had lived a long time in Washington and knew the climate well. With the permission of the Canadian government, I asked her for a new garden design, which she submitted shortly thereafter. The government was furious because the fee for her design was a couple of thousand dollars. They refused to go ahead with it. That was the end of the grand redesign of the embassy's garden.

When I left Washington in 1989, the garden at the residence remained more or less as I found it when I arrived in 1981. My efforts led nowhere and I left no imprint. Nor did I improve my knowledge of gardening in Washington. There was one thing I did learn, however, through all the entertainment we engaged in. The only flowers that showed up at night, if we were giving a reception or dinner outdoors, were white. In midsummer, the flowers that would withstand the heat and the rain were upright white petunias that I placed in planters on the terrace and low-standing walls. I also put white alyssum and silvery curry plants in vast clay pots supplied by the embassy. I always tried to keep the flowers white and silver and as fragrant as possible, with some degree of success. If we ate out on the terrace we could see and we could smell. Arranging for those sights and scents was my only memorable gardening experience in Washington.

20

Other People's Houses

W HILE ALLAN WAS SERVING IN Washington, we were occasionally asked to stay as house guests in grander houses than we had been accustomed to when Allan was an insignificant civil servant in Ottawa. A friend of ours—Robert Duemling, an American diplomat whom we knew when he was serving in Ottawa—had married Louisa du Pont Copeland Biddle, the daughter of Mrs. Lammot du Pont Copeland. Mrs. Copeland owned Mount Cuba, an estate near Wilmington, Delaware.

Recently, Louisa's mother died in her mid-nineties and her rare American antiques and Chinese export porcelain were sold at a single-owner record-breaking auction at Sotheby's in New

York. The proceeds will fund a foundation at Mount Cuba dedicated to the protection and propagation of native wildflowers. Mrs. Copeland's wildflower garden at Mount Cuba was the largest of its kind in the United States.

Staying with the Duemlings and Mrs. Copeland at Mount Cuba was a little like living in an Edith Wharton novel—we slept in heirloom beds, ate from antique American silver, and were surrounded by furniture of the finest Philadelphia cabinetmakers. Mrs. Copeland's lifestyle was luxurious, but very different from other places we stayed as house guests—Walter Annenberg's art museum home in Palm Springs, Kay Graham's sprawling summer house on Martha's Vineyard, Polly Fritchey's modest home on Fisher Island, Evangeline Bruce and Marietta Tree's merry widows' retreat in Tuscany, among others.

Entering Mount Cuba was like walking back into the nineteeth century, and not only because of the furniture. Louisa's mother was a strong-minded matriarch who thoroughly enjoyed her style of life. While maintaining a certain aloofness, she was determined that her guests would be well treated and have a good time. Shorter and plumper than her daughter, Mrs. Copeland's gaiety contrasted with what I thought was a rather gloomy house. She was apologetic about the problem of keeping staff in the country, although she did have a chef, butler and maids. What was bright and light about the house, and stirred the gardener's heart in me, were her working greenhouses, the most I have seen outside of Kew. But I'm no expert. The only greenhouses I'd ever seen before Mount Cuba were commercial or publicly owned. Our visit took place in late February, just before the Philadelphia Garden Show, the largest and best in North America, where Mrs. Copeland's plants habitually won a large share of the prizes. She was a passionate gardener and her greenhouses were filled that month with what seemed to me to be all 425 species of the primrose—*Primula auricula*, *candelabra*, *denticulata*, *capitata*, *frondosa* and on and on. The only primrose I had ever seen before was the common polyanthus. Mrs. Copeland told me that she kept her gardeners, the most precious members of her staff, searching the country for rare plants and seeds. If I were to be born again, I would like to be Mrs. Copeland.

The greenhouses filled with primroses should not be confused with her conservatory, where plant girls displayed her finer specimens just before we arrived to sip Bloody Marys or martinis late weekend mornings. These gatherings were, as Louisa explained "one of Mummy's traditions." As soon as we arrived, the girls who placed the plants quietly disappeared. Mrs. Copeland's other passion, she explained, was travelling, and though well into her eighties she was planning an ambitious cruise through Alaskan waters on the then luxurious Viking Line.

Besides Louisa and Bob, we were joined by members of the painting Wyeth family and other family friends. Saturday night, Mrs. Copeland was in a long dress, while the rest of the women wore short, made from synthetics from duPont factories. The food was typical of WASP-land (not very good), but the drink, again not a surprise, was of the finest. The late Mr. Copeland was a collector of the grape and the grain and had an enviable cellar that Mrs. Copeland generously shared with her guests.

Saturday night was a bit of a haze for me. Allan's fault as usual. He kept saying, "Taste this wine, you'll never taste it again." When the cognac was served—a 1906—I passed, but as he told me, "It goes down like cream." I wondered if some of the guests were in the same alcoholic haze as I. No member of the family contradicted the matriarch in our presence. The du Pont family had the discipline and the vices of a very Victorian household. Sunday lunch was in honour of a non-family member, the CEO of duPont, a worldly, self-possessed man who handled Mrs. Copeland and family with diplomacy and a certain bemusement.

On our way back to Washington, Bob, Lousia, Allan and I took a tour of Winterthur, the leading museum of Americana, long supported by the du Ponts. At the museum shop Louisa bought a little pot of slightly wilted *Primula auricula* for $7.95. "I don't have any at home," she said. I thought of the hundreds of specimens at Mount Cuba. Mothers and daughters. Why doesn't Louisa ask her mother for one? But then what do I know about Edith Wharton-land?

Sunnylands in Palm Springs, a contemporary house with an Aztec-style roof, stands in the middle of Walter Annenberg's private golf course. It contains, for part of the year, his collection of Impressionist masterpieces, now owned by the Metropolitan Museum of Art in New York. Allan spent a large part of his time gawking at the van Goghs and the Monets, but being a visual idiot so far as art is concerned, I was drawn to the white oleander hedges surrounding the golf course. No golfer, I wandered around the grounds of the course, looking at the rare trees, some centuries old and transplanted at great expense from the desert. Mrs. Annenberg nervously watched me, fearing that I might be hit on the head by a golf ball.

At Sunnylands, I faced the same problem that worried me before we visited the du Pont estate and which always confronts the house guest. What to wear? Preparing for Mount Cuba, I was told, "just informal dinner dress." Before visiting Katharine Graham at her summer home in Martha's Vineyard, I was advised by her social secretary, "Oh, it's very informal, casual" and Lee Annenberg informed me before I left Washington, "Very informal, California-style, casual but elegant." I know enough not to take literally the words "informal" and "casual." They usually mean you can expect anything. But the words "California-style, casual but elegant" terrified me. I decided to take everything I owned to Sunnylands, except my ball gowns. (My husband tells me I still do that wherever I go, except to Winnipeg.) In a state of anxiety, I borrowed a glittery silk top and pants from another Washington hostess, Jennifer Phillips, who informed me that she thought the outfit was "California-style, casual but elegant."

Jennifer proved to be correct because, when I wore the outfit on the Friday night of our arrival, I noticed a couple of the other ladies also wearing silk pants and glittery blouses. Lee Annenberg, a highly organized and warm-hearted hostess, always beautifully dressed, cast her eyes on me without disapproval. For dinner st Sunnylands on the following night, I could have worn a ball gown—some of the other guests decided to be "dressy."

Unlike Mount Cuba, Sunnylands was definitely sunny, no gloomy corners or colours, lots of contemporary yellow and green comfortable chairs and bathrooms fitted out like spas. When the waiter asked me what I wanted to drink, I said champagne. "That's my girl," Walter said, "that's my girl." (He usually repeats everything twice.) He told the butler to open a bottle of vintage champagne which he poured into a large water glass. "I hate those flutes," he said. "You can't get the taste of a good champagne."

Katharine Graham owned a large, rambling beach house on the shores of Martha's Vineyard. It was separated from the long, deserted beach in front of the house by a large stretch of wild land covered with shrubs, berries, wild roses, indigenous grasses and reeds. Katharine had erected a little structure close to the beach where she would give picnic lunches prepared by her chef. The beach house was all white and furnished with white down-filled sofas and chairs that you could sink into, read a book and not be disturbed. The only thing that disturbed the paradise was the endless socializing on the Vineyard. Except for Jacqueline Onassis, who lived at some distance in an isolated part of the island, Katharine Graham was the Queen of the Vineyard. She entertained guests during the summer almost every weekend and, of course, the Vineyard was the playground of the liberal left. In Edgartown, where Republicans resided, Katharine said, with a sniff, "They wear ties."

Despite her friendship with Nancy Reagan, Kay was a Democrat. In Washington, she entertained every president and their cabinet secretaries. During one of our visits to the Vineyard, we arrived the weekend before Nancy Reagan, then the president's wife, was coming to stay with her. Mrs. Graham was in a tither. She plotted out each place on the Vineyard Nancy Reagan might like to see or visit, testing our reactions and asking for our suggestions. She was very nervous about Mrs. Reagan's visit. "She isn't even bringing a personal maid," Kay said to me. "Do you think I should find one for her?" (Kay, of course, did not have a personal maid at the Vineyard.) I suggested not. "She doesn't want her own, so leave her alone." I was amused by the idea of Mrs. Reagan socializing in the middle of hate-Reagan-land. I didn't want to ask Kay who she was planning to have for dinner in her honour. The people that Kay usually entertained at Martha's Vineyard—Bill and Rose Styron, Arthur Miller, Vernon and Ann Jordan, Bob McNamara, legal scholar Ronald Dworkin, Bob Silver of the *New York Review of Books*, Art Buchwald, Jules Feiffer, Walter Cronkite—were all dyed-in-the-wool liberals. But Kay was always seeking balance in her relationships and her weekend guests often included Henry and Nancy Kissinger, Joseph

Alsop, and former high-ranking Republicans. I knew she would get just the right mix for Nancy Reagan.

In Washington, Kay was often thought to have a stiff and almost Germanic manner. She rarely smiled—to get her to smile, a certain amount of courting had to take place—and she could be censorious. A regular guest at our embassy dinners throughout our stay in Washington, she did not hesitate to offer unsolicited opinions on some of the fellow guests she met there. Once, staring at the editor of another newspaper, she said to me, "Sondra, how could you have that man in your house?" On another occasion, she looked at a prominent guest with a dubious business background and scolded Allan for having invited him. I liked her candour. But I would never dare to say the same sort of thing in her house.

In Martha's Vineyard, Kay was much more relaxed but always a conscientious hostess. On our first visit to the Vineyard, she gave up her ritual morning tennis game (she had her own court) to show us around the Vineyard. She stressed informality at all times, but one thing scared me to death. There was a slip of paper on the table beside our bed when we arrived. It listed the guests, all very well-known, coming for lunch and dinner during the next two and a half days, as well as where we were to be taken for cocktails or dinner. This was casual and informal Martha's Vineyard where you went to escape from it all. I wondered what it would be like staying in Edgartown where not wearing a tie was a faux pas. I never did find out.

When Evangeline Bruce heard we were going to Europe one summer while we were in Washington, she asked us to join her and Marietta Tree as guests for a week at their villa in Tuscany. Marietta Tree told me that when their husbands died, she suggested to Evangeline that the two widows rent a villa in

Tuscany where friends could visit. The villa they chose, relatively modest by some standards, was extraordinarily pretty and
well kept up. It was situated in the rolling Chianti country
amidst villages that had not changed in centuries. During the
decade and a half they had lived there together in the same
house, two magic maids did everything from carrying baggage
up three flights of stairs to making the beds and cooking all the
meals. A more cheerful pair of women I had never met.
Without them, the widows could not have managed because
there were visitors for lunch almost every day, as well as a
steady stream of house guests. The villa was in the midst of
what was known as "Chiantishire" where English toffs and aes-
thetes liked to gather under the Tuscan sky. They lived in their
own isolated villas but the social life, like that on Martha's
Vineyard, was intense. The widows' neighbours included Sir
Harold Acton, Stephen Spender's son and his wife, Ashile
Gorky's daughter, whom Evangeline referred to as "that witch,"
and Sir Woodrow (later Lord) Wyatt, the ex-journalist whose
posthumous diaries rocked London. A snaggle-toothed snob,
he was bursting with gossip the day he came to lunch and entertained the ladies with vicious and malicious tales, as only an
Englishman can do. When Allan was introduced as the
Canadian ambassador, Sir Wyatt said, "Oh, Canada, what an
interesting idea." After lunch, I stayed on with the ladies to
listen to his gossip—and pretty low and delicious it was—but
Allan had had enough and went to sleep. Other house guests
were favourites of Evangeline—Nicko Henderson and his wife,
and a minor, very minor, English poet who read his latest verses
to the ladies under the pergola to great approbation.

It was the pergola that made the strongest impression on me.
At lunch, under the shade of the grapevines, we ate different
pasta made each day by the Italian maids and drank tumblers of

Chianti. Even the high-strung Evangeline, with her eighteen-inch waist, relaxed by allowing herself a second portion of the pasta and a third tumbler of the wine. She said, "I gain ten pounds in the summer and then I take it off before I go back to Washington." Marietta Tree, although as beautiful as Evangeline but not as thin, ate and drank seemingly without comment. They both claimed not to have dinner in the evening and that was true while we stayed with them. The Italian maids cooked superb osso bucco, veal piccata and divine Italian desserts unknown to me. The two widows each took one nibble and then crossed their plates with their knives and forks while Allan and I cleaned up. Aside from the pergola, the greatest attraction to me was the swimming pool. It was the first "infinity" pool I had ever seen and is still the most beautiful in my experience. The water appeared not to be contained in the pool as it perpetually poured over its edges and drained back into the pool through invisible pipes. It was set on the top of a hill near the edge of the property. As you were swimming, you could look down over the hills of Tuscany. There seemed to be no barrier between you and the deep rolling valleys below.

If you wanted or needed anything, it was best to consult Marietta. She rented the house, organized it, hired the help and had convinced Evangeline to be her partner. Marietta was the activist, planning expeditions to Arezzo to see the frescoes by Pierro della Francisca, to Siena to see the Bellinis, to restaurants in the surrounding villages and even to the local hairdresser an hour and a half away, where she sat quietly without complaint for a couple of hours because the hairdresser forgot she was coming. Evangeline was the passive one, disappearing for hours in her room to read. She disappeared so much I thought that we got on her nerves. I asked Marietta if something was wrong. "Don't pay any attention," she said. "She's always been like that. Even when David was alive and she lived in all those grand embassies, she only appeared at dinner."

Both the merry widows are now dead—first Marietta from cancer and then Evangeline, who one day woke up blind in her home in Georgetown. On a visit to Washington, I went to her home. She was sitting, beautifully dressed by her maid, wearing dark glasses. Her strong visual sense—her love of beautiful clothes, furniture, rugs, gardens and museums—made her blindness especially tragic. I asked her, after the usual chit-chat, how she was managing. "I'm not," she replied. "I really want to die." I knew she had completed her book on the letters of Napoleon and Josephine just before she went blind and there was now talk of a promotion tour. I urged her to try to do it. She said nothing but gave one of her sardonic smiles. Her only response was to ask her companion to give me a signed copy of her book. She was in a deep depression, although she made pretense of normality in social conversation. Not long after, before retiring one night, she reached out for a book on a shelf nearby to hand to her companion to read aloud, and died instantly.

Marietta died in her early seventies, Evangeline in her late seventies. With their deaths, and those of Pamela Harriman and Kay Graham not long after, the era of the hostesses died too.

21

Jarvis Street Blues

*T*HE LAST YEAR I SPENT IN WASHINGTON, I pretty well knew who my friends and enemies were or at least thought I did. I no longer felt stressed by being in the eye of the media. Allan's tensions were also subsiding after the feverish free-trade negotiations were brought to a successful conclusion and above all our daughter Rebecca was recovering her health after a perilous operation in Pittsburgh. Allan felt, after thirty years in government, he had enough, and it was time to take his father's advice (who probably didn't know it came from Lord Rothschild) that "in a capitalist country, be a capitalist." I loved Washington so much I asked him why he couldn't be a capitalist in the Capital. "You don't understand," he replied. "I'm a lawyer and lawyers in Washington are really only lobbyists." Sometimes he would say, "Who wants to be a small fish in a big pond?" It wouldn't have bothered me because I believed that swimming with the small fish in Washington might be more enjoyable than swimming with bigger ones in Canada. I had met a few Canadian big fish when they ventured into US waters. They reminded me more of sluggish carp than leaping dolphins. But Allan was determined to return to Canada. He had seen too many retired diplomats hanging around in Washington, waiting for party invitations from people they would have ignored when they were in office. "You can stay in Washington in winter if that's what you want," Allan said. "After I make some money, we can buy a small house in Georgetown, but I want to move to Toronto, it's the commercial centre of Canada. That's where I have to be if I want to make a living."

I had never thought much about money in Washington. I had been living with a butler, chauffeur, chef and maids for over seven years without any money. In the political and bureaucratic world, money provided no status, power did. During all the years of my married life, I lived in societies where one's rank or position in the system was important, but money never was. In Ottawa, where I had spent over twenty years, the mandarins were the cocks-o-the-walk but their pay was very modest.

Admittedly, while I was in Washington the finger of Mammon did touch me at times. I longed for a Judith Lieber purse. Nancy Reagan had a number of Judith Lieber purses that she displayed like objets d'art in her private apartments in the White House. A uniquely designed Judith Lieber purse, encrusted with beads and crystals, could cost between three and fifteen thousand dollars. Of course, no one actually needed a Judith Lieber purse and I certainly didn't. But the Reagan era was to me symbolized by these gaudy eye-catching bags. They were the true emblems of the Reaganite ladies. Nancy Reagan, of course, wore one when she went out to social events. When I attended receptions I could see them carried about like trophies by the socially ambitious and prominent.

Travelling officially as ambassador and his wife in the United States, we were often entertained by people of great wealth, whose style of life included multiple mansions, couture clothes and great art collections. I knew with absolute certainly I would never be able to afford such a lifestyle, including the ultimate and only necessary luxury of a rich man, the private aircraft. The only thing I really wanted, as the symbol of a life I would have to abandon, was The Purse. Wherever they sold them, I would stand Allan in front of the counter, ask him if he liked the look and strongly hint that one of those purses was what I really wanted as an anniversary or birthday present. He stared at their bizarre shapes and colouring and thought I had lost my mind. "You like these?" he would ask. "I don't like them." He would move on. "Women collect them," I would tell him, "like you collect art." In the end both Nancy Reagan and I lost in our quest for Judith Lieber handbags. The press found out about Nancy Reagan's collection of Judith Lieber purses, all presents, presumably, of Judith Lieber, and she had to return every one. I, for my part, lost because I left Washington without one of these diamant trophies. But you might also say I won. Had I acquired such a purse, it would have been totally useless to me in my new life back in Canada. In Toronto, there are no doubt women who have Judith Lieber purses or long for them. But they don't touch my life or I theirs.

Neither of us ever lived in Toronto before, but we were impressed by all the publicity it was receiving at the time in the United States as "the city that works." Nevertheless I had this idea of living in Washington. I saw myself in Georgetown and, like Voltaire, cultivating my own little garden and intellect. I would entertain people who were in and out of politics but all good conversationalists and all drawn to the Washington forum like the ancients were drawn to the agora in Athens. When I grew up in Winnipeg, I was attracted by the high-minded milkman's son, my first love, because of his passionate conversation about politics and ideas. I was still attracted to this kind of person. They were to be found in the print media (more often on its edges), the independent think-tanks, universities and sometimes in the administration and Congress. They had one thing in common—no money. I saw myself as a minor hostess to small-time intellectuals discussing big ideas. That was good enough for me. I also thought that, as a writer, this would help keep me in contact with other journalists and editors and provide a ready market for my writing in the United States. In the end, we bought no little house in Washington, because we had no money.

It was Barbara Walters who summed up my situation at a going-away lunch for me in New York. I told her I was going back to live in Toronto after Allan completed a teaching stint at Berkeley and Harvard. "Toronto? Why would you do that?" she asked. "Nobody you know in Washington or New York will visit you in Toronto. Toronto's off the map. What about your writing? Nobody wants to read a journalist from Toronto." Marietta Tree, who was sitting on my other side, was a little more sympathetic, when I said, defensively, that I lived twenty years in Ottawa, with nobody visiting me from Washington or New York, and I managed to survive. But I knew Barbara Walters was right. Toronto, in most of my glamorous acquaintances' eyes, was tundra land, without the interesting wildlife and unusual native customs.

My vision of our future life was very different from Allan's. In our years in Washington, he never once mentioned that he was in debt. It seems we had spent too much money of our own keeping up with the Judith Lieberniks. He knew he would have to pay off that debt but refused to do so by working in Washington because of his distaste for lobbying. "My work as ambassador to the US made me chief lobbyist for Canada," he said. "I had enough. I don't feel like being chief lobbyist for some steel-pipe manufacturer or Canadian tree-grower, even if it's lucrative." Then he would make his clincher statement, "I'm a Canadian and I'm going back to Canada. Period." So I was dragged to the strange, emotionally cold city of Toronto, and I reverted to my role as *La Malcontenta*.

In Toronto, I went from princess to bag-lady in twenty-four hours.

Since I didn't know the city, I assumed we could find a house in a few weeks. For a great sum of money we rented a three-room furnished flat, not counting the room with a giant red Jacuzzi that didn't work. The apartment was on Jarvis Street in downtown Toronto. It was the late 1980s and prices were sky-high for renting and buying. I didn't know that Jarvis Street was not considered a good address by Torontonians. A hundred years ago, yes. I was soon to learn that Toronto had one very peculiar difference from other places where I had lived. In England, if people don't know you they ask, "What school do you go to?" In the United States they ask, "What do you do?" Toronto people ask, "Where do you live?" Sometimes even, what side of the street do you live on? I was about to find out that the address is everything. Toronto was almost the opposite to Washington because in the US capital just about everyone you met was a transient or not intending to remain permanently in the city—even if they did. Most Torontonians I met were born in the city and never left. As the saying goes, there is no one more self-important than a local celebrity on his own dung hill.

In our flat in Jarvis Street I felt as if I had rented the worst rooms in a halfway house, albeit one with a very pleasant door-man who told me where to find the best malls. Because we had a certain notoriety at the time, people in the block recognized us but did not greet us, which was sort of unnerving. It turned out that we remained in the flat for over a year. When we real-ized it would take us a long time to buy a house that we both liked and could afford, we farmed out poor Archie to live with my daughter and I went out to buy a bed, mattress, armchair and comfortable sofa that I could sit on. The chairs and bed in the flat felt as if they were stuffed with cornhusks or kapoc. My chronic arthritic back had flared up, aggravated by our wander-ings to Berkeley and Harvard. Allan had taken short-term teaching assignments, which he hated, to cleanse himself from the taint of government before trying to make money in the private sector. I could have stayed in Berkeley for its climate and Canbridge for its intellectual environment but, never mind, Toronto was Allan's goal.

I was anxious to settle because I had a book and other writ-ing commitments that I had to fulfill. On Jarvis Street, using a laptop computer with an intermittently flickering screen that needed the neck of a goose to be seen, I wrote the book and ruined my spine.

When I told Torontonians I was living on Jarvis Street, I was met with disbelief, disapproval or silence. Jarvis Street was the favourite address of prostitutes, drug addicts and chicken hawks (a phrase I had not heard before, chicken hawks were young country boys selling their bodies to cruising city men). They were particularly attracted to the front of our building and the seedy park across the street.

I had no dog. I had no house or garden. I had no husband

because Allan was constantly travelling. I had no close friends because I had not lived in Toronto before, and I had no car ("Who needs a car when you live in downtown Toronto?" Allan asked). I was a displaced person, with a giant, non-working red Jacuzzi.

Amidst a sea of concrete, I heard the siren call of house and garden—especially garden. It grew louder every hour.

23

Birth of a Garden

SATURDAY WAS HAPPY DAY. Our amiable and patient real estate agent would drive us around in her comfortable Cadillac sedan and show us other people's houses. After a year of fun snooping and sightseeing, we eliminated everything that was practical and affordable, such as a house in the suburbs. We were determined to find a home in a central and well-treed location that would not be impossible for Allan to finance.

Our search was prolonged because Allan was an inside man, while I was an outside woman. His concern was the inside of the house, especially whether it would have enough wall space to hang his pictures. I kept looking at the lot, which was invariably too small for my gardening ambitions. After a year of disagreement, I was so fed up I was ready to move in anywhere, including houses in the suburbs or city houses with tiny gardens. In desperation, we made reckless bids for houses we hated and were saved from our folly only by the greed of the owners who wanted more money. Eventually our agent took me to a contractor-built, Arts and Crafts turn-of-the-century brick house of the type that dot the city. It took William Morris fifty years to reach this remote part of the colonies. A divorced doctor lived in the house with his many sons—so many that his Rosedale neighbours told us they thought it was a frat house. It had not been renovated since the 1950s. The house had the largest backyard I had seen in our search, and because of its condition the price was conceivably within our reach. I told Allan, who was travelling when I first saw it, that the house was the shambles and would take years to fix up. But I had to escape from Jarvis Street, the doctor's wife needed her alimony, the real estate market was softening and the price wasn't completely ridiculous so, after eighteen months in Toronto, we bought it. Allan warned that we would have to move into it while it was being renovated. We arrived with the plasterers and painters, the plumbers, the carpenters and the foremen.

We chose a contractor who called himself "The Black Swede." He came highly recommended by someone we trusted. "I like building strip malls better than renovating old houses," he told us. That should have been a warning. But he was anxious to get the business and gave us a reasonable estimate. I became so upset by him that I complained about him at a party to a prominent Toronto psychiatrist. I told him I was having nightmares about a contractor who, out of sheer perversity, always did the opposite of what I wanted. "You know," the psychiatrist said, "there is a new subspecialty in psychiatry—treating people who want to kill their contractors."

He also told me I was suffering from "immigrantitis." "Why immigrantitis?" I asked him, "I'm hardly an immigrant, like my father." "Because you moved from one world into another," he replied. "Lucky for you, in both worlds everybody speaks English." The doctor's diagnosis was right. Toronto was a foreign place to me. People walked too slow, talked too slow, and what they talked about—their summer cottages, their boats, their cars, their houses, did not interest me. The big-money men whose names they dropped had no meaning for me. I found it a glum world. Our comedians had mostly gone south and left us with glum cineastes, writers and bankers. Torontonians were a gloomy and parochial lot. Their icons were even gloomier. If you had some doubts about the humourless writings of Margaret Atwood, Timothy Findley or Michael Ondaatje, you had best keep them to yourself or risk being blackballed from the CanLit club.

While we were beginning to renovate, a couple of people I knew in Toronto who had visited our home noticed that we did not have a separate dining room and they agreed that we did not need one—a separate dining room, they said, would not add to the value of our house. Allan, who had never eaten in a kitchen in his life, told me to change my friends. There was no way he was going to live in a house without a dining room. However, the only place to put the new room was at the back of the house, which, to my great resentment, would take up precious garden space—garden space being the only reason I wanted to buy the house. Allan's view prevailed and my gardening ambitions suffered a major setback.

The Black Swede and I for once agreed on something—if there had to be a dining room, a second-floor deck on top of its roof would be an attractive feature of the house. The deck would be adjacent to our master bedroom and I could see

myself arranging pots of flowering plants and stretching out on
a divan on a summer evening. The building of the deck pro-
voked our next-door neighbour into a frenzy of letter writing
and lobbying to prevent us from doing so. From what we were
able to ascertain, it seems that he was convinced that we were
going to hold an endless series of cocktail parties on top of the
dining room. This, I suppose, was because we were known to
have entertained a lot in the embassy in Washington. Because
the idea of having cocktail parties on a second-floor deck off
our bedroom was ludicrous, we didn't take him seriously until a
kindly neighbour behind our property told us he had a history
of being difficult.

After we received lawyers' letters and enquiries from municipal authorities, Allan shot off his own warning missiles. They
didn't do any good. The neighbour demonstrated real talent in
finding ways to annoy us. When my youngest daughter got
married, just as the bridal party was entering the garden on a
beautiful spring day, he began to mow his lawn. He surpassed
himself when a group of old ladies visited our property on an
organized garden tour. As they walked down the narrow path
adjacent to his driveway between our houses to pass through
our garden gate, he hosed down his cars, spraying the women at
the same time. He had a particular aversion to Archie. If the
dog barked after 8 p.m. more than once, he would telephone us,
without identifying himself, and say, "Get the goddamn dog to
shut up." He moved off the street when his marriage broke up.

Despite it all, he was legally unable to prevent us from
building the deck. It was splendid and spacious and I hated it. If
we wanted to grow anything, we had to haul pails of water from
the bathroom onto the deck. Worse, we had to hall up bags of
earth from the garden. On the way back, we would trudge dirt
all over the bedroom carpet. It was far too hot to sit or lie on

the deck and I wasn't going to add insult to injury by building a trellis there to provide some shade.

I did manage to grow nasturtiums from seeds in the half-dozen window boxes I installed. If I did not examine them every day, an army of aphids would mow them down. The Heavenly Blue morning glories I planted would only stay open a few hours in the morning. They closed up promptly at noon, true to their name. My cleaning lady who came in the morning was most appreciative but they were not seen by anyone else. I still haven't solved the problem of what to put in the window boxes. I tried cascade petunias, the fragrance of which I thought might waft through my bedroom door. The most fragrant were the many-petalled bluey-lavender petunias but their growing habit was erratic. The newer showier wave petunias came in colours that did not appeal to me and had little fragrance. Because I was so keen on odours floating into my bedroom, I tried flowers such as evening stock with its strong spicy smell. The three that bloomed lasted a week. My worst venture was with something I saw blown up on the cover of a magazine called "poached eggs" (*Limnanthes douglasii*). Never trust a picture of flowers unless it says actual size. I thought they would look absolutely gorgeous flowering from the window boxes. When I planted the seeds, I failed to notice the actual height of the flower. I had ignored the small print on the package. If I had not, I would have seen that it didn't say trailing or cascading. In fact, all the poached egg plants flowered. They were an inch and a half tall, their normal height. If you leaned over and stuck your nose into the window box, you could perceive a sweet tiny yellow plant. I still have dreams for the perfect plant for my deck and through a process of elimination, I'll get there yet. What I want is simple—a stunning trailing flower with an almost overpowering fragrance.

Shortly after the dining room went up I stood at the rear window and looked at the big old brick garage, constructed early in the last century, which was set back in the garden more than a hundred feet from the street. I realized I would never be able to back our Toyota down the long narrow driveway from the garage to the front thoroughfare. I can't even drive forward in a straight line, let alone back up. I told Allan that the price of his dining room was the destruction of his garage and he reluctantly agreed. When the Black Swede, in his good time, had dismantled three-quarters of the structure and then disappeared to work on another job in the manner of all contractors, I made a stunning discovery. I liked the look of the almost destroyed garage. "It's a ruin," I said to Allan, looking at the long high brick wall still standing and the crumbling brick buttresses supporting it, "and I want that ruin." I knew it would be good for vertical gardening, which I was just beginning to read about. I imagined climbing roses, clematis and honey suckle.

While we were still embroiled in arguments over renovating and decorating, I went to a dinner where some people interested in gardening were present. A witty woman with an English accent dominated the table. She told me she was a landscape architect. I liked her immediately and asked her to look at my backyard. When Penny Arthurs inspected our front and back gardens, I hesitantly asked her about an old garage ruin. "Good idea," she said, "the wall will give you a lot more gardening space. We'll use the wall to make rooms in the backyard, just like Sissinghurst." She was only being slightly ironic. The notion of comparing Sissinghurst with its exquisitely kept garden rooms to our backyard made me laugh. "Don't laugh," Penny said. "You have potential here. Except for one terrible thing. You should have brought me in sooner. It's too bad you built such an awkward exit from your new dining room into the

garden. Instead of being able to make a natural entrance into
your garden from the rear of the dining room, you have these
pokey off-centre stairs going down to your garbage cans. If I
had been in the picture earlier [a phrase I was to hear often
during years to come], your exit would have fit into a practical,
symmetrical, welcoming indoor-outdoor garden scheme." This
was my first lesson in gardening design. I only thought of flowers. I never thought of the form and structure of the garden.
And I never thought about how you get into the garden from
the house.

The next thing Penny said to me was, "What kind of garden
would you like, high-maintenance or low-maintenance? Give
me an idea of your ideal garden." I knew exactly what I wanted.
I showed her a picture of a rural English cottage garden, a
seemingly careless scattering of flag stones here and there and a
riot of flowers growing all over the space from the rear wall of
the house to the fences on the side and back, interrupted only
by a brick walk. "You don't live in England," Penny said. "You
can't grow half the flowers in your picture because of the climate and it's totally impractical unless you have the money to
hire two full-time gardeners to keep the invasive plants from
killing the others." "And what about trees?" "You need order,"
she said. "You need a blueprint and while I know you don't
want grass, some here and there will help to give the garden
form. Sondra, you are a spontaneous person and you want to
have a spontaneous garden. I'll control you. Both you and the
garden need to be reined in."

I had been living with a control freak—my husband—for
about forty years. I worried about having another one in my
life. But I knew she was right. I knew I had no strong sense of
design. Margaret Trudeau once complained to me about the
rigidly conventional design of the gardens at the prime minis-

ter's residence at 24 Sussex Drive. "Why can't I just drop the seeds anywhere, scattering them around and let the flowers grow?" she asked. "Why does the garden always have to look so boring?" I agreed with Margaret Trudeau that a lot could be done to enhance the prime minister's garden, but not being as romantic as Margaret, I knew that throwing a bunch of seeds around randomly would get you nothing. I was somewhere between Margaret Trudeau's unrealistic romantic approach to garden design and Penny Arthur's controlled vision. I dislike neatness and rigidity but I began to realize that a garden without control and discipline would have more in common with a hayfield than my ideal cottage garden.

I was deeply impressed with Penny's observations about the clumsy entrance into our yard as well as about building a garden of separate rooms. I told her I would like to hire her. "When can we start?" I asked. "How about tomorrow?" She answered in her clipped, professional English manner that she needed to draw up blueprints for the front and back and that would take time. She gave me a price for preparing the blueprints and for her time. A few weeks later, she spread out several large scrolls on our dining-room table showing cheaper and more expensive options for the garden. I stared at the scrolls and felt I was back in my grade nine geometry class. Penny soon realized that, unlike Allan, I could gather no idea of what she proposed to do from looking at the blueprints on our dining-room table. I made her walk around outside and show me precisely what she wanted to do on each spot where we stood. That is how, from that day on, we worked together during the next four or five years.

Penny and I have opposite personalities. What we had in common was that we both loved gardening and we both liked to laugh. But our contrary characteristics led to many arguments.

I always felt Penny would never admit a mistake and Penny felt I was too impractical in my approach. In the long run we made an ideal combination.

To my initial dismay, Allan began to take an interest in the garden, something he had never done before. He was a tree man of sorts. But like his father, he had a hard time distinguishing between a tulip and a rose. Back in Ottawa on Lisgar Road and Ellesmere Place, he ignored the gardens but did like to plant a birch tree or mountain ash from time to time. I think his new-found interest was my fault. It was the old garage wall that was the source of his attention. Why not seek out some architectural antiques to complement the decaying garden wall and ruined brick supports? He always had an interest in Victorian tiles and had begun collecting them in England. In Toronto he found a group of large old terra-cotta tiles that were removed from the side of a building in Chicago. Why not insert them among the flagstone paths and the stone patios we were laying down, to add colour and reinforce the design? Then he became interested in antique stone statuary and he began to haunt places that sold cherubs, urns and fountains. He found some rickety wooden garden chairs that no one could sit on except Marcel Proust in the Tuileries Gardens in Paris.

The garden eventually emerged as a product of my passion for flowers, Penny's relentless focus on the "bones" of a garden—the hedges, parterres, patios, walls and hedges—and Allan's growing obsession with antique architectural objects of any shape or kind except gnomes.

24
——

The Tale of the Trees

A FEW MONTHS AFTER we completed our renovations, the garden began to take shape. A symmetrical flagstone walk led down from a two-tiered stone patio, separated from each other by a low stonewall, to a row of tall cedars at the rear of the garden. The brick garage ruin defined the eastern part of the garden and a rectangular grass space dominated the western portion. Additional patios were laid down, interspersed with gravel. Old red bricks and large green terra-cotta tiles led the eye to different areas of the garden and knit it into a balanced whole. Thanks to our landscape gardener, and Allan's purchases, the bones of our garden were solid and elegant.

At this point, I began to concentrate on what I wanted to

grow in my new so-called Sissinghurst-style garden. I longed to grow the old-fashioned roses I grew in Ottawa, which I first saw at Sissinghurst. But they have faults; they are non-repeating. Reine Victoria, Mme Isaac Pereire, Rosa Centifolia, Cardinal de Richelieu, the moss roses—they never bloomed more than once in my Ottawa garden during the whole summer, no matter what the catalogues said. And they take up a lot of space. They needed Sissinghurst, or at least Lisgar Road in Ottawa, which was much larger than my Toronto space. The English grower, David Austin, had been successful in reproducing the scent and the flower shapes of the Old Roses. Some had a centifolia look; others were blowsy and bourbon. David even managed to create that little green eye in the quartered petalled Old Roses. Above all, he bred a repeating gene in most of them. A number of Austin roses bloom many times during the season like modern roses, yet they have much of the charm of the Old Roses. I decided to use Austin roses as a compromise. I also had been reading up on clematis—tearing away at the tangled Ramona on Lisgar Road in Ottawa had begun my new love affair with the many varieties of this fascinating vine.

But Allan was becoming very preoccupied with the front of the house. Although the front garden was far from being my priority, we did agree on one thing. We thought we should plant a row of four crabapple trees facing the street. The front of the house being rather drab, the blossoms and fruit would liven it up. We began to wander through Rosedale and peer into people's gardens to see what inspired us. It was late autumn when we began our reconnaissance. In front of a handsome old stone house not far from us, we noticed four sturdy crabapple trees that were densely packed with clusters of bright red fruit. As the winter set in and snow began to fall, those trees miraculously retained all of their fruit. The thick crowd of deep-red crabapples, set against the barren branches, lit up not only the front of the house but the whole street. From a distance, on a winter day, the trees looked like four misty red clouds. For some reason, the fruit on this particular variety of crab trees did not appeal to the birds so it was not picked off by them, unlike all the other crabapple trees in the neighbourhood. We wanted those trees.

I explained to Penny that we wished to plant that particular species (and no other) in front of the house. Coincidentally, I got to know the discriminating owners of the house who gave me the precise name of the crab trees and where to buy them. This was important because, as I was to discover, mislabelling of shrubs and trees is a great hazard of wholesale and retail gardening centres. Penny agreed that the trees would do wonders for our front garden. She said she knew the species, *Malus* Angel Wing, and didn't need any help in locating and purchasing them. I was dubious because, when accompanying her on previous excursions in search of trees for the back garden, all the trees were dormant and it was thus difficult to judge one from the other. I had to rely on the grower's label and Penny's eye and knowledge.

Both Allan and I urged Penny to make sure she got the right trees. She was positive that she had found them. Four large dormant crabapple trees arrived the next spring and were placed in perfect symmetry in front of the house by the highly professional duo she worked with, Stuart Maclean and Dirk Wenzel. The following year, not only did the trees bloom, the blossoms were as thick as snowflakes in a storm and brilliantly white. We were the envy of our neighbours. Come autumn, huge clusters of small red crabapples appeared and remained on the trees until autumn set in. We were very proud.

One splendid autumn morning, I looked out my bedroom

window—the fruit had vanished from the trees. Not a single crabapple remained on the branch. I ran to Allan. "It's the birds," he said. "It's the damn birds that have done it. I'm going to shoot them." Of course, Allan had never owned a gun in his life and the crabapples were all gone by this time so it wouldn't make any difference. I had a better idea. I walked over to the property where I first saw the trees that inspired me to buy ours. They were covered with fruit. Not one crabapple lay on the ground. I noticed another thing. The branches of our neighbour's trees were growing more horizontally, while ours were growing straight up. Was it possible Penny bought the wrong trees?

I called her immediately and asked her to have a look. She examined both sets of trees. "Your trees are still young," she said, "wait." Even Dirk, who had planted them and had been so impressed with the gorgeous flowering of the trees in the first year that he planted one on his own property, told us, "I'm sure they are going to be all right. You should wait." Waiting, of course, is what gardeners are supposed to do. Patience is all.

The following year, only two of the four trees bloomed and then rather sparsely. When I complained to Penny, she said, "You have not pruned them properly." Since they were only in their second year, I thought it was a bit soon to trim but Penny was the expert. She recommended an experienced tree man who would trim them properly. The tree expert came, trimmed, told us not to worry and left with eight hundred dollars.

Fall came around. It was the same story. Little bits of fruit appeared for a little bit of time and one day in early autumn, with or without the help of birds, they transferred their fruit to the ground. Meanwhile the fat fruits on our neighbour's trees remained healthy, as they had during the previous autumn and through the winter. By this time, Allan was consulting a medical man for irregular heartbeat. He blamed his condition on Penny and the trees.

The following spring, the trees grew straight up another six feet and were obscuring the second floor windows of the house. There might have been a half-dozen blossoms on all the trees. Allan said, "They're not trees, they're gigantic weeds." Dirk snuck around to see us. "Don't tell Penny, but my trees haven't bloomed at all and have no fruit." Then he whispered, "I think they are the wrong trees." In fact, there wasn't a scintilla of similarity between our trees and the ones we originally had wanted. Penny urged us to wait yet another year. "You've lost your guarantee by now, anyway," she said helpfully, "so why not wait another year and see what happens?"

But we had lost faith. In addition, we were starting a new garden project, having bought some land adjacent to our own. Because of the additional land, we needed to do a redesign of the garden. Despite our tree distress, Penny was still our first choice to help us design the new project. She bit the bullet and agreed to remove the trees and find the ones we originally wanted. She didn't charge us for the additional time and expense, but we did have to pay for the trees and the planting.

Four years later, the fruit of our trees is lighting up the street in the dead of winter. Allan stands in front of the house so he can pick up the compliments from strollers passing by. Everyone on our street installs Christmas lights and keeps them on during the winter. We are the sole exception. One passerby was particularly admiring and asked Allan if the crabapples were a new design of Christmas lights. He was thrilled.

Penny is still my ultimate adviser on any new project. I think she gets bored with clients who want instant, no-maintenance gardens. My garden, high-maintenance and constantly in flux, may elicit approval or disapproval, but it's not a boring place.

25

Mama's Not Cooking Anymore

*D*URING MY FIRST YEARS IN TORONTO, before dealing with
contractors that I wanted to murder, trees with no fruit,
outdoor steps that led to garbage cans, and gingerly trying to
educate myself about the habits and customs of the local residents, I wrote a book titled *Washington Rollercoaster*. Happily, it
had the shelf life of smoked fish rather than fresh fish. It
appeared near the top of the best-seller list, and disappeared
after a few months. I shouldn't complain. I had my moment of
fame.

As I had written a column for the *Washington Post*, I thought my best hope for continuing to write was as a columnist for a Toronto newspaper. Because I was known as a hostess, many journalists and others believed I knew a lot of people in Toronto (I didn't), that I gave or went to numerous glamorous parties (I didn't), and that I was carrying on my ambassadorial "wife of" role in my new life and house (of course, I wasn't). I was approached by a prominent editor who said, "Sondra, I've got the perfect job for you. Write a gossip column for our newspaper. We've had no one since Zena Cherry passed from the scene." I tried to explain that the life I once led in Washington was dead. I had no chef, no upstairs and downstairs maids, not even a butler. It's true, of course, I had a dining room but that was because my husband refused to eat in the kitchen. More important, I had no will or desire to be a hostess or to entertain. The idea of reporting on social events was, to use Nancy Mitford's phrase, "vomit-making." I quoted George Bernard Shaw's line about Frank Harris, a writer and man-about-town in London at the turn of the century who wrote deliciously and scandalously about parties he attended: "Frank Harris is invited to all the great houses, once." I never in my life reported in my columns what happened at other people's private parties. For a gossip columnist to be asked back by the same hostess, you have to be a sycophant (like Suzy) and/or extremely well connected (like Liz Smith). You kick only the people who are down, that is, who can't be of any use to you anymore. Well meaning as the editors were, I told them I wouldn't write gush or slush or give a push to those already sliding down the hill.

The *Toronto Sun*, under then publisher Doug Creighton, gave me an opportunity to write a weekly column, which I did for a period of time, but their readers were not my audience. With its Sunshine girls, hockey fights and lurid murders, my little ironies wilted among its pages. After a couple of inglorious years, I was terminated without notice immediately, after Creighton was pushed aside.

As my interest in gardening increased, I visited the Chelsea Garden Show in London and found it marvellous, overwhelming and appalling, all at the same time. Even though I visited the show when it was least crowded—opening night when the toffs attend and the public is kept out—the great domed tent was as claustrophobic to me as the old souks in Istanbul. Commercial displays exhibited everything from exotic mushrooms, Rembrandt tulips and ruffled tetraploid lilies in full flower to delphiniums, fountain grass, foam flowers and the latest methods in organic gardening. Outside the big tent, champagne glass in hand, I wandered through the various corporate garden displays, with contrived water features, attempts at the forest primeval, Persian gardens and miniature eighteenth-century parterres. This is what they do at garden shows and Chelsea does it best of all. Arranging rocks, water, grasses, flowers, shrubs, trellises, statuary, parterres, all together in different gardens in such a small space, each designer trying desperately to be unique, was a remarkable feat but a bit self-defeating because the effort was too obvious. I decided to write a drollish piece about the show and sent it to the *Globe and Mail*, which put it on its editorial page. Eventually, this led to a fairly regular spot in the paper, but not that often and I was never on staff. The point of my columns was to make people smile, or even laugh. I wrote about dogs, fads, food, spas, gardening, vacations, my husband's quirks, the blunders and the follies and foolishness of everyday life.

Allan would often be asked at solemn board meetings dealing with aluminum, timber, tar sands and the like, whether he minded being the butt of his wife's jokes. "Call me the foil" he would tell them, ambiguously. At least that's what he told me he said when he got home. "Better make fun of yourself or me, but don't make fun of anyone who supplies my income," Allan warned. His life consisted of working for a number of companies and people who supplied us with the loonies with which to live. I kept a list of Gotlieb income-providers beside my computer. On top of the sheet, I wrote "Lest I forget who pays for my garden." Many on the list were ripe for parody. But the stories remained in my head and not my computer.

When I returned from Washington, my interest in cooking was practically nil. Trying recipes, going to restaurants, digging out places to buy bagels, sausages and smoked salmon—these activities played an enormous role in my pre-Washington life. My interest in food was disappearing for reasons I still can't quite understand. Although I got fatter, my gastronomic passions waned in Washington. I thought it was because, at the embassy, the kitchen was the chef's domain and not my own. Now I had my new kitchen in my new house. When the Black Swede asked me what kind of new kitchen I wanted, I said, without even thinking about it, "Build it fast and build it cheap." The ultimate kitchen was not part of my dream. I was not the same person who wrote *The Gourmet's Canada* and *Cross Canada Cooking* and co-edited *Where to Eat in Canada*. Was my lack of interest reinforced by finding eating in one expensive restaurant in Toronto as similar and banal as eating in another? Like their hefty expense-account counterparts in the same city, I found the much- vaunted ethnic restaurants in Canada's multicultural capital to be unexceptional and overpraised. I don't know whether the fault lay with me or the restaurants, but there was not one, cheap or expensive, that I wanted to go back to. I did not envy the job of a restaurant critic in Toronto.

Obviously, I had changed physically and emotionally from

my earlier years. When I wrote professionally about food, I ate what I liked and remained relatively slim. I never dieted. My son-in-law kept staring at photos of me in my food books. "I can't believe this pretty young hippy girl with long hair is your mother," he said to my daughter. He was the one who could never keep his mouth shut. I looked at my pictures and recipes with regret. Staring at the rather glamorous pictures, I sadly acknowledged that I was thirty pounds heavier than during my gastronomic heyday. Five pounds for stopping smoking, five pounds for menopause and ten for genetics. But what about the rest? If you want to lose weight at my age, you need an hour a day on a treadmill. This I cannot do. I blame it on my arthritic spine. No more aerobics, jogging or jumping up and down for me.

Speaking of genetics, my mother also lost interest in cooking as she aged. She still liked to cook but she didn't like to cook anything different. She stuck with her old specialties. I bought her a Cusinart for her seventieth birthday. Big mistake. A Cusinart meant she had to make something new with a weird piece of equipment. She exchanged it for a freezer to store knishes, noodle puddings, cottage cheese pie, brisket and sweet and sour spare ribs that she could make at her leisure and serve months later, when the whole family finally gathered round her table in Winnipeg. At that time in her life, my mother liked to cook what she liked to cook and only what she liked to cook. Novelty was never her preoccupation; plenitude was. With the freezer she was always on the ready. The day after she died I opened the freezer. It was stuffed with foil-wrapped packages, carefully dated as far back as two years. She was legally blind and could write but couldn't read the labels.

She liked to make poppy-seed cookies and she ground the seeds herself in a special hand grinder meant only for poppy seeds, an instrument I have never seen before or since. It was stolen from her apartment while her family and friends sat Shiva after she died. I know who took the grinder and I hope the lady is putting it to good use. Mother also used an old-fashioned hand-turned meat grinder. It definitely made the tenderest hamburgers, meatballs and meatloaf. She did like the old-fashioned Mixmaster for her sponge, chocolate and bundt cakes. Cusinarts, blenders and coffee grinders were all techno trash in Mother's eyes.

When we moved to Washington eight years earlier, I brought with me a large, eclectic collection of cookbooks that I had painstakingly assembled when I wrote my own. Some were hard to find and long out of print. Somehow, when we returned to Canada and our household goods were shipped back by the government, my collection of cookbooks disappeared. I had my suspicions about where they were—in the chef's hands in the kitchen in the embassy. Except for all my Julia Child cookbooks, I didn't care about them.

My children, remembering the old days when I was in my gastronomic prime, were sorely disappointed when they came to my house for dinner in Toronto. They would get imperfectly cooked roast beef without the puffy, crispy Yorkshire pudding I used to make, osso bucco without the gremolata, and fruit salad instead of frozen chocolate-rum supreme surrounded by homemade lady fingers. They always felt let down but only my son, who inherited the family's gastronomic gene, would pick up the frying pan. Now, when the family gathers around the table for dinner on birthdays, holidays and other family events, my son and daughter-in-law cook the special dishes. They marinate, macerate, knead yeast dough, and will even make fresh foie gras (if we pay for the ingredients).

I cook, but without my former dash. When my grandchildren

come for dinner, they, of course, like different things. With one exception. They are all crazy about smoked salmon. However, they like only the best quality. My three-year-old granddaughter, appropriately named Sally after my mother-in-law, can devour a dozen slices of smoked salmon in two minutes. We don't even need to waste crackers. Cooking for my grandchildren is not a gastronomic challenge. It requires no skill or interest. They like Kraft Dinners, chicken fingers and fish fingers. Macaroni and cheese will sometimes serve as a substitute. Unfortunately, their parents, my children, have more sophisticated tastes and are not satisfied with what their children eat. My children get overcooked roast beef or underdone turkey unless my son and daughter-in-law take pity.

Yet a little bit of the hostess remains in me. This town of a hundred solitudes, Toronto, likes large receptions, fundraisers, cultural openings, celebrity lectures, events in cavernous convention halls, private clubs and drafty museum atriums and hotel ballrooms. Such occasions seem to me the only time when doctors, writers, professors, business executives, designers, accountants, lawyers, local politicians and bank presidents mix. At home, people go back to their collective solitudes— doctors dine with doctors, bank presidents with bank presidents, Hungarians with Hungarians and, like the rest, journalists seem comfortable only with their own kind. Occasionally, the vestiges of my hostess instinct rise up and I try to form a bridge or two among the solitudes by combining people in small groups at my home from different backgrounds and professions. Sometimes it works and sometimes it doesn't.

How do you entertain without cooking? Well, of course, there are caterers. If Allan is feeling flush or somebody else is paying, a good caterer, not easily found, is my first choice. Other than that it's Mercy and me. Mercy has been coming to my house every weekday for the past seven years and I never give a party without her. She cooks three things: curried shrimp, basil shrimp and Filipino noodles with little bits of chicken. My role is to make the dessert (sometimes), usually an easy apple betty or fruit pie. Not very exciting but the excellent patisserie around the corner where I used to shop moved away. I have not yet descended to the dinner parties of Clare Booth Luce's last days in Washington where a waiter would pass each guest a Dove bar (a chocolate-covered ice cream bar) for dessert (in Winnipeg, we called them revels). My only other culinary effort at my dinner parties is to prepare, for starters, an avocado dip. I mash the avocado with a potato masher and add whatever takes my fancy.

My cooking days are over so why do I still miss my Julia Child cookbooks? Why do I still subscribe to *Gourmet* magazine. Not only do I subscribe, I read it from cover to cover. A strange but short-lived urge comes over me. I decide I will make an elaborate dessert for my next dinner party—gingered pears in a toasted Madeira cake with meringue and hazelnut toppings, en flambé. My friends and family are still waiting.

As my love of cooking waned, my interest in gardening became an obsession. God knows, in my new garden I'll grow any flower, but I have no desire to plant a single vegetable.

26

My Sloppy Sissinghurst

GARDEN ONE IN TORONTO was my learning curve. I had blundered about in the two gardens I had owned in Ottawa, knowing nothing, reading little and planting on impulse. In other words, see a pretty flower, kill a pretty flower. Never mind about "bones," design, attractive colour contrasts, leaf and textures. I was determined not to make a garden in Toronto as I did in Ottawa. When we arrived in the city, I replaced my missing library of cooking books with gardening books—without nostalgia or regret. Julia Child was the past, Anne Raver, garden writer in the *New York Times*, was the future. I did prefer the prose of the English writers— Christopher Lloyd (opinionated but amusing), Anne Scott

James (snobby but practical), Beth Chatto (also informative but with an annoying Goody Two-shoes style), Penelope Hobhouse, John Brooke (the common man's garden adviser). Later on, I read Robin Lane Fox (in the *Financial Times*), an Oxford classics don who actually loved flowers, unlike his brother, Martin Lane Fox, the garden architectural expert with whom I spent an hour in a friend's garden deciding whether an Ali Baba jar was at the correct distance from the hedges on either side. The English books were more literate and wittier than the North American ones, but often useless for the climate in which I lived. The English books were for knowledgeable daydreaming.

When I returned to Canada, there was a new zeitgeist; gardening was in. There were now two garden magazines in Canada, one edited by the no-nonsense Canada-centric Liz Phimean; and two Canadian gardening books published shortly after I arrived were much talked about. One was by Marjorie Harris, who had a racy and interesting style and whom I knew before only as a journalist, not as a garden writer. The other was a gorgeous book about Canadian gardens co-authored by two prominent, well-connected women, Nicole Eaton and Hilary Weston. Toronto was more attentive to gardening than Ottawa with its harsh climate. Unlike Ottawa and even Washington, Toronto had a wide choice of small and large garden centres in the area that grew and sold a varied selection of perennials and annuals. Some gardeners look down their noses at annuals, but I believe they are as necessary to a garden as worms and ladybugs. As Martha Stewart says, annuals are "a good thing." I dragged a reluctant Allan to my pleasure palaces of perennials and annuals on the outskirts of Toronto and would dash up and down the aisles of potted plants, knowing that his patience was limited and he was consoling himself by patronizing the local hot dog stand or Tim Hortons. Let him get fat; I wanted to stay there all day, to look, smell the flowers, take notes and buy, buy, buy.

I was determined not to have an amateurish garden, nor one, God forbid, full of vulgar plants—"bedint" in Vita Sackville-West's code word for vulgar people as well as plants. Yet on the other hand I didn't want to go in for ghastly good taste—bluey-pinky shades for ladies who don't like to take a chance in love or gardening.

The role of my garden designer was to inhibit me from my greatest weakness, impulse gardening. Impulsiveness is part of my general character and has led me into deep waters too many times. I knew the kind of control I needed would cost money. Penny Arthurs of The Chelsea Gardener charged a fair rate, but I was frightened by the knowledge that I had to spend serious money for a decent garden (i.e., one with bones). I was already afraid of Penny. But I didn't want to waste money on cockamamie ideas that I read in gardening magazines, such as growing gunnera—huge green platelike plants that do well near bogs in Ireland and Syon Park in England but wouldn't survive in my backyard. (Three of them would have taken up a third of my space. They do say one should buy plants in threes.) I also wanted to plant ceanothus, a glorious blue climber that I first saw in Sissinghurst—which a more knowledgeable person told me would die instantly in this climate. Garden One had a great advantage; it exposed me to my own ignorance.

I was also determined that everything I planted was going to survive and then grow forever in the plant zone in which I lived. But that was a stupid idea too, because I soon found out that some perennials last longer than others, no matter the zone. And one becomes bored with certain plants. Some plants are like some people—we don't want them to last forever.

The first year Penny and I chose all the plants together, loading them into her SUV and carting them back to my garden. Nobody knew how to load plants better than Penny—the helpers at the garden centres stood and gaped in admiration. Every plant I attempted to put in the van, Penny reinstalled to make space for more. Ten years later, half had disappeared from my garden, either because I pulled them out accidentally or on purpose. Sometimes they refused to bloom because they were in too much shade. After three or four years watching my garden grow, I knew what it was to hate a plant. I am not one of those who like an unchanging garden with box or yew parterres filled with pink Queen Elizabeth roses or begonias, and perhaps a "water feature." Sometimes the only change in such a garden might be substituting white Iceberg roses for the pink Queen Elizabeths, or, God forbid, the Peace rose.

Penny controlled me with box parterres and periwinkle and ivy in the beds in the front. This was the handsomest and least fussy part of our garden. But I subverted the classical look by sticking tree peonies and wild roses, daffodils and *Muscari* in the parterres. I don't think Russell Page would approve and I'm not sure about Penny either. She kindly kept her mouth shut. But I have this problem. I never met a flower I truly hated (at first) even *Pelargoniums*. So where was I going to put the tree peonies that I liked so much? And a few bulbs within the box parterres in spring can't look all that bad. I never put big tulips there, only the small species kind. Actually, there are no rules. Prince Charles puts big tulips in his parterres in Highgrove.

Penny and I had many arguments about what plants to put where. I thought she favoured shade too much and she thought I favoured the sun. But roses, and I wanted plenty of them, need six hours of sun daily. I read in a gardening magazine that certain roses did better than others in the shade. This is not only a lie, it's a damn lie. The more sun the better for roses. So I planted my David Austin shrubs near the kitchen window, which we thought was the sunniest part of the garden. Unfortunately, we were wrong. As the years passed, I noticed shade creeping in from our neighbours' trees and our own. The blooms of the David Austin climbing Heritage rose, which at first blossomed so well for me, became smaller and fewer.

I made another mistake. Instead of mixing roses with other plants, I planted smaller David Austin roses in the back and larger roses in the front. I also planted Ballerina roses, which are pretty indestructible, in the same bed. Too many roses planted in a bunch do not a garden make. I have been playing around with the rose bed by the kitchen for some ten years now, and I still find it unsatisfactory. Penny stuck a dwarf crabapple in the middle, which is pretty in season but acts as a kind of shuddering support for all the climbers I added. I introduced six different kinds of clematis in that bed that thread through the rose bushes and the railing of the stairs nearby—fairly successful. I planted lavender underneath, which did not survive, in an attempt to hide the skinny legs of the rose bushes, so despised by garden designers. Then, instead of lavender, I put in sage, nepeta, alliums and ladies' mantel that overgrew each other and created a not inglorious mess. Eventually, most of the roses in the garden by the kitchen sighed for sun but the Ballerinas in the front are flourishing and Heritage is still fighting. The clematis vines, which I put in as an afterthought, are doing exceptionally well and smother what's left of the rose bushes. Remember, like all wonderful flowers, most clematis take at least three years to look good enough to receive visitors.

In England, clematis vines are thrown over rose bushes and fruit trees all the time, and even climb up oaks. The host trees always seem to survive. This is not the case in our climate. My clematis vines do better over the ruins of my old brick garden wall and the tall brick pillars adjacent to it, but they don't flourish on the trees. Or rather, the clematis flourishes, but the trees don't. English clematis gardeners such as Christopher Lloyd do not approve of clematis growing up house walls or fences. They prefer to fling them over plants, shrubs and trees and even let them grow in the grass. I have tried all of this, but never with the kind of success the English gardener enjoys. For me it's always a fight between the magnolia tree and the climber, the rose shrubs and the clematis. In the battle of the shrubs and roses in my garden, I sometimes let the shrubs win and sometimes the clematis. Once in three years, they look good together. I still do look for the perfect bush to carry a clematis.

For a gardener like me, who wants more space but lives in the middle of the most expensive city in Canada, "land, lots of land" (as the song goes) seemed to be "the impossible dream" (in the words of another). The nice neighbour to our immediate east, who owned a gigantic old brick house in which she lodged several elderly ladies, unexpectedly died. The good news was that the real estate market was tanking, thanks to a steep recession, and the house was being sold cheaply. But not cheaply enough. A friend suggested we borrow the money from a friendly bank and buy the boarding house, which was a wreck, tear it down and build the ultimate city garden.

There was a housing law at the time that provided that when someone bought a house in which rooms were being rented, he could not eject the tenants without finding them a similar place nearby to live, and to which they agreed to move. No small hurdle. We had enough bad headlines in our life and Allan saw a new one looming, "Gotlieb puts old age pensioners out on street." Apart from this consideration, we could not afford to buy the house or carry a second huge mortgage. A developer bought the house and, one night not long after, it disappeared. To this day we don't know what he did with the old ladies. Did he find them a suitable place to live in the neighbourhood or are they buried in the rubble? Contractors and builders have business shortcuts unknown to former diplomats. But Allan knew one thing. The builder believed he could construct two houses on the lot in place of the one that existed there before. Allan found out that the developer was three and a half feet short of his right to do so. Allan passed on to the builder his little nugget of information and assured him, in the most diplomatic way, that, if he tried to go ahead, it was more likely that the neighbours would lynch him than waive their rights.

The market took a turn for the worse, the builder seemed to need money, and our youngest was getting married and wanted the wedding in our backyard, which was not big enough for the number of guests she planned to invite. I saw my chance for more land. I knew it would be cheaper if we could buy a portion of the builder's property rather than a new house with a larger garden, assuming we could ever find one. We bought a slice of the developer's land, which gave us not only room in our yard to put up a tent and hold the wedding but space for Garden Two. Behind a garage and sunroom that Allan wanted to build on our new property, I had almost four thousand extra feet to play around with. The bride was happy, Allan was happy, I was happy and Penny was happy because I told her she was going to get the assignment to design Garden Two.

When I surveyed the new piece of land, it reminded me of a dog run. It was long and thin, 25 feet wide and 160 feet long, suitable for racing Bichon Frises. But Penny looked at it with different eyes. "You have room here for three different gardens. At the top, behind the garage, you have lots of sun. You can have that checkerboard garden you've always wanted."

Checkerboard gardens have existed since medieval times. Monks grew herbs between the square stones near the cloisters. Russell Page, the great classical gardener, wrote that if he ever had a garden of his own he'd use a checkerboard design. In Canada, Marjorie Harris, the gardening writer, was the only person I knew who had one, although at the time I had never seen it. Checkerboards lend themselves to experimenting with new plants and chopping and changing without disturbing other plants whose roots might be in the way. So, using squares of bluish limestone, we laid down a checkerboard garden with surrounding borders in the sunniest part of the new property. This time we paid attention to getting from the house to the garden in an attractive and practical way. The theory was that you could step down directly into the garden from the new tiled sun room and pass by all the gorgeous plants held in tight control by the square paving stones.

The first three years, I planted large bushy things—six-foot oriental lilies, heleniums, rambling roses, artemisias and tree peonies, that eventually grew over the paving stones and made the bones, the square paving stones, invisible. The big, blobby bushy things had to go—even a tree peony that cost $145 and blocked the view from the sun room. The tree peony was more evidence that you cannot trust pictures or descriptions in catalogues. I thought I was ordering one of those rare kinds with blotchy colours at the base of the flower, *Paeonia rockii*, but when it finally bloomed after a three-year wait, a banal pink blossom half-opened, without deep blotches around the stamens. I saw the same plant at a Korean grocery store for $15.

There were some tall plants I could not sacrifice, a Graham Thomas yellow rose, three five-foot-high Leandor roses (strictly speaking, they were in the surrounding border just outside the checkerboard), and some extraordinarily expensive ruffled tetraploid lilies, apricot and deep red, which bloomed in August for almost a month. But I pulled out the rest of the plants without remorse and went low and small. I was even ready to plant tiny pink begonias as long as they didn't break the pattern of the checkerboard. Several years later I planted *Iris reticulata* in one square for early spring showing, and small species tulips and fritillary, each in their own squares. In fact I went overboard, as I usually do. A year ago, I decided to spend as much on bulbs as the Americans do on their defence budget. I planted early-flowering Dawn and species tulips and a variety of allium bulbs near my late-blooming lily-flowered tulips, along the borders of the old and new gardens. Alliums, which belong to the onion family, are supposed to keep away the squirrels. We shall see. The squirrels in my backyard were trained by the Taliban.

Penny had put down some pebbles and steps to separate the checkerboard from the rest of the garden. Allan discovered a Victorian railing which Penny enhanced with a brick foundation—this design effectively removed the space for dog racing from my mind. We erected more brick walls, to continue the idea of different rooms in the garden. A hostess of one of those American television garden shows called up and asked to do a feature on our garden. When the lady on the telephone asked me to describe the design of the garden, I said, "It's made up into different rooms, separated by brick walls, cedars, and wooden fences on either side." "Rooms?" she asked. "What do you mean by rooms outside?" I flapped about, trying to explain that we grew different things in these separated areas. "But what do you do in them? Is there a media room?" "No," I said, "but we keep one for orgies."

Stepping down from the Victorian brick-and-iron railing fence, you enter what I call the Middle Kingdom. I have a lot of trouble with this half-shade, half-sun, part of the garden. It has a raggedy undecided look, because the shade and sun change, and what grew last year dies the next. And snails (also Taliban-trained) like to eat my purple fleshy leafy *Ligularia* Othello and Desdemona. *Rodgersia* do grow nicely in the shade, near the brick, but the rest is a jumble-jamble of leftover irises, peonies, and of course, when in doubt, clematis. Penny planted some *Corydalis lutea*, which has taken over all my garden like a weed and I love it. The more desirable blue varieties have sighed and died on me. I have as yet, no satisfactory solution to the Middle Kingdom. It's a bit like Hector, the Airedale I owned in Ottawa, that I could never train. Someday I'll figure out what to do with it. But unlike Hector, I will not kill it. That's what gardening is all about.

27

The Yoghurt and Moss Garden

"*A*nd what should I do with the end part of the new garden where it's so boggy?" I asked Penny when we were in the midst of planning. "What about a miniature Canadian forest? You know, some big rocks, ferns, birches and trilliums?" she suggested. "Why would I want a miniature Canadian forest when all I have to do is step out into the ravines, two minutes from my house?" I replied. Anyway, I hated big rocks jutting out of a flat terrain. I called this the Flintstone school of gardening and it is bedint. "A rock pile does not a garden make," I told Penny. "I won't do it." "Well, we can try some delicate shadbush trees, ones that give off only light shade," Penny replied. "They have a full blossom in the spring and pretty berries in the fall. You need some verticals at the bottom of the garden." I was dubious but let her go ahead. I'm still of two minds about those serviceberry trees but they do bloom briefly in spring—they don't give much shade, which I do not need, and they have a certain delicacy about them. Obviously, they attract birds because the berries only last two days. So perhaps I have to thank the shadbush trees for the many red cardinals in my garden. But these trees are too common. Contractors and builders seem to have placed them in every front- and backyard in the area. But Penny was right about needing verticals in the dog run.

Then came the battle of the rocks. I knew my rock refusal wouldn't go far with Penny. She said, "Sondra, I'm going to get smooth, flat rocks. Dirk Wenzel will dig them into the ground so that they are level with the earth. All you will see is the flat tops—and just a few here and there, sort of randomly placed." Then she gave her clincher. "I'm thinking moss garden." Moss garden. I immediately liked the idea.

I asked, "How do you grow moss?" She said, airily, "You gather up some moss in the forest, put it in your Cusinart with some yoghurt, grind it up and then plaster it against the rocks. The moss will grow." She advised me that I could buy small packages of Scotch moss and Irish moss for a good sum of money at a garden centre. "And," she said, "you can add a few ferns here and there, but it won't be a miniforest, it will be a moss garden. If you want, it can also be a spring garden." This got me excited. I longed to plant wild narcissus—pheasant's eye—in the spring, the kind I saw in the markets in Switzerland that smell so sweet.

In the first three years, the moss garden was a mess. Due to the usual ordering difficulties, I never did get my pheasant's eye narcissus. The moss I bought at the garden shops mostly died. It needed more sun than it could get in my backyard, thanks in part to the shadbush trees. Then there was a lucky break, literally speaking. A gigantic willow in the backyard of one of our neighbours in the rear projected a huge, drooping branch over virtually all my potential moss garden. A tremendous electrical storm tore off the offending branch, which was so big it reached our house eighty feet away. I wasn't sure whose responsibility it was to remove the monstrous thing but it seemed to me only fair that it belonged to the owner of the tree rather than the victim. But safety comes before valour. Some Russians had recently moved into the house and rumour on the street was that they were Mafia. On one occasion the neighbours said they heard gun play and then saw the police remove some men from the house. I got the branch hauled away at my own expense and left the Russians alone.

Not long after, the moss began to grow, but very slowly. Now that I had more sun, I was more optimistic. Penny was too and she brought me some moss that she had dug up in her place in the country. She said, "Grind it up with the yoghurt," and drove off. I tried the recipe again and managed to cook up enough moss-yoghurt to cover one-half of one rock. At this rate, it would have taken me a month of grinding and stirring, and much more moss from Penny's forest bosk, to make any sufficient inroads in the project. In desperation, I took to asking anyone I knew with a country place to bring me moss if they were coming to our house for dinner. Then I learned that there was a video on how to make a moss garden. It recommended large quantities of acidic fertilizers (the kind you use to make bombs?). I bought and spread the stuff all over the garden. It led to a few more patches of moss here and there but the moss garden wasn't right. It still looked bald. I kept planting violets, creeping jenny, low-growing herbs and some wildflowers and ferns to fill in all the bare spaces.

One day an organized group went through the garden and I said to a lady on the tour that the moss garden was my biggest failure. She said, "I have just seen the most magnificent moss garden right here in Toronto. It's as large as your whole garden and it's all moss. All the owner wants in his garden is moss and that's what he has." "What's his secret?" I asked. "He waters the garden three times a day," she replied. "He keeps it as wet as possible. He has an underground sprinkler." I too have an automatic underground sprinkler, and the next summer I sprayed only the moss garden every night. It worked. The combination of wet and more sun transformed the most forlorn part of the garden into what I consider a star attraction. But a lot of people, I discovered, don't like moss. They don't like it on bricks or stone or anywhere. They think it is something that needs to be scrubbed away. But it is my husband's favourite place in the garden and I like it even though it is nowhere near the impeccable carpet that one sees in the gardens of Kyoto.

Our last major project was the water feature (I do hate that phrase). My arthritis was getting worse and the thought of a warm small pool, just big enough in which to do aquatic exercise began to appeal to me more and more. This was going to be expensive but, as Allan pointed out, we didn't have a house by the lake, or any kind of summer place, because I have to stay home and watch the garden. I was concerned that the pool would take away from the beauty of the garden as well as planting space. But there was one particularly unsuccessful room or space in Garden One. It was a shady, scraggly part covered with gravel. Plastic was placed under the gravel in order to keep down the weeds, as Penny explained to me, but it had the effect of caking the soil below to such an extent that it was totally inhospitable to planting new shrubs. It was the perfect place for my pool because it was shady (I loathe swimming in the sun), it was off-centre and did not immediately draw your eye to it. I brought in Penny to design the perfect pool. She made it in the form of a simple rectangle that echoed the shape of the lawn on the other side of the walk and reinforced the original bones of the old garden. On one side of the pool was the old brick wall, which created a sense of privacy. On the other side I planted shrubbery fit for shade.

Nothing repels me more than turquoise or light blue–coloured pools. They ruin the appearance of gardens. I wanted the pool to be dark black but in fact it ended up showing a tinge of Prussian blue. One day the eminent English gardener, Martin Lane Fox, was visiting Toronto on a commission for a friend who brought him around to see our garden. He walked through the garden and said absolutely nothing. Then he made two comments. "Your gravel should be yellow, not white" and "I like the colour of your pool."

28

GardenMiscarriages

A S A GARDENER, I'M SLOPPY, lazy, imprecise and forgetful. I only know a few Latin names of flowers. Since correct pronunciation has never been my strong point in Latin or English, I tend to slur over the names in conversation with people more learned than myself. For many years I used to say "foilage" instead of "foliage." I always take a deep breath before I say "clematis." The first vowel is the longest, I've been told—many times.

Even before I started gardening, I knew that the good gardener keeps a diary and writes everything down. This is a must, saves money, saves time, saves repeating mistakes. I still don't do it because sloth is one of my major vices. Friends, knowing my hobby, send me garden calendars and diaries as gifts and I swear, by God, I'm going to crack one open tomorrow. Instead, I scribble things down on bits of paper, when I think of them, shove them into a pocket where they fall out or get washed out in the laundry. But when I do start my fantasy diary, this is how it should be done.

1. A diary should note the full name of the plant in Latin because there are so many varieties and then the common name, so you can recognize what plant you're writing about.

2. Note where and when you planted it, so you can keep your eye on it if it sickens—this will remind you of the kind of soil you put it in, and how much sun it wasn't getting.

3. Do a postmortem when the plant dies. Did you place it too close to another plant that took over? Study the diary, and if you like the plant enough, try it again in a different place and soil. I grew beautiful tall lupins in the harsher climate of Ottawa but couldn't grow them at all in Toronto. I tried three times in three successive years to grow them, but each year I never wrote the precise details about location and soil so I may have been repeating my mistakes. I love lupins. If I had more persistence and kept a postmortem in my non-existent diary, perhaps I would have had them blooming all over my garden. Or perhaps not.

4. Keep name tags somewhere but not near the plant. If they are made from paper they will rot or if they are metal the dog will pull them out. At first I never kept any tags or even wrote down what I bought. I have these beautiful Leander rose bushes (bred by David Austin) in the new back garden just outside the borders of my checkerboard. Actually, I'm not really sure their name is Leander but that's what I tell everyone. I know I planted three varieties of Austin rose at the same time—Ellen, Leander, Hero or another Austin rose

with similar colour and growing patterns. Mind you, I'm not always that stupid. There are many David Austin roses I planted for which I don't need the label. I know where I planted the low-growing Sharif Asma because it's the most fragrant of my roses, or maybe Evelyn is.

I can recognize certain other varieties of plants by smell, such as the variegated *Daphne burkwoodii*, Carol Mackie and *Viburnum carlesii* because, although quite different plants, they both have such an intense fragrance. When a plant smells wonderful I have to know all about it. And I have no difficulty retaining its name. But there is a problem. So many plants are said to be fragrant—the large tobacco plant *Nicotiana sylvestris* and the smaller variety, *Nicotiana alata*, the trumpet-shaped *Datura*, purported to be used for hallucinogenic purposes in the American Southwest, and the night-blooming Jasmine. None of these plants ever smelled for me, although I grew them all. The sure smellers are oriental hybrid lilies, like Black Dragons, Regal lilies and Casablanca lilies.

Beware the lilies. I like to lean over them and draw their scent as a pick-me-up. I have a habit of doing this just before we go out to dinner and I am wearing my best clothes. At the party, someone is sure to point out hideous yellow marks on my silk dress or signs of leprosy on my nose. "Did you spill mustard?" they ask. "No," I reply as I look down at my clothes. "It's the saffron from the stamen on my lilies. The spots will stay there forever." This happens to me every summer and on my anniversary and birthday. Allan sends me a dozen of my favourite Casablanca lilies on our anniversary on December 20th, which always last exactly ten days—until December 30th, my birthday. In ten days, I do a lot of smelling and ruin a lot of clothes.

The stains on my clothes are sure signs of a sloppy gardener as is my tendency to forget exactly what it is that I planted. So I decided to be more careful, and last year I resolved to save all the labels from the plants I bought. I put them carefully in a clay pot that I kept on a shelf in the garage. By this time I knew the name would prod a memory of where I put the plant. I planned to write all the names down later in one of my growing collection of empty garden diaries. That was the only year since we built the garage that Allan decided to clean it out. Neither of us can explain what led him to behave so out of character. But he was very thorough and since the clay pot was cracked, he threw it out along with all the labels.

In my garden diary, I also resolved to list all my gardening blunders. As everyone tells me, I have too many peonies. They have a short flowering life and take up too much space. I include tree peonies in this category. They are gorgeous but they have little aroma. The ordinary peony like Bowl of Beauty, which doesn't smell either but stands up well to the rain, takes up too much room. So why did I plant some more peonies last year? Because Margaret, at the garden centre, swore on her life that her new purchase had a fragrance that would make me swoon. She sold me a four-stemmer for very little money. The next year two stems bloomed and I did exactly as she predicted, I swooned at their perfume.

I am a plant person. Plants always trump design, planning, discipline and order. The flower and the fragrance come first. That's my biggest blunder.

29

Archie Exits

T HE LAST THING A GARDENER NEEDS is a dog. But Archie, the embassy dog, came before the garden. Archie appreciated the garden because every spring—it really should have been every fall, but that's another one of my blunders—we spread horse manure over the garden. Archie was fond of its odour. He would roll himself over and over wherever the mounds were the thickest, usually near a newly planted shrub, which he would occasionally dig up just for the hell of it. Tibetan terriers are not true terriers and don't go in for too much digging. Archie would rather bark at a mole hole than go in for real investigation. But the manure rolling did try my patience. I would sheepishly take him to the canine cleaners for deep dog fumigation, which often required a shave down to his skin. When Archie returned bald, he looked like a worm on four legs—you'd never mistake him for Yul Brynner.

Although Archie liked the garden and left most of my flowers alone, he had a particular dislike for *Campanula carpatica*—a kind of a clump-forming bluebell—and got rid of it as soon as I planted or replanted it. Luckily, he never liked to stay in the garden by himself so I kept an eye on him as he strolled towards this hated plant. Archie never went into the garden alone, unless he wanted to do some mischief. If he stayed in the garden by himself I knew he was doing the forbidden—stealing lamb shanks or ribs of beef from the kitchen and burying them in the garden, uprooting freshly planted rare specimens in the process. He also disliked anything I ordered from a place in Puget Sound with hard to find metre-high Japanese Maples and tiny rare grasses.

Archie despised water. When we put in the therapy pool, he never got closer to it than a yard or two. If you were in the pool, he would stay sufficiently far away to avoid any splashing water. Nevertheless, nothing would fascinate him more than watching someone, from grandpa to grandchild, swim in the pool. Archie could swim (naturally we threw him in the pool to find out). But the only other time he ever did so was when he accidentally fell into the pool while chasing a squirrel at top speed.

As in the case of most dogs, there were certain spots in the garden that Archie preferred. He would settle under the shade of the star magnolia in the old garden, with lots of manure underneath, not too far away from where people might be sitting around, having drinks and eats. The perch under the magnolia was perfect because it was equidistant from the two exits from which food might be carried out to people in the garden.

Although I never saw him dig, every morning when we would wake up in spring, summer and fall, we would see new holes in the rectangular expanse of grass in the back. It was the bane of our grass experience. We would fill them with new earth, reseed, or put in new sod. Our garden helpers, Mr. Suzuki and Blair, who came in every so often, were sure that Archie had done the digging. (They were the ones who had to cut the grass and do the heavy lifting.) "You'll never get rid of the holes in the grass until you get rid of Archie," they would say.

Archie was going on sixteen years old, a great age for a Tibetan terrier, and had had a successful operation for cancer, failing heart and various other ailments. But he maintained his greatest interest in life—food that humans ate. He also adored our grandchildren when toddlers and never jumped on them. I thought it was a kind of nice grandfatherly affection until I realized that the reason he constantly stuck close and kept an eye on them was in case they dropped a half-eaten cookie or Eskimo bar. Archie was old enough to realize he didn't need to nab the sweet or chicken finger directly from their hands. The wisdom of the years taught him that toddlers rarely finish anything and that a slow but safe place behind was sufficient to enable him to pick up the droppings.

Chocolate proved to be the death of Archie. You might say he was the only dog killed by Nestl . Allan was on the advisory board of Nestl in Canada. As far as I could see, they paid him largely in chocolate bars (not stock options, alas). When he came back from meetings, instead of a briefcase stuffed with cash, he brought a briefcase stuffed with miniature bars of KitKat and Coffee Crisps, as well as Smarties and other newer-brand Nestl chocolates. Management would pass these confections around in great quantities at board meetings, to be washed down with Nescaf . Allan, ostensibly collecting them for his grandchildren although he really liked to eat them himself, would stuff dozens into his briefcase.

One night he came home from a meeting late and tired. Knowing the dog's affection for chocolate, he made sure his briefcase was locked, but instead of placing it on a safe spot high on his dresser, as he usually did ("Archie-proofing" he would say), he threw the briefcase on the sofa in the bedroom. The next morning there was a trail of chewed-up and torn chocolate wrappers and vomit throughout the house. By Allan's count, Archie must have devoured twenty bars.

But where was Archie? I could find him nowhere in the house. Then I saw a shadow in the garden. For the first time in his life, Archie had pushed open the glass doors leading to the garden and gone out alone. I called to him but he refused to come back in. In all the years of his life, whether in Toronto or Washington, I never saw him not agitating to get out of a yard if he was in one by himself. I knew he must be terribly sick.

Somehow, we got him to a vet who told us he was dehydrated from diarrhea and vomiting—no surprise as I had seen our carpets. But not to worry, our vet said, the cancer had not returned, his ticker was working and, after taking many tests and X-rays, including an MRI, he told us that Archie was okay. To be on the safe side, however, he said he would keep him on an IV for four or five days in his clinic. A week later, when the vet told us we could pick him up, Archie was standing on his own four feet and seemed to be his old self, if a little shaky.

But as soon as he got into the house, instead of rushing upstairs and curling up on my bed or his favourite sofa, he insisted on going outside into the garden. Bizarre behaviour. He stayed in the garden three nights and days and we could not get him back into the house or to eat or drink anything. I read somewhere that when dogs die, they want to die alone. This was the first and only time in Archie's life that we could not get him to stay in the house. He curled up under his favourite magnolia tree and remained there. Allan even waved a Nestl chocolate bar in front of him to see if he could get a response. Archie just lowered his head.

"He's dying," I said to Allan, as he was leaving the house to go to England. "You're leaving me with a dying Archie. What am I supposed to do?" Resourceful, I am not. What are husbands for? Allan called the Humane Society who helpfully said that when the dog died, I should pick him up, put him in the car, bring him over and they would bury him. I was physically and emotionally incapable of picking up Archie's corpse. After much hysteria from his wife, Allan called the vet and told him Archie was suffering greatly and was on the point of death. Although it was the vet's day off, he told Allan to bring Archie over and he would put him to sleep.

A few weeks after Archie died, three enormous holes appeared in our grass. I said to Mr. Suzuki and Blair, "I don't believe in ghost dogs. Archie is gone. It's the raccoons that have been making these holes all along." They looked sheepish, as well they should. They were hardly cheered when I told them I wanted another dog. "Not yet," I added, "maybe in another year. But there's going to be another dog and I know the garden will suffer."

30

Enter Paxie

W HY WOULD AN OLD WOMAN, in her forty-seventh year of marriage, want to buy a dog? There are lots of reasons. A pet deflects anger, dissipates anxiety and takes her husband for a walk. Perhaps you want to say something nasty to your nearest and dearest. You can deflect confrontation by mentioning the problem to your dog. Generally, you do this in the presence of the spouse who has the choice of getting involved in the conversation or decides to leave the matter strictly for the ears of the dog. When you practise saying to your dog first what you really want to say to your husband, the dog absorbs your frustration and anger. The subject of the conversation with your dog that you want to have with your husband is exactly the same. It's all in the tone. When I complained to Hector the Protector, the Lion of Rockcliffe Park, about something annoying Allan was about to do, I would usually speak of it with a certain lightness. You might call it doggie-talk. A dog is a dog, after all. It has the intelligence of a baby. When the thorny problem is reduced to baby-talk, using the dog as an intermediary, it eases immediately and may even dissolve. In the great movie *Dinner at Eight*, when Jean Harlow wanted an emerald necklace or to go to a fancy party, she'd ask the pooch, making sure her husband, Wallace Beery, overheard.

The presence of a dog is a kind of mood alterer, like Prozac or other anti-anxiety pills. I could have named the dog Prozac, Zoloft or Halcion. But I decided that, if we could only agree on what kind of dog we wanted, I would call it Paxil, a drug which was lifting the spirits of a close friend of mine. So we had the name for the dog but there was a problem. We couldn't decide on the breed.

Allan said, "Why not another Tibetan terrier? Nice temperament, right size. They look wonderful when they are all brushed out." Allan was particularly fond of Archie's looks on his few good days. One afternoon, he was driving Archie back from the coiffeur. Archie was sitting beside him upright in the front seat of our Toyota, looking straight ahead. Suddenly, Allan heard a police siren. A cruiser flashed behind him and signalled for him to stop. It was a warm sunny day, the windows were open and Allan was driving in his usual slow way, about twenty miles an hour in a thirty-mile zone. No other cars were around. The six-foot-three policeman lumbered up to the driver's door with a smug look on his face, ticket book in hand and stuck his head inside the window. Before Allan could open his mouth, the policeman did a double-take and burst out laughing. "I thought you had a little girl with long blond hair sitting beside you without a seat-belt. That sure is a good-looking dog," he said, and walked away, embarrassed. Allan has had a few moments of triumph in his life. This one he particularly savours.

"No Tibertan terriers," I said. "I can't deal with the hair matting problem. Archie's haircuts cost more than mine. And I always feel guilty. Every time I take Archie to the coiffeur's, I get a bawling out. I don't want that in my life anymore, unless, of course, you are prepared to comb out the new Tibetan every day, all by yourself." We both knew this was unthinkable. Allan backed off.

"How about a Yorkie?" I asked. "What's a Yorkie?" he responded. "You know," I said, "They're small and only come up to your ankles. Real lap dogs. Or maybe we should buy a Papillon. They're the same size as a Yorkshire terrier, but they have cute little butterfly ears." Allan was horrified. "I want a dog because I need a reason to go for a walk. I will not be seen walking a dog that only comes up to my ankles." My daughter had recently bought a Bichon Frise. Because of its tiny size, Allan was against it and didn't want to be seen with it. When I nixed the Tibetan terrier, he proposed its cousin, a Wheaton, the ultimate yuppie or boho dog. In our neighbourhood, every second dog seems to be a Wheaton terrier—even our younger daughter owns one. That was reason enough for me to want something different. "And besides," I said, "Wheatons are too big. I have to have a dog I can lift in case he gets sick or I have to control him. You keep forgetting my old arthritic spine. Strange because I mention it to you every day."

When I wrote a newspaper article about looking to buy a new dog, I received many suggestions. My book agent, Bruce Westwood, brought his Portuguese Water Dog for us to admire. I got other calls from Portuguese Water Dog owners who refer to themselves as "Portie-people." I discovered that there is something about Portie-people that makes them want to extol their dog's beauty, character and virtues. I never did get one call from a schnauzer owner. Bruce's dog was a beauty, but a big beauty, too big for me.

There was a mysterious caller who telephoned my husband near midnight. The man claimed that the dog for the Gotliebs was a Norwegian Buhund. "Wash and wear hair," he said, "a connoisseur's dog, easy temperament, intelligent and the same size as a Tibetan terrier." I looked up the dog in my local breeder's book and found a man who raised Buhunds less than a couple of hours away from Toronto. I organized an expedition with Allan, my son-in-law, daughter and grandchildren to see a live Buhund mother and her litter. The breeder also raised Labradors and the first thing my grandchildren saw were frolicking Labrador pups. Believe me, there is nothing cuter than a Lab pup. Allan inspected the Buhund and whispered to his son-in-law that he wasn't crazy about dogs with pointy faces. Like my grandchildren, he adored the Lab pups but knew they grew big. He jocularly said to the breeder, "If you could transplant the Labrador's head onto the Norwegian Buhund's body, I'll buy one." The breeder was not amused. We left dogless.

About a year had gone by and we still had not bought a dog. We checked out Jack Russells (too fierce, need too much training), Kerry blue terriers (too big, too fierce and too much hair), and Cockapoos (a mix of poodle and cocker spaniel). "The trouble is," one vet told us, "you might get more cocker than poodle." And cocker spaniels were, in the experience of our youth, not the brightest of breeds. Fox terriers and wired-haired terriers were other possibilities. But we were told that they were diggers, had steel-hair problems and needed a lot of exercise—more than Allan wanted.

I don't know how I came to choose a poodle. I considered them sophisticated city dogs with a reputation for intelligence. I knew they came in all sizes and shapes. My main reason for not choosing one was Allan's resistance to owning a dog with a pointy head. Thumbing through the breeder book one day, I saw an ad for a "Marmalade Miniature Poodle" about Archie's size. When I telephoned the breeder, a brisk English voice told me her dog had just given birth to fourteen marmalade minia-ture poodles. "Pick out the biggest one for me," I said, having in mind Allan's aversion to runts. Two months later, we brought home Paxil, a ten-week-old female, the biggest of the bunch. I overcame Allan's dislike of pointy heads by promising him that I would let her hair grow thick around her nose. On the way back home, it dawned on me that this was the first time in my life that I had bought such a young pup. Hector, Sweet Pea and Archie were all about six months old before they came into my life. I was a sixty-five-year-old arthritic mother with a newborn baby.

After two months at home with the dog, I realized I had given her the right name for the wrong reason. Far from being a substitute for Paxil, I found that I needed a prescription for the pills. I was up during the night and at dawn, I was listening to her whine, moan and bark, I was watching for suspicious wet spots all over the house, stepping on tiny turds, and displaying the results of Paxie's teething problems on my wrists and ankles. I was as exhausted as a new mother. Allan never dia-pered his children or paid them much attention until they could walk and talk. If he didn't do it for his children, he wasn't going to do it for his dog. Once he tried to take Paxie for a walk and complained that "she behaves more like a miniature bull than a ladylike poodle." The only satisfaction he got was that several pretty girls admired the exceptionally rich caramel colour of her hair.

I even resorted to hiring a trainer, something I never did with my other dogs, because Paxie couldn't stop jumping up and scratching. The dog never stayed still. The trainer told me she was high energy and needed a lot of exercise. "What are we going to do?" I asked. "People like you and your husband [she meant our age]," the trainer replied, "are best off with King Charles Spaniels. Nice lazy dogs, not too big. You bought the wrong dog." Too late. No one ever mentioned King Charles Spaniels to me before.

I stared at Paxil. Paxil stared at me fondly. She loved me dearly. My children said, "Be patient. She's just a puppy. She'll quiet down." I hope so. She's not a good listener. She doesn't sit beside me quietly and give me comfort when I complain about my husband. Like Archie, she won't go out in the garden alone, but unlike him, she likes water. The pool is covered in winter with a tight-fitting top that acts for Paxie like a sort of trampoline. Archie would never go near the cover. Paxie's favourite activity, when we go outside with her into the garden, is leaping and bouncing on it like an acrobat. She can leap six feet as she races back and forth across the cover. Poodles like to swim, I'm told.

A lazy old couple with a young energetic dog, hardly the perfect combination. Nor the ideal result of a year of cogitation. She hasn't tasted chocolate. But she has eaten socks, underwear, sofas, dried flower arrangements, an entire flowering maple, my new prescription glasses, an electric cord, gloves and a brown velvet hat. She sticks her nose into the fridge every time I open the door. So Paxie is my mood-altering drug? Will the she-devil take my mind off other things to worry about?

31

Paxie Nine Months Later

MY HUSBAND, A SEPTUAGENARIAN, has become a chick magnet. To put it more accurately, he is a chick-magnet walker.

None of the dogs I ever owned achieved the supermodel attention that Paxie receives. My husband can't take this dog for a walk without attracting nubile young girls, wearing T-shirts that don't quite meet their belly buttons, who swoop down and embrace Paxie, exchanging tongue-kisses with her. It is only then, it must be admitted, that Allan becomes the centre of their attention. He is swamped with questions about the dog. "I've never seen such a beautiful dog," they say. "What breed is it?"

"A very unusual one," Allan replies. "She's a poodle." They don't quite believe him, but continue to kiss (the dog) and make baby poody sounds. "But she doesn't look like a poodle," they say. "She's a miniature marmalade poodle," he adds. We have had this "what-is-this-breed?" question from bikers, screeching their machines to a stop at the sight of Paxie, and now, during the garbage strike, substitute garbage guys who stop their pick-ups in mid-street and drool over Paxie. One woman, who didn't stop jogging while asking about Paxie, hit her head on a tele-phone pole.

Sometimes on a Saturday Allan walks to the local Starbucks with Paxie. He ties her to a pole and sips his coffee on the out-side patio, while she stands on her hind legs, her forepaws flail-ing until she attracts the crowd. People cluster about, petting her, allowing Allan to peruse one whole article in the *New York Review of Books*. He knows she'll be good as long as those com-pliments on her looks keep coming. She preens before the cam-eras, even offering a paw for autographs. "Not a sign of that petulance we know so well," Allan says. "It's like taking a walk with Naomi Campbell. Everyone wants to meet her."

Paxie, like Naomi, is a high-strung prima donna. The flat-tery she gets during her walks makes her more difficult at home. She demands constant attention, bitching if there isn't a coterie of flunkies to applaud her when she responds to a "Sit!" demand. Left alone, she does things in order to attract atten-tion to herself, like bouncing off walls, eating my plastic eye-glasses (anything plastic is tasty), or leaping several feet in the air and hitting me in my esophagus while I'm reading.

Actually, it's me, not Allan, who is the centre of her universe. She worships me as the top goddess, the main man, a mystic guru, her charismatic CEO. She knows I am corruptible because I sneak chicken nuggets into her kibble. Fridge food is like an inside trade to Paxie. She believes that anything I handle or wear will give her my magic power and so she has to touch it too. My prized, pricey clematis that took me a half-hour to plant is torn up and paraded in her mouth as a sacred trophy. No item of my clothing is safe; according to her religion, the closer the thing is to my body, the more precious the object is to her. Panties, brassieres, the aforementioned glasses, socks and, of course, shoes, are totemic. They are chewed and even eaten.

One morning I saw a ten-inch turd coming out of her rectum and I thought she had tapeworm. When I pulled it, I found my knee-high stocking. I've learned to pile most of my clothing on top of a highboy, but if there's nothing around except my husband's socks, she'll hide them away just in case. We do leave doggie stuff—chew bones, chew rags—around and about but they don't appeal as much as old panties from the Bay.

Paxie also wants to protect me from harm. She barks at anyone who approaches, from my smallest mobile grandchild to the person I am most in need of at the moment—the man I pay to pick up my garbage while the sanitary engineers strike. Allan believes she is hard-wired with an electric cord stretching from her bum to her throat that keeps her constantly on the move, barking, jumping, leaping onto available laps, promiscuously indulging in any caress offered.

Now when Allan and I both take Paxie for a walk on a Sunday afternoon we feel like the Queen and Prince Philip doing a royal walkabout. At present we have unique status due to a dog. But this will not last. Mercy, our executive assistant who types my manuscripts and irons Allan's shirts, takes Paxie with her when she shops at the local grocery or goes to the nearby park so Paxie can socialize with her peers. About three weeks ago, Mercy tied Paxie up to a bike rack in front of the grocery store not far from where the local ladies park their SUVs. When Mercy left the shop, she was filled with trepidation because Paxie, though calm, had an unusual audience— three women with pen-and-paper in their hands. Had her little paws scratched a Mercedes SUV? Paxie has been brainwashed at home with anti-SUV sentiments. The women handed Mercy slips of paper with their phone numbers. "We want to know the name of the breeder," they said. "Call back and tell us where we can buy a dog like that."

My feelings are ambivalent. Imitation is, of course, the highest form of flattery. But do I want copy-dogs in the neighbourhood? Breeders of marmalade miniature poodles are easily found in the local dog magazines. Last week we knew that Paxie's fame was finished. Mercy, getting off the bus, thought she saw me taking Paxie for an early morning walk. But it wasn't me, it wasn't Paxie. It was a clone. The invasion of the Red Poodles in Rosedale has begun.